Uniforms Exposed

Dress, Body, Culture

Series Editor: **Joanne B. Eicher**, *Regents' Professor, University of Minnesota*

Books in this provocative series seek to articulate the connections between culture and dress, which is defined here in its broadest possible sense as any modification or supplement to the body. Interdisciplinary in approach, the series highlights the dialogue between identity and dress, cosmetics, coiffure and body alterations as manifested in practices as varied as plastic surgery, tattooing and ritual scarification. The series aims, in particular, to analyse the meaning of dress in relation to popular culture and gender issues and will include works grounded in anthropology, sociology, history, art history, literature and folklore.

ISSN: 1360-466X

Previously published titles in the series

Helen Bradley Foster, *"New Raiments of Self": African American Clothing in the Antebellum South*
Claudine Griggs, *S/he: Changing Sex and Changing Clothes*
Michaele Thurgood Haynes, *Dressing Up Debutantes: Pageantry and Glitz in Texas*
Anne Brydon and Sandra Niessen, *Consuming Fashion: Adorning the Transnational Body*
Dani Cavallaro and Alexandra Warwick, *Fashioning the Frame: Boundaries, Dress and the Body*
Judith Perani and Norma H. Wolff, *Cloth, Dress and Art Patronage in Africa*
Linda B. Arthur, *Religion, Dress and the Body*
Paul Jobling, *Fashion Spreads: Word and Image in Fashion Photography*
Fadwa El Guindi, *Veil: Modesty, Privacy and Resistance*
Thomas S. Abler, *Hinterland Warriors and Military Dress: European Empires and Exotic Uniforms*
Linda Welters, *Folk Dress in Europe and Anatolia: Beliefs about Protection and Fertility*
Kim K.P. Johnson and Sharron J. Lennon, *Appearance and Power*
Barbara Burman, *The Culture of Sewing*
Annette Lynch, *Dress, Gender and Cultural Change*
Antonia Young, *Women Who Become Men*
David Muggleton, *Inside Subculture: The Postmodern Meaning of Style*
Nicola White, *Reconstructing Italian Fashion: America and the Development of the Italian Fashion Industry*
Brian J. McVeigh, *Wearing Ideology: The Uniformity of Self-Presentation in Japan*
Shaun Cole, *Don We Now Our Gay Apparel: Gay Men's Dress in the Twentieth Century*
Kate Ince, *Orlan: Millennial Female*
Nicola White and Ian Griffiths, *The Fashion Business: Theory, Practice, Image*
Ali Guy, Eileen Green and Maura Banim, *Through the Wardrobe: Women's Relationships with their Clothes*
Linda B. Arthur, *Undressing Religion: Commitment and Conversion from a Cross-Cultural Perspective*
William J.F. Keenan, *Dressed to Impress: Looking the Part*
Joanne Entwistle and Elizabeth Wilson, *Body Dressing*
Leigh Summers, *Bound to Please: A History of the Victorian Corset*
Paul Hodkinson, *Goth: Identity, Style and Subculture*
Michael Carter, *Fashion Classics from Carlyle to Barthes*
Sandra Niessen, Ann Marie Leshkowich and Carla Jones, *Re-Orienting Fashion: The Globalization of Asian Dress*
Kim K.P. Johnson, Susan J. Torntore and Joanne B. Eicher, *Fashion Foundations: Early Writings on Fashion and Dress*
Helen Bradley Foster and Donald Clay Johnson, *Wedding Dress Across Cultures*
Eugenia Paulicelli, *Fashion under Fascism: Beyond the Black Shirt*
Charlotte Suthrell, *Unzipping Gender: Sex, Cross-Dressing and Culture*
Yuniya Kawamura, *The Japanese Revolution in Paris Fashion*
Ruth Barcan, *Nudity: A Cultural Anatomy*
Samantha Holland, *Alternative Femininities: Body, Age and Identity*
Alexandra Palmer and Hazel Clark, *Old Clothes, New Looks: Second Hand Fashion*
Yuniya Kawamura, *Fashion-ology: An Introduction to Fashion Studies*
Regina A. Root, *The Latin American Fashion Reader*
Linda Welters and Patricia A. Cunningham, *Twentieth-Century American Fashion*

Uniforms Exposed

From Conformity to Transgression

Jennifer Craik

Oxford • New York

English edition
First published in 2005 by
Berg
Editorial offices:
1st Floor, Angel Court, 81 St Clements Street, Oxford OX4 1AW, UK
175 Fifth Avenue, New York, NY 10010, USA

Berg is the imprint of Oxford International Publishers Ltd.

Library of Congress Cataloging-in-Publication Data

Craik, Jennifer.
    Uniforms exposed : from conformity to transgression / Jennifer
Craik.—English ed.
        p. cm.
    Includes bibliographical references and index.
    ISBN 1-85973-898-2 (cloth) — ISBN 1-85973-804-4 (pbk.)
    1. Uniforms—Social aspects. 2. Clothing and dress—Social aspects.
I. Title.
    GT25.C737 2005
    391—dc22
                                                  2005010964

British Library Cataloguing-in-Publication Data

A catalogue record for this book is available from the British Library.

ISBN-13   978 1 85973 898 6 (Cloth)
            978 1 85973 804 7 (Paper)

ISBN-10   1 85973 898 2 (Cloth)
            1 85973 804 4 (Paper)

Typeset by JS Typesetting Ltd, Porthcawl, Mid Glamorgan
Printed in the United Kingdom by Biddles Ltd, King's Lynn.

www.bergpublishers.com

Contents

Part IV Uniform Culture

Illustrations

Acknowledgments

I have always been fascinated by uniforms – by their arbitrary yet repetitive elements and by the strict rules about how to wear them, or, rather, how they should *not* be worn. Uniforms seem to have a life of their own. People wearing uniforms often report feeling different in a uniform. In effect, the uniform wears them! So, what is the magic power of uniforms? This book investigates some aspects of uniforms in contemporary culture. It is not a definitive history of uniforms but is more interested in how they are worn, why they are popular (or unpopular) and why we have such a fascination with them.

The book explores the development of uniforms in modern and contemporary culture, arguing that they have become an integral body technique of how we construct and perform our identities and social roles. Indeed, rather than declining in importance or number, uniforms have proliferated in a culture that ostensibly embraces individualism and personal choice. Following an introductory chapter in Part I outlining this argument, the book is divided into three further parts. In Part II, *Uniforms and Authority*, I explore the centrality of military uniforms in shaping modern uniforms and persona, specifically taking the example of school uniforms and women's uniforms. Part III, *Uniforms for Work and Leisure*, looks at the proliferation of uniforms in occupational roles and in leisure – particularly sporting uniforms and sportswear. Part IV, *Uniform Culture*, examines uniforms in popular culture and the transgressive uptake of uniforms.

This book has a long and short history. Intrigue about uniforms played a part in my book, *The Face of Fashion* (1994), and was reignited by a request from the Australian Broadcasting Corporation's Radio National programme *The Comfort Zone* in 2000 when producer Mark Wakely asked if I knew anything about the design of school uniforms. This led to an interview on why school uniforms looked like they did, with subsequent broadcasts on the design of military uniforms and the transition from sports uniforms to sportswear. Many thanks to Mark, co-producer Kerry Stewart and host Alan Saunders for their interest in this topic. Thanks also to colleagues in the Centre for Cross-Cultural Research, Australian National University, Canberra, who fanned this interest and contributed ideas and feedback on the first papers I wrote about uniforms. Special thanks to Joan Kerr, Barbara Campbell and Penny Edwards.

While writing this book I have presented parts of the manuscript to colleagues in seminars and at conferences: in the School of Film, Media and Cultural Studies (FMC), the School of Politics and Public Policy (PPP), and the School of Arts, Media and Culture (AMC) at Griffith University, Brisbane and delivered two lectures at the Queensland University of Technology (QUT), Brisbane. Many thanks to all the diverse contributions, reminiscences and critiques from colleagues involved in those seminars including Annita Boyd, Melissa Connell, Nadine Wills, Michael Meadows, Trish Fitzsimons, Cathy Jenkins, David Adair, Helen Lancaster, Wendy Keys, June Cullen and Maureen Burns from FMC; Pat Weller, Haig Patapan, May McPhail, Robyn Hollander, Patrick Bishop, Glyn Davis and Ciaran O'Faircheallaigh from PPP; Ian Henderson, Martin Travers, Kay Ferres, Regina Ganter, Tamsin Kerr and David Saunders from AMC; and Lucie Camenzuli and Kathleen Horton from QUT.

I have also presented the material on uniforms at work at the "Making an Appearance Conference" at the University of Queensland, Brisbane in July 2003, and greatly appreciated the post-paper discussion and feedback from many colleagues. Margaret Maynard has been particularly supportive in the final period of writing the manuscript and, in the process has become a valued friend. For resource support from the Political Sciences Program, Research School of Social Sciences of the Australian National University, Canberra, many thanks too to Rod Rhodes, Mary Hapel, Susan Hanson, Gail Radford and Marian Sawer.

I am grateful to the Griffith University Research Grant Scheme for a grant to complete the writing and preparation of the book. Thanks also for research assistance provided by Melissa Connell, Ashley Lavelle, Tracey Arklay, Bernardo Ceriani and Jonathan Richards. Very special thanks to Gillian Evans, who painstakingly tracked down copyright permissions and images. For generous assistance in providing images and illustrations, sincere thanks to Olwen Schubert and Gail and Dawn Johnston. Sheryl Williams has ably smoothed the administrative pathway while Bruce Wuth, Sean Batt, Bryan Shanahan and Darren Boyd have provided invaluable technical support.

Many others have helped – knowingly and unknowingly – in the gestation process and I have been most grateful to them all: Morgyn Phillips, Audra Colless, Don Adams, Evert Lindquist, Prudence Black, Helen Sutton, Verity James, David Harris, Sharon Peoples, Jeffrey Minson and Anne Freadman. The encouragement of the families of the Bardon Allstars since 2002 has been much appreciated: thanks to Lara and Roy Cassidy, Tina and Ewen Thompson, Susan and Bruce Wuth, Miriam and Graham McNee, Mary and Amir Shoshani, Cheryl and Bryce Cleary, Sally and John McKillop and Bernice and Michael Duke.

Sincere thanks to colleagues elsewhere who have been supportive, especially Valerie Steele, Kathryn Earle, Joanne Eicher, Elizabeth Wilson, Sandra Niessen, Marie O'Mahony, Carol Tulloch and Chris Breward. The team at Berg have been highly professional and efficient; special thanks to Hannah Shakespeare and Ken Bruce.

Above all, I must thank John Wanna for his many diverse contributions to the material and ideas in the book, unofficial fieldwork, superb editing, and inspiration and perseverance in seeing this project completed. Erinn Wanna has followed the project with interest and encouragement. Finally, our twin sons, Aidan and Sean Wanna, have trained up to become an enthusiastic cheersquad ("Mum, there's another uniform for you . . .") as well as experts about epaulettes, legal wigs and robes, fastskin suits, shakoes, hussars, zouave flair, fishnet stockings and black leather catsuits. At least dinner conversations have not been boring!

Part I

Uniforms and Culture

Figure 1
Staff at the Old Carleton
Hotel (Shanghai, 1920)

1

Uniforms, Body Techniques and Culture

Why Do Uniforms Intrigue Us?

This book speculates on the pervasive motif or theme of uniforms in clothing and fashion more generally. To approach the topic I ask a series of questions. Why do uniforms hold such a fascination in modern and postmodern cultures? Is the fascination to do with what they say or don't say; what they mean or how their meanings might be bent; where we find them and where resonances of them crop up? What is the relationship between the aesthetics of uniforms and other clothing styles? Why do certain canonical elements of uniforms – such as brass buttons, braid, frogging, epaulettes, tailored clothing (jackets, coats, trousers), headwear, exaggerated collars – so insistently recur in fashion and contemporary culture? The answers to these questions can be found in the *ambivalent* connotations associated with uniforms in western European culture. While ostensibly uniforms signify order, conformity and discipline, uniforms also are a fetishized cultural artefact embodying ambiguous erotic impulses and moral rectitude.

Uniforms shape who we are and how we perform our identities. As well as becoming a leitmotif of our clothed self, uniforms have equally shaped our ways of seeing and become central to the visual language and spatial conventions of photography. Aesthetic conventions such as the use of light and shadow, colour contrast, gold, silver and metallic embellishment, movement, synchronicity and repetition are keynotes of looking and seeing evoking the spectacle of the uniformed body. Uniformed and quasi-uniformed bodies (people dressed individually but in similar ways – e.g. business people, clubbers, sports spectators) constantly proclaim a uniformed self (cf. Joseph 1986).

Uniforms are intriguing. Uniforms are all about control not only of the social self but also of the inner self and its formation. Uniforms send out mixed messages – some of these are obvious but others less so. Often it is those other subliminal messages that make them so intriguing. Those mixed messages are a combination of "not" statements (rules of wearing and not wearing that are often unstated or only partially stated – or arbitrarily applied) and transgressive messages. Rules about uniforms are highly detailed and fastidious. Wearing a uniform properly –understanding and obeying rules about the uniform-in-practice and turning the garments into communicative statements – is more important than the items of clothing and decoration themselves.

Enforcement of uniform practice is central to the social life of the uniform. Enforcement involves both rewards and punishment for transgression. Punishment can take many forms: loss of privileges, repeating uniform practice until perfect, humiliation and physical or psychological discipline. Although we think of the public face of uniforms as coterminous with order, control, confidence and conformity, we also know about the *other face* of uniforms as subversion, transgression, punishment and shame. It is this double character of uniforms that makes them so intriguing.

An element of the intrigue comes from personal experiences with uniforms. Most people recall vivid experiences with uniforms and these encounters are often highly memorable. Anecdotes about uniforms usually involve polarized opinions, highly charged and often hinting at the other face of the uniform. Memories are full of images of humiliation, pride, embarrassment, ritual, fitting in, shame, rebellion, transgression and punishment.

So, we find that uniforms – and the enforcement of rules about them — are imprinted on our techniques of self-hood through techniques of the body (sociological, psychological and biological). There is a disjunction between the ostensible meanings of uniforms – as embodying sameness, unity, regulation, hierarchy, status, roles – and the experience of uniforms. Often, anecdotes about uniforms involve formative moments of self-hood, especially associated with breaking out or away from normative codes, rebellion or subversion, about individual interpretation or difference in sameness.

The uniform, then, is not as obvious as commonly thought. Uniforms have *overt* and *covert* lives and it is the relationships between these two dimensions that are the subject of this book. There is a profound difference between the *Oxford English Dictionary* (*OED*) definition of uniforms (not changing in form or character; unvarying; conforming to same standard or rule; dress worn by members of same body, e.g. soldiers, sailors, police officers) and the attributes associated with them. The study of how uniforms are represented – in art, photography, film, performance art and music – also deserves attention. Indeed, the aesthetics and connotations of uniforms and uniform practice have significantly shaped our aesthetic codes.

They have also shaped our political regimes. Uniforms are a specialized form of clothing that is used "to demonstrate the authority of individuals or groups and to transform this authority into the power of government" (Langner 1965: 124). The rank, functions and power of the uniformed person is often "supplemented or superseded by badges or insignia which may also serve the same person" (Langner 1965: 124). The uniform, then, is a radical form of clothing that is employed to announce a particular type of identity that acts both as shorthand of the kind of behaviour exhibited by the wearer and expected by the observer. Uniforms convey specific structural relations (via types of uniforms and titles of wearers) that form the framework of interpersonal relations that are possible with the uniformed person (cf. Stone 1970: 399). According to Stone (1970: 403), appearance generally – and uniforms in particular – prescribe a range of responses: "identities are placed, values appraised, moods appreciated, and attitudes anticipated." Uniforms (formal and informal) are thus strategically used to play the games of social life by allowing people to conform to groups they are part of (school friends, relatives, religious groups, ethnic groups, occupational categories and so on) as well as moments in rites of passage (playmates, teenage rebels, romance seekers, homemakers, parents and retired people). In other words,

Figure 2
Archbishop and Cardinal.

people use dressing as a game in which to maximize the fit with one's peers and, equally, let spectators know "what game they are watching" (Stone 1970: 413).

So uniforms are ambiguous masks of appearance, on the one hand, intending to unambiguously place the attributes and role of the person, yet, on the other, part of complex social play that can be deliberately appropriated, subverted or rejected. Because uniforms have another face, we find that uniforms have been appropriated in a range of transgressive and subversive contexts – such as in pornography, prostitution, sado-masochism, transvestism, cross-dressing, vaudeville, mardi gras, gay cultures, subcultures, choirs and strippergrams. In other words, there is a constant play between the intended symbolism of uniforms (sameness, unity, regulation, hierarchy, status and roles) and the informal codes of wearing and denoting uniforms (subversion, individual interpretation and difference). Uniforms that are worn in extreme regimes or in developing countries seeking modernity and international recognition often use highly elaborate uniforms as a demonstration of their actual or desired power. In such cases, encounters with uniformed people may be less a reassuring sign of order than a sign of intimidation, threat – even corruption. We might ask: do people wear uniforms or do uniforms wear people? Certainly, the wearing of uniforms constitutes central body techniques in the actualization of persona and habitus.

Techniques of the Uniformed Body

This book adopts the approach of Marcel Mauss (1973, 1985), who developed a "triple viewpoint" to understand techniques of the body as a nexus of sociological, psychological and biological attributes that combine to produce the social body through persona and self. Body techniques are learned – there is nothing natural, argued Mauss, but certain fundamental trainings become so second nature that we think of them as instinctive. In fact, body techniques are arbitrary yet contingent, a product of cultural specificity and historical variability. Techniques are learned through prestigious imitation to perform in very precise ways that become internalized. There are no natural or essential human body techniques.

Uniforms are an example of body techniques *par excellence*. They are acquired by prestigious imitation of those we admire or who are in authority. As argued above, most of the body techniques associated with uniforms entail the acquisition of "not" statements – that is, what to avoid or repress. Uniforms are extremely effective indicators of the codification of appropriate rules of conduct and their internalization. Arguably, it is this set of rules and the manner of their enforcement that is more important than the elements of uniforms themselves.

Yet, the rationale for uniforms often seems arbitrary or bizarre. This is because they are highly specific and deliberately calculated to produce a certain array of body techniques. For example, a tie that is part of a uniform symbolizes constraint, neatness, public persona (the social "front" of the self), while the choice of colour, pattern, width and knot indicates further social and cultural attributes of codes and conventions (Hart 1998). Furthermore, choosing a different type of neckwear – for example, a bowtie or cravat – may indicate a different set of attributes, such as an artistic temperament or effeminacy. It is essential that the wearer and onlooker share a common code about the meaning of the item and how to wear it in order that a tie – or indeed – any piece of uniform can "work" as a social marker.

Traditionally in Anglo-Saxon countries, such as England, Australia and New Zealand, surgeons downplayed their high occupational status by using the title "Mr" rather than the more prestigious "Dr", but at the same time, typically choosing to wear a bowtie rather than a necktie, thereby conveying high social status associated with cultured cognoscenti. Moreover, outside the operating theatre, surgeons frequently eschewed wearing a protective uniform worn by mere doctors, nurses and attendant staff. In an American study, Roth (1965) found that medical specialists treating the highly contagious disease tuberculosis were much less likely to wear protective clothing (cap, gown, mask) than other staff; in fact, there was an inverse relationship between the wearing of protective gear and occupational status.

Roth (1965) accounted for this as a form of magic, where the protective clothing is attributed the magical ability to ward off disease yet the senior medicos possess a more efficacious magical charm that renders the need for protection unnecessary. Moreover, even among staff who did wear protective clothing, this was more likely to occur in procedural contexts but not in the more intimate social contexts (for example, when visiting patients). Nowadays, Anglo-Saxon surgeons are embracing the title "Dr" but abandoning the bowtie, perhaps a sign that their occupational status has declined and they need a title and recognizable occupational uniform to compete in the highly diversified medical field.

The connotations of the surgeon's choice of bowtie differs from the connotations of the bowtie worn by a "confirmed bachelor" where the tie operates as a semi-secret code of sexual preference and social position. The bowtie worn by the conductor of an orchestra – or author – indicates flamboyance, creative flair and professional authority while the bowtie worn as part of a dinner suit is a sign of formality and sartorial restraint. Codes associated with uniforms are highly elaborated and precise, indicating fine gradations of status, rank, role, occupation, character and performativity (cf. Finkelstein 1994).

Sometimes these are articulated only by uniform "failures", that is, wearing the wrong uniform, wearing uniform inappropriately, mixing different uniform codes, and so on. I recall a conversation between a Swiss banker and a German financial entrepreneur as to why a cousin of the former was not getting ahead in another bank. "Well, he always wears a brown suit," said the banker. The entrepreneur responded: "Doesn't he know that you should only wear a black or navy suit?", as if the inappropriate choice of suit was a sufficient explanation of his professional failure.

A different kind of example is discussed by Margaret Maynard (2004: 25–6).[1] Intrigued by a press photo of the Zambian High Commissioner meeting Queen Elizabeth II in 2001, she researched the background to the outfit he was wearing. Although the Queen may have been used to meeting foreign dignitaries on their home turf in their traditional – or customary – dress, the High Commissioner had decided that he should combine "customary dress, a modern adaptation of past ceremonial dress and lastly current western dress".

He chose a version of the ceremonial costume worn for the annual *Kuomboka* ceremony by the Lozi people of western Zambia.[2] With his wife advising him, he chose a traditional cap (a red *lishushu* rather like a reggae cap), white business shirt, a *siziba* (a pleated skirt, made in London with a fabric chosen by his wife) and a traditional "kanga" cloak (*malesu*) over the top. He had been planning to go barefoot, but, as it was cold, his wife purchased long socks and neutral-coloured Clarks lace-up shoes specially for the occasion. This outfit compared with other accounts of the customary costume:

> Men, like women, were wearing long multicoloured skirts and large berets tilting on one side (like Basque berets) made of red cotton. The king alone distinguished himself by wearing a splendid admiral uniform of the century British royal navy, with British crown's permission. (Embassy of France to Zambia and Malawi, n.d.)

Figure 3
Academic dress.

The wearing of the *siziba* is traditional although it is now worn with a white shirt as opposed to topless (as recorded in Francois Coillard's 1897 photograph, cited by Milbourne 1997). The admiral's suit was a gift from Edward VII to the then king when he attended Edward's coronation in 1901. The outfit of the High Commissioner seemed somewhat comical, yet it was, in reality, a carefully negotiated compromise and mix of two very different ceremonial uniforms.

However, even the traditional component was not quite what it seemed for the Lozi have been adept at adapting the festivity and its costumes over time, building a special royal barge to a design provided by a missionary, adding masks (*makishi*) for impact, incorporating the much-prized admiral's uniform, abandoning the royal dance (the *Lishemba*) and adding royal drums (as recently as 1975) (Milbourne 1997; Libakeni 2004). Milbourne (1997) concludes that these changes "indicate the ongoing creativity of kuomboka" as an "invented tradition" or rather, "*a continually inventive tradition*" (my italics). At different times, European influences have been accommodated. For example, when British administrators "appropriated" the ceremony as an "aquatic dis-play" for visiting dignitaries, the Lozi accepted this as part of political negotiating.[3] The flexibility of the festivity and its costum-ing would, in the High Commissioner's eyes, have made it the perfect vehicle – or mask – to accommodate British royal protocol even though this may not have been recognized for what it was by the Queen or press.

On the other hand, the dowdy-looking floral shirtdress worn by Queen Elizabeth II (in a fabric eerily similar to that of the Ambassador's *siziba*) may have been interpreted by His Excellency as a lack of appropriate ceremonial occasion on her part. As Maynard (2004: 26) observes, despite occurring in 2001, her dress and "almost ritualised hairdressing" (a coifed off-the-face perm) was "a lasting tribute to British style of the 1950s", institutionalized as royal uniform yet strangely anachronistic and a far cry from the more dynamic "royal" dress codes adopted by Diana Princess of Wales and European royals, such as Denmark's Crown Princess Mary (cf. Beaton 1965; Hurlock 1965b).

As this example suggests, there can be complex forces at work in the performance of uniform codes and opportunities for misunderstandings and incomplete interpretations. The rationale of uniforms is highly specific to an institution, organization or group because it embodies precise calculations designed to distinguish members of that uniformed group by their acquisition of distinctive body techniques. In this process, learning to wear the uniform in the prescribed way – or rather, learning what *not* to do – is an integral part of the role of uniforms as an extension of the habitus of the individual. The acquisition of a uniform's codes becomes internalized at the same time as other body techniques particular to the institution are being acquired.

In other words, *how to wear* the uniform becomes "as if natural" and unremarkable because of the power of sanctions for transgressions. Wearers of uniforms learn to behave as corporate automatons, following the rules with precision. As Okely (1993) recalled on analysing her experiences at boarding school:

> Children cannot articulate their experiences in the language of adults. Only after childhood can it thus be expressed. When young we found the school world the reality, the norm, the only rationality. That was its power. My mother has often said since, "But why didn't you tell me?" We, my sister and I, could not discriminate that which now seems bizarre. (Okely 1993: 95)

Generally, school students obey the uniform code up to a point, although minor deviations are common. Any discussion of uniforms immediately sparks memories of how students rebelled or subverted the rules – by hitching skirts up, wearing non-regulation socks, loosening the tie, battering the hat, shaving their head, wearing jewellery or nail polish, and so on. Much can be told about the nature on enforcing uniforms from rules about how they should be worn. Until the 1970s, many Australian state schools carried out daily inspections of girls to see if they were wearing regulation school bloomers over their underpants. The elaborate lengths that some schools adopt to enforce uniform rules often seem ludicrous to an observer. For example, consider this set of guidelines on "Personal Appearance" issued by one Australian grammar (private) school anxious to preserve standards:

> The College has clear expectations of the way students are to wear their uniforms. Shirts are to be tucked in, top button done up under the tie and long socks held up with garters worn with shorts. Students are also expected to have hair cuts which suit the College guidelines and older students are expected to be clean on each school day. All items of uniform are to be in good condition. . . The hat is a part of the uniform and is worn at all times and especially on camps and lunch-time. . . near enough is not good enough. . . Grooming is an important life skill and good habits must be created early. (St. Joseph's Grammar School Gregory Terrace (Brisbane) uniform policy, cited in The School Uniforms Galleries, 2002, www.school.uniform.freeuk.com/st_josephs.htm)

Yet, attempts to be subversive depend on a precise knowledge and tacit acceptance of the rules and also of what extent deviations will be tolerated (Dawson 1997). Beyond this limit, a student risks suspension or – if too deviant – expulsion. Thus, the uniform is an extremely effective way to monitor the success of the training in body techniques and to identify and isolate those who have not acquired the requisite techniques. We can infer that uniforms exemplify the main elements of Mauss's (1973) argument since then uniforms are an essential component of the body techniques being instilled by the occupant of the uniform.

In the case of uniforms for men, there is a close fit between the attributes of normative *masculinity* as inscribed in uniform conduct and normative masculine roles and attributes. However, for women, there is a discrepancy between the gendered attributes of uniforms and normative *femininity*. For example, skirts that are part of female uniforms encode seemingly familiar messages about uniforms – regulation, restraint, discipline, practicality – but also convey certain attributes of femininity – tailored modesty, neatness, demureness – but not others – loose morals, sexiness, slovenliness or precociousness – that is connotations of sexual desire or attractiveness or disregard for social and moral conventions.

Body techniques inscribed *in* uniforms contain a series of oppositional attributes: discipline versus spontaneity; group identity/conformity versus individuality/expressiveness; formality versus informality; compulsion versus choice; sexuality versus sexuality; and sexual innocence versus sexual perversion.

The traditional rationale for wearing uniforms emphasized the former set of attributes. Contemporary debates about uniforms, however, frequently evoke the rhetoric of the culture of individualism that relates more to the latter set of attributes. This is especially so in the context of debates about the retention, reintroduction and redesign of school uniforms. There is an incompatible dimension to such debates. In the mid-1990s, for instance US, President Bill Clinton (1996) argued for the compulsory introduction of school uniforms across the United States as a means (body technique) to combat disciplinary problems, antisocial behaviour, gang domination and poor academic performance. This argument transformed the attributes of uniforms and rules about wearing them into a set of behavioural correlates (US Department of Education and US Department of Justice 1996). Uniforms were perceived to produce better schools by producing more docile bodies and better performing students.

Clinton's campaign was in effect borrowing the strategies of the French court as discussed by Norbert Elias (1983). He traced how the body became *the* key component of establishing and maintaining court society in the ancient regime of pre-revolutionary France. The development of court society was structured around precise body protocols and statuses, roles and rituals. Over time, clothing-body relations became key elements of French court and civil society. Clothes acquired symbolic values as tradable commodities. Just as ordinary folk emulated the manners and modes of the aristocracy, so too the aristocracy emulated the consumer habits and modes of the burgeoning business and middle classes since customary social status was not the sole recipe for success in the emergent mercantile economy. In sum, uniforms became an extension of the

Figure 4
Libyan leader Muammar
Gaddafi.

social body and its techniques; making training visible; constructing a particular habitus; and negotiating identity and the self.

The Emergence of Uniforms of Modernity

Uniforms have a long history charting the development of social forms of distinction and distinctiveness. Rules about uniforms stem from rules about dress more generally. Rules about how people should dress are so fundamental to human society that they are frequently encoded in legislation or codes of conduct (e.g. by professional bodies, schools). Of particular importance in European society was the existence of *sumptuary laws* that regulated civil conduct concerning, among other things, who could wear what under what circumstances.[4] Restrictions might be placed on the type of garment that certain groups or people could and could not wear; gold and silver fabric, jewellery and ornamentations were often restricted; expensive fabrics (e.g. silk, lace, velvet) might be restricted.

In Southeast Asia, Reid (1988: 75–90) has traced a variety of techniques of regulating the body that were used to denote rank, status and role. These include filing or blackening the teeth, boring or distending the earlobes, tattooing, styling the hair, manicuring fingernails, wearing certain types of jewellery particularly gold, prohibitions on wearing certain textiles, and so on. Reid (1988: 78) concluded that "as a means of ensuring that each man stayed in his allotted place, tattooing was even more reliable than sumptuary laws on clothes." Some of these regulations were informally enforced while others were formally inscribed in sumptuary laws.

While sumptuary laws had also existed in antiquity – for example in Ancient Greece (600 BC), Ancient Rome (300 BC to AD 300), from the T'ang period in China (AD 618–906) and the Tokugawa period in Japan (AD 1600–1868) – their longevity in European countries between AD 1100 and 1700 coincides with the emergence of modernity (Hunt 1996: 17–38).

European sumptuary laws existed in Italian cities, France, Spain, Swiss cantons, England, German provinces and Scotland and straddled the "fundamental divide between the premodern and the modern" (Hunt 1996: 28). Rather than waning, sumptuary law and dress codes were fundamentally tied up with the mercantile revolution that fanned conspicuous consumption and the consequent need to preserve social hierarchies. As a result, sumptuary laws proliferated at this time. They became increasingly concerned with dress codes, formal codification, the preservation of class distinctions and the denouncement of extravagance and luxury. Alongside this codification was the emergence of dynamic sartorial sensibilities that became known as fashion. Dress became a means to subvert the social order and negotiate the neophyte consumer culture. Sumptuary laws were therefore of two types: on the one hand, the imposition of expenditure limits; on the other, the reservation of particular kind of cloth or style for certain groups – either as a privilege or as a negative prohibition (Hunt 1996: 27; see also Hurlock 1965a; cf. Quataert 1997 on clothing laws in the Ottoman Empire). Yet, the nature of these laws suggested that they were a response to challenges to existing hierarchies, that is, to elite social anxieties about changing social realities.

It was in this context that uniforms became entrenched as a sartorial way to differentiate people as to role and status. As Hunt (1986) put it:

> Uniforms work through codes; they may exhibit a precise
> (and potentially complex) code that makes possible very
> precise readings. Military, medical and clerical uniforms
> make possible the close reading of rank, grade, function, etc.
> Such codes are capable of extensive expansion when com-
> bined with the additional semiotic diversity facilitated by
> ornamentation and other semiotic devices of which heraldry
> provides an expanded system both of differentiation, for
> example, by status, and individual recognizability. (Hunt
> 1986: 61)

Different kinds of ornamentation permit infinite variation of basic
codes alluding to "power-laden" references, "the most obvious
being the use of military symbolism in buttons, braids, epaulettes
and other details or the use of symbols of precious metals, of gold
and silver finishes to detailing in buttons, clasps, etc" (Hunt 1996:
61–2).

While military uniforms are the subject of Chapter 2, the other
formative type of early codification of dress shaping the sensibilities
of modernism was ecclesiastical dress which created separation
from the laity on the basis on spiritual – and sometimes moral –
superiority as well as elaborate codifications of status and role
within religious orders. Although not usually defined as uniforms
– but as a distinctive kind of dress – it is clear that the precise
codification and elaboration of types of garments, choice of fabric,
ornamentation, colour and difference from lay dress means that
ecclesiastical dress conforms to the definition of uniforms – albeit
ones concerned with spiritual well-being. Equally, however, the
attempt to create a distinct social group with high spiritual values
has spawned a counter-culture of transgression – the "not" statements of the meaning of ecclesiastical dress. This is the subject of
Chapter 9.

Hence, we see that while sumptuary laws framed the modern
sensibilities that underpinned uniforms in contemporary culture,
these rules were less about enforcement and more about the
regulation of behaviour and control of excess and displays of luxury
and conspicuous consumption. This stemmed from social anxieties
surrounding the major changes going on socially and economically
in the early modern period. Dress became a coda both for self-
presentation as well as what Hunt calls "individuation" (Hunt
1996: 395) in an attempt "to secure a stable connection between

appearance and entitlement" (Hunt 1996: 396). The postmodern understanding of uniforms, then, relates to their role as the visible signs of self-governance of individual sensibilities, responsibilities, status and specialist roles.

To understand this role of uniforms, this book distinguishes *formal prescribed uniforms* from *quasi-uniforms* and *informal uniforms*. Quasi-uniforms refer to modes of dress that are consensually imposed as appropriate while informal uniforms are individual combinations of clothes and looks that seek to project an individual and construct the visible signs of a "unique" identity but in fact conform to informal rules and fads that percolate through civil society. Examples of quasi-uniforms include business suits for men and women, smart yet modest casual outfits for teachers, chinos and check shirts for weekend yuppies, or black outfits for funerals. Examples of informal uniforms include what university students wear to class, social protesters clothes at demonstrations, après-ski wear, surfers' wear, or socialites' party wear. This typology is elaborated with regard to occupational uniforms and dress in Chapter 5.

Whereas formal uniforms are more rigorously managed by external impositions and codification – for example in the military or police forces – informal uniforms are "managed" by other forms of approbation and censure from word of mouth (among school or university students) to gossip columns and celebrity magazines in the case of stars, sporting heroes, popular musicians, socialites and actors. We can see this a modern form of sumptuary law where "high intensity governance" of dress behaviour reflects social anxieties and "low intensity governance" (Hunt 1996: 397) indicates less critical issues and concerns. Accordingly, the final part of the book explores uniforms in popular culture and everyday fashion to show how deeply ingrained uniform culture has percolated our very social being.

Part II

Uniforms and Authority

Figure 5
Ray at Sheungshui
Railway Station, 1958.

2

From Military Uniforms to Codified Civility

From Identification to Indulgence to Utilitarianism

Almost all uniforms we see nowadays in whole or part derive from traditional military or ecclesiastical uniforms and dress. These were the main precursors of the modern application of uniforms in various contexts. They also embodied the double-faced character of uniforms that has accompanied the development of uniforms as a generic form of dress, that is, how uniforms have shaped clothing codes more generally and been adapted to different functions and meanings. This double face refers to the disjunction with the ostensible meaning of uniforms as signifying order, stats, role and hierarchy but, at the same time, encoding the seeds of the obverse.

This chapter traces the ambivalence and its replication in the take-up of military "lookalike" uniforms in civil society. Examples are numerous and include the following: school uniforms; scouting and Boys' Brigade uniforms; professional uniforms (for example, in the medical profession, police, security forces, park rangers as well as door keepers and concierges); and quasi-uniforms (including men's "white-collar" suits; white or khaki "safari" suits in subtropical and tropical colonies; professional photographer's multi-pocket vests and trousers; and professional women's suits – often Hussar-style jackets and tailored skirts). Even anti-authority subcultures have been influenced by military uniforms in devising their distinctive dress codes – such as American rappers' penchant for camouflage fabric, bikers' use of "bomber" jackets and rock musicians' partiality for wearing ex-military gear. So how did the transition from military dress to partially codified civil dress occur?

Uniforms have been an essential element of human society especially where *group identity* has been crucial, as a mark of distinctiveness (e.g. religious orders), as markers of social status (e.g. rulers, aristocrats, castes, those in authority or wielding power – and those subjugated) and as markers of group membership (e.g. as citizens, clans, occupations, party members). Differences in dress, protective devices and distinctive emblems have been common in organized military formations even in ancient China, the Middle East and the Roman Empire (Wise 1981; *The Collins Atlas of Military History* 2004). Highly elaborated uniforms were used and modifications made to make uniforms and protective gear more practical, for example, the Romans' use of tunics with skirts of separate panels to enable soldiers to ride horses and fight more easily than conventional armour permitted. Indeed, there are also examples of the early use of camouflage. There are two types of camouflage: colours of dress (e.g. red dye or blood, blue woad, face paint, animal furs of Scots, Maoris, Zulus) that are meant to scare the enemy and colours or dress that are meant to disguise the attacker or help them blend into the background (e.g. the modern camouflage fabrics, use of blackened faces, hiding the body under branches).

During the republican era (509–27 BC), Roman light infantrymen called *velites* wore wolf pelts over their helmets as they harried and dispersed groups of soldiers (Newark, Newark and Borsarello 1998: 8). The aim was to threaten the enemy and boast their prowess. Hannibal used North African "crack" troops dressed in leopard skins and masks to disperse and rout the beautifully turned out and precision formations of Roman soldiers. Another use of animal disguise in military action occurred in the fourteenth century when Balkan scouts (called *delis*) of the Ottoman Turkish

Figure 6
Civilian and naval officer.

army resorted to wearing feathers and fur over their uniforms. Other European soldiers wore bearskins and other animal furs as part of their ordinary dress – e.g. Danes, Norse, English warriors (and later English royal palace guardsmen).[1] Subsequently:

> This elaborate 'hunting' costume later evolved into the furs and feathers worn by hussar cavalry regiments [in the fifteenth century]. This however, has clearly developed into the very reverse of its original disguising purpose. (Newark et al. 1998: 9–10)

These early examples of camouflage combine hunting techniques and displays of prowess with the associated pre-modern forms of shamanism. Camouflage in the sense of blending into the background was – perhaps surprisingly – less common, although

> Vegetius records, in the 4th century, Roman efforts to counter barbarian pirates with camouflaged scouting craft which had their sails and rigging dyed blue and their crew similarly

disguised in blue tunics and painted faces. (Newark et al. 1998: 10)

As we will see, the concept of camouflage as a defining feature of military dress came quite late. Initially, the development of military dress in modern Europe developed alongside the emergence of civil society so military functions (attack and defence) were only one role of the military. They also symbolized the character (and health) of the political regime and of the authoritative command of the state. Equally important was the role of regulating civil conduct. Perhaps even more surprising was the fact that there has always been a connection between military uniforms and fashion. This was partly because the uniform was a relatively recent military device. After the fall of the Roman Empire, for centuries fighting men had worn everyday dress or dress that signified allegiance to their lord or monarch.

Glamour was often a characteristic of such dress with military garb heavily influenced by contemporary fashions and, in turn, the dress of the dashing soldier influencing civil fashions. Countless references can be found to the "dandy" element of soldiering gear where soldiers, commanders and units competed to outdo each other sartorially. When (hunting) green became a popular choice for soldiers in the late eighteenth century, the Duke of Wellington warned that "the soldiers will become conceited, and be wanting next to be dressed in green, or some other jack-a-dandy uniform" (quoted by Newark et al. 1998: 11). According to Ruth Bleckwenn (1978: 9) the rise of mercenaries (paid soldiers with no allegiances) led soldier's dress to blossom "into the realms of the fantastic". Heavily influenced by contemporary fashion, it consisted of a doublet, shirt, tight knee breeches, stockings, heel-less shoes and cap: "But it was the details that characterised the soldier."

Other armed forces followed this example. When the Swiss beat Charles the Bold, Duke of Burgundy, in 1476, the victors seized the booty of silk and luxury materials, "slashed it to pieces and used it to patch their own ragged clothes" (Laver 1995: 77). Later, slashing was refined as the practice of cutting slits in the material to expose inserts of colourful luxury fabrics. This practice became an art form that "imitate[ed] and surpass[ed] the *mi-parti* of court dress" (R. Bleckwenn 1978: 9). By slashing the fabric, the coloured inserts could be revealed:

This idea too was borrowed by the soldier from civilian fashion, but was exaggerated to the extent that it became the hallmark of military style. . . Doublet, hose, vest, even shoe and cap could be decorated in this way. . . Thus every outfit worn by every soldier had its individual character. (R. Bleckwenn 1978: 9–10)

Slashing became popular among German mercenaries and then spread to the French court. By now it had become fashion. With the marriage of Henry VII's sister Mary to Louis XII of France, the English emulated "the *landsknecht* fashion also" (Laver 1995: 78). Other European states followed suit. Sleeves, breeches, skirts and cloaks were slashed to reveal extravagant panels. The fad was long-lived.[2] A self-portrait by Dutch artist, Frans van Mieris, painted between 1657 and 1659, depicts him as an officer wearing a black hat with blue satin trim, feathers and gold rim, and a "magnificent velvet doublet with . . . satin lining" and slashed sleeves revealing a white satin shirt (Middelkoop 1997: 96–7). Clearly there is an overlap between the artist's self-projection not only as an important person of substance but also as one of style and good taste.

It was not until the beginning of "model armies" and modern methods of warfare showed the advantages of "absolute uniformity" among soldiers that the idea of dressing them the same took hold: "so essential a characteristic of military dress that 'uniform' has become the everyday term for it" (R. Bleckwenn 1978: 9). Already there were differences in the dress of different kinds of military. Officers – usually on horseback – still wore armour and surcoat while senior infantrymen wore plainer unslashed surcoats. While the cavalry were still elaborately dressed, their military role was becoming less important.

In the second half of the sixteenth century, soldiers' dress changed along with a new approach to military tactics. Discipline, drill and formal procedures replaced the individualistic "cavalier" approach to soldiering. Infantry dress became plainer though still copying civilian fashion while other branches – pikemen,[3] musketeers and cavalry – each had a distinctive uniform (Carman 1977). This more basic approach was elaborated in the seventeenth century with more fashionable cuts and the addition of finery – "ribbons, rosettes, lace trimmings and buttons" (R. Bleckwenn 1978: 12). Officers remained more dashingly outfitted proudly displaying a coloured sash representing their commander and often wearing

Figure 7
Four naval officers.

different dress on the battlefield – the beginning of multiple dress codes for the military. According to Bleckwenn:

> This manner of dress, a mixture of a baroque love of delicate detail with a common-sense reaction to the harsh realities of warfare, became the model for male fashion in Europe between about 1630 and 1650. (R. Bleckwenn 1978: 12)

As the century progressed, the uniform of the infantry became plainer with less colourful garments and less decorative trimming: "with the benefit of hindsight, we can see here, already, the beginnings of modern military uniform" (R. Bleckwenn 1978: 12).

Military uniforms of the eighteenth century were shaped by wider economic and political forces. The idea of mass production of military gear had been pioneered in the Thirty Years War that dominated European politics and numerous countries from 1618 to 1648, and this inevitably led to the standardization of uniforms and dress codes. At the same time, European monarchs were exerting supreme authority and what better symbol than the existence of a standing army. Professional soldiers were supported by volunteers and pressed men, and all kitted out in the uniforms of the regime. France played an especially important role in the emergence of specialised military dress:

> Style in military uniform is strongly influenced by military success, as surely as in civilian life it follows fashion. Because France emerged from the Thirty Years' War as the undoubted victor, from 1670 the European soldiers adopted the *justau-corps*, or long woollen coat. (H. Bleckwenn 1978: 16)

This "remained the basis of military dress" and was popularized in civilian fashion as well. Coats came in white, red or blue and were set off by colourful facings and linings of cuffs, collars, lapels and coattails with embellishments in the form of buttons and trimmings of lace, braid and embroidery.

Glamour, Discipline, Modernity

One of the most intriguing aspects of the emergence of military dress is the incorporation of aspects of what Thomas Abler (1999) has called the ethnic fighting gear of "hinterland warriors". Not only did European armies enlist local warriors and fighters to assist their campaigns in unfamiliar locations and contexts, but also the clothing of the "natives" changed over time as did that of the European armies. The former gradually adopted a "stylized military" garb that retained the most distinctive elements of their hinterland dress but combined that with key elements of imperial military dress. Equally, the military uniforms of the imperial forces adopted aspects of hinterland dress, such as headdresses, animal furs, knee-length boots, feathers and the like. Dictionaries of items of military dress show the diverse cultural origins of uniforms. But why the uptake of "hinterland" and "native" dress by these supposedly "civilizing" forces? Abler (1999: 6) argues that it related to the ambiguous European stereotypes of 'frontier peoples" as both "noble savage" (the positive concept) and "merciless savage" (the negative concept). According to Abler, this ambiguity produced significant sartorial and strategic advantages for troops decked out in "frontier" splendour – not to mention seductive connotations (Abler 1999: 14–15).

The most spectacular example of military fetish can be seen in the idolatry of the Hussars – Hungarian light cavalry with striking or showy uniforms (cf. Abler 1999: 23–46). Hussars emerged in the early fifteenth century as elite roving cavalry soldiers circulating in central Europe. They quickly became renowned as "dazzlingly uniformed" (H. Bleckwenn 1978: 40) in ever changing but stunning colourful *dolman* jackets with two rows of gold buttons and decorated with colourful white, red or yellow braid. As well, they wore a cape (*pelisse*) sometimes made of panther or other animal skin and worn over the left shoulder. The dolman had a stand-up collar and pointed cuffs in contrasting colour. Calf-length leather boots, a cap with cockade and leather satchel (*sabretache*) completed the look. Hussars were well trained in "defence, reconnaissance and skirmishing" (H. Bleckwenn 1978: 42) and were much in demand for their reliability, skill and intelligence. Hussars became components of "most nineteenth century European armies" including the French, Italians and English, who had several regiments of Hussars or Corsairs "each attired in a differently hued and trimmed uniform" (David 2003: 12). Abler (1999: 28) identified Hussar regiments in Austria, Bavaria, France, Prussia, Wurttenberg, Russia, Sweden, Saxony, The Netherlands, Great Britain, Argentina and Mexico each dressed in highly colourful yet individually stylized uniforms (Abler 1999: 30–1).

These quintessentially glamorous uniforms complemented the amorous and fast-paced lives of the Hussars – reality and fantasy were inextricably mingled:

> The fact is that with their fur-lined coats, jackets, skin-tight breeches in showy colours, in many hues: sky blue, maroon, silver-grey, light green, royal blue, dark green, adorned with tresses, embroidery, braids, strips, *fourrageres* [fur trimming]; their silk belts in lively shades, coifed with their colbacks[4] . . . these young men well-cinched in their fashionable uniforms had a truly proud air. (Michel Ney, cited by David 2003: 12)

So stylish were the uniforms that they seemed to preclude any military engagement. Hussars became fashion icons rather than military heroes. Young men who had "absolutely no intention of risking themselves on any battlefield further away than the Palais-Royal, affect[ed] high military collars *a la hussarde* and tightly buttoned topcoats" (Steele 1988: 54; cf. Roche 1996: 243). Although denounced as frippery and a source of degeneracy, many men adopted the decorative excesses of military clothing while some bought second-hand officers' uniforms to cut "a dashing figure" and strut around (Myerly 1996: 149).

Figure 8
Derek Hughes, 1947.

As Daniel Roche (1996: 222) has argued in his seminal study of clothing in the Ancient Regime in France: "The history of uniform . . . deserves our attention since it is at the heart of the encounter between appearances and social discipline." The military uniform emerged in seventeenth-century France, initially as a means to readily identify opposing sides in battle. Soldiers wore clothes of the same colour tied at the waist, with similar headgear and other signs of membership on the hat and coat. From the outset, the uniforms of officers reflected trends in fashion as much as the practicalities of military engagements. They were inspired by an impulse to display elegance and indulge in adornments that changed in accordance with stylistic shifts.

Gradually, military leaders saw the benefits of extending standard uniforms to all soldiers as an apparatus to instil discipline by training the body and mind in specified ways (Roche 1996):

> The need to shape minds and bodies finds in uniforms a valuable aid: it is a training, an element in the education of controlled individual power . . . It is an instrument in a process designed to shape the physique and the bearing of [an] individual, whose autonomy conditions his docility and whose obedience transforms individual strength into collective power. (Roche 1996: 228–9)

So too, the military recognized the value of the uniform as a force of collective regulation in civil society. Ex-soldiers often chose to wear (part of) their uniforms in civilian life because they were of better quality than other clothes they possessed. Moreover, the uniform signified attributes of discipline and reliability, attributes that enhanced their employment and other prospects. The uniform "wholly identified the person with the social personage suggested by the costume" (Roche 1996: 224). The uniform was the visible lexicon of social characteristics, skills, attitudes and habits valued in civil society.

The uniform not only conveyed attributes of docility and repression, but also was an ideological instrument. In Maussian terms, the uniform created a persona in individuals and a powerful collective presence. The uniform became a means of shaping actions – both physical and mental – and instilling new habits, including movement and posture, developing an aesthetic sensibility and inculcating new habits of cleanliness. Roche (1998) argues that the uniform was a potent force in the transition from the Ancient Regime to the court society and its imposition of elaborate modes and manners that was intended to distinguish the court from the rest but in fact produced an embryonic civil society (cf. Elias 1983). In other words, it transformed manners in general.

Reforms in uniforms aimed at aligning movement and posture between body and garment. But it also reflected a new sense of public space, new ways of communicating between and within emerging class fractions, and new aesthetics associated with these changes. Colours became increasingly important to distinguish different units and offset the main colour – usually white, grey, blue or red. Facings and trimmings came in a multitude of colours, though over time the number of permitted colours was reduced although a complex taxonomy of which people were entitled to wear certain colours, fabrics or garments remained. Despite these variations some constant elements emerged, such as the preference for brass buttons and leather that required regular polishing and maintenance, the introduction of buttoned pockets for practicality, and the use of badges, pins, braid and gold thread to indicate status.

The design of the military uniform was central to its effectiveness both as a means to distinguish different sections of the forces, to denote rank and to instil very particular modes of caring for and presenting the uniformed personage. But, often uniforms proved to be "expensive and unsuitable, inconvenient and inefficient":

> Here we see the gulf between the ideal of the theoreticians and the reality of the barracks and the military tailors, where the decorative fought a constant battle with the utilitarian, and the desire to cut a fine figure was sometimes transformed into a passion to be different, hence, the misuse of collars, lapels, buttons and trimmings. (Roche 1996: 231)

Many of the elements found in *school uniforms* made an appearance during this period and became firmly entrenched as the epitome of uniforms as a clothing genre. These became the vestimentary signs of a modern sensibility and civil persona (cf. Elias 1983; see also Mauss 1973, 1985). Maintaining good uniform practice required a disciplined approach to their upkeep and etiquette. Over time, this radically altered attitudes to clothing among the ranks and prompted something of a consumer revolution. The concern with clothing and appearance gradually leaked into civilian life in which the aesthetic of military uniforms became an influential factor in the manifestation of ideas about style, fashion and elegance.

As we have seen, the uniform became a primary force in the establishment of the military as a political and administrative power in France. As soldiers circulated within civil society or re-entered civilian life, the power of uniforms also shaped the emergence of the pre-revolutionary populace. During the revolution, uniforms again played a key role. Although rejecting existing military colours and styles, wearing revolutionary colours was gradually absorbed into new outfits that announced the revolutionaries. Thus, by their ability to shape the habits of the body and the mind, uniforms "could serve to tame violence and be a tool of progress" (Roche 1996: 256; cf. Martin 1978; Wrigley 2002: 68–74).

Britain, too, developed military uniforms during this period and these designs gradually shaped male civilian dress. Breward (1995: 86) argues that British men's fashion in the 1690s stabilized as a knee-length coat, waistcoat and breeches adorned with "discrete decorative buttons and occasional military frogging" that would become "a sober patriarchal model for gentlemen interested in, but not obsessed by fashion, through much of the succeeding century". By the late eighteenth century, there was an "increasingly military appearance of elite masculine dress" (Breward 1995: 118). While military-style fashion declined after 1815, many military motifs have become staples in the language of fashion. As Hollander (1978: 474) notes: "lapels, cuffs, straps, pocket flaps, extra buttons, buckles, and sometimes rings have become traditional decorative elements in tailored informal clothing for both sexes during two centuries of stylistic modification." Gradually, then, we can see that military motifs circulated in representational forms as both a symbol of social status and authority and came to be encapsulated in fashionable looks that were emulated in non-military dress, gestures and looks (cf. Spicer 1993; McDowell 1997). As Myerly (1996) concludes:

> The overall impact of military design on civilian dress has thus been most significant, and gentlemen's fashions in

Figure 9
American soldiers and
civilian.

> Britain (and Europe as a whole) have been fundamentally
> influenced by the clothing of officers or huntsmen. (Myerly
> 1996: 149)

However, this military influence did not mean that men's fashion
was dreary and staid. On the contrary, David (2003) has argued
that fashionable sensibilities shaped the design of uniforms in post-
revolutionary France (1790s) and that fashionable uniforms not
only made military personnel highly desirable but also heavily
influenced civilian fashion: "Decorated and decorative men were
an integral part of the landscape in the latter half of the [nineteenth]
century" (David 2003: 4). Moreover, contemporary military dress
celebrated rather than renounced extroverted display: "flamboyant
exhibitions and fantasy were central to the identity of the
nineteenth-century military man" (David 2003: 5). According to
Martin (1978: 77), "the French had a tendency to treat clothing
regulations of the day with a lassitude, amounting almost to a
native *fantaisie*, in the decoration or transformation of various
details." David cited a contemporary art historian, Charles Blanc,
who observed that:

> Soldiers and their officers are still compelled to avow, by their
> different coloured uniforms, their original purpose, as shown
> in their style of dress, of slaying their fellow creatures. (Blanc,
> cited by David 2003: 6)

Comments like this suggest that the influence of military uniforms
became increasingly pronounced from the Napoleonic era 1795–
1815 (cf. Hollander 1978: 228; Steele 1988: 54). The officers
commissioned their own uniforms both from military tailors and
civil tailors leading to extraordinary competition among officers
for the most elaborate and outstanding outfits.

The Napoleonic era itself was the crowning glory of military
uniforms, composing "the most elaborate display of pomp in the
whole history of the military dress" (Klessmann 1978: 101).
Observers were stunned by the extravagance, attention of detail
and visual impact and allure of military uniforms. At this time more
than any other, military uniforms – not only in their singular
elegance but especially in their massed display – became the focus
of aesthetic sensibilities. The military uniform – in all its splendour
– represented the *zeitgeist* of post-revolutionary Europe and a
mainstay of aesthetic sensibilities more generally.

Under this mesmeric influence, the design of military uniforms
in Europe underwent considerable change in the nineteenth century. The association of colours with nations was already established – blue (Prussia), red (Great Britain), white (Austria and
Russia) and white or blue (France). But this period saw greater
standardization of uniforms and the elimination of individual
proclivities of commanders – for example, different coloured
linings and facings were, in part, replaced by "regimental numbers
on buttons and on head-dress" (Klessmann 1978: 101). At this
time, it also became standard practice to issue three uniforms: dress
uniform, active service uniform and barracks uniforms (Klessmann
1978: 108). This diversification of uniforms became the spring-
board for the adaptation of uniforms to particular military circumstances later on.

Despite the trend towards standardization, some individuality
still remained. One of Napoleon's marshals, Bernadotte Berthier,
for example, sartorially competed with his leader by commissioning
an extravagant special uniform for his regiment. The designer,
Louis-Francois Lejune, chose a black coat, white dolman with gold
braid, scarlet breeches and shako (with heron feathers) and black

silk sash with gold barrels. Their horses – "after the manner of the hussars" – had panther-skin saddlecloths "with scalloped red and gold edging" (Klessmann 1878: 113). Others, too, cherished individuality – some, like Joachim Murat (Marshal of France, Grand Duke of Berg, King of Naples and head of the French cavalry), wore a different uniform every day like "a brightly coloured parrot" (Klessmann 1978: 113). The Hussars continued to display their difference by their distinctive uniforms.

Things were not quite as splendid as existing historical records seemed. Troops, *en masse*, tended to make a poor picture with uniforms faded and dirtied by sun, rain and mud. Dyes were only partially colourfast and faded: "In reality the colours of contemporary battles are misleading: in reality, the colours of most scenes of carnage must have been a dirty grey-brown" (Klessmann 1978: 133). Over time, military uniforms became even plainer although some retained "tiger-skin saddle cloths and leopard-skin helmet trimmings" persisted (Klessmann 1978: 136). In fact, many of the essential features of the Napoleonic period became integral features of military uniforms of the subsequent era.

Napoleonic uniforms turned the muscular upper torso into a peacock-like display of colour and power. Uniforms were the ultimate in glamour. Hollander (1978: 228) observes that naval and military uniforms in the 1800s were "admirably suited to the rather sexually explicit display of men's bodies." Above all, the tight white doeskin trousers drew attention to the crotch. Not only were women attracted to men in uniforms, but also they were attracted to the sharp silhouette created by uniforms themselves. Some women wore "actual uniforms" such as canteen women in the Second Empire (1852-70), namely "knee-length skirts over full-length trousers . . . [with jackets matching] the regiments they followed" (David 2003: 14). Some fashionable women wore female versions of men's uniforms. Later on:

> Fashionable women wore clothes derived from the popular rifle regiments' uniforms, such as green-velvet rifle dresses and hats, and from hussar uniforms and headgear, of which the pelisse (originally the hussars' braided outer jacket, richly laced and lined and faced in fur) is now a much-altered survival. This trend continued into the Regency, and in Scotland noblewomen reflected the pride taken in the highland regiments' performance at Waterloo by wearing highland

Figure 10
Dick and Jack in
China, 1931.

jackets and plumed bonnets; a new colour, "Waterloo blue,"
was also adopted for high fashion. The Crimean War later
inspired another new colour, "Alma brown," and in 1856,
leather belts, thick military heels, and jackets modelled on
dragoons' dress became fashionable. The cardigan sweater
and raglan sleeve proved to be more enduring contributions
to ladies' fashions. (Myerly 1996: 149–50)

After Napoleon's crowning as emperor (1804), court dress elaborated military derivation for men combining "military stiffness with
aristocratic luxury. Napoleon's own clothes tended toward uniforms, both civil and military" (Steele 1988: 54). In response to
this sartorial – as well as military threat – Britain created its own
vestimentary icons. According to McDowell (1997: 56): "The cult
of the modern hero was spun round Nelson and Wellington as the
perfection of masculinity: the romantic man of action." The link
between masculine ideals and military power was conveyed through
dress and style codes in which the uniform was deeply embedded

(Hume 1997). There was a gradual decline of styles of the Ancient
Regime and republic replaced by a return to romanticism and the
neo-Gothic (Steele 1988: 54).

The earlier emphasis on bold colours gave way to a focus on cut.
Officers' uniforms retained small colourful trims for offsetting
effect or to denote rank. Over time, uniforms conveyed authority,
status and hierarchy through predominantly subdued colours –
black, grey, blue, white and khaki – with the use of contrasting
bright colours for neckties, linings, headwear, decorative effects and
medals. This striking combination made French military dress "the
envy of Europe" and sparked a design war among European
nations to make their military dress "more dazzling, multicoloured
and glittering than before" (McDowell 1997: 78–9):

> Chests were padded, waists whittled, thighs encased in
> skintight breeches and calves in shiny leather boots. Then
> came the trimmings: silver aiguillettes [ornamental tags], gold
> epaulettes, fringing, piping, complicated intertwined sword
> knots, velvet facings, silver and gold buttons, frogging, lacing,
> silk lapels and, above all, bearskins, shakoes,[5] crested helmets
> and waving plumes.
>
>   The colours were just as extravagant. Jackets, pelisses and
> trousers could, it seemed, be any colour under the sun: cherry
> red, sky blue, brilliant yellow rich green, crimson, dove grey,
> indigo. (McDowell 1997: 78–9)

McDowell suggests that this love affair with the spectacle of the
uniform and display of masculine attributes stemmed from the
heady alignment of heroism, muscularity, sexual prowess and
titillation: men in uniform became sex objects. The Napoleonic
period had institutionalized the uniform in European societies not
only as a weapon of power and might but also more importantly
as the key component of contemporary aesthetics of display,
spectacle and fashion (cf. Myerly 1996).

This trend continued. In 1870, Tissot painted the military hero,
Frederick Gustavus Burnaby, "as a male fashion plate, resplendent
in the authority of his dress uniform, lolling elegantly at his ease"
(McDowell 1997: 68). According to McDowell, this image captured "archetypal male flamboyance – controlled, understated but
unmistakable – using flashes of gilding and colour to enhance and
flatter the shape and proportions of the man." He argued that this

"impressive sartorial presence" created an *esprit de corps* in the military creating a camaraderie, which gave military uniforms "appeal" as fashion. For example, military uniforms reappeared in London's Swinging Sixties (see Chapter 8). For David:

> The number of military fashion influences is not surprising, for few forms of clothing, male or female, could compete with the visual impact and sexual allure of the officer's full-dress uniform. (David 2003: 16)

Functionality, Sexuality, Colonization

Military uniforms themselves became highly elaborated with different uniforms for different occasions and highly specific meanings attached to particular elements of uniforms. These circulated initially in the military but soon informed general fashion trends. The nineteenth century saw challenges to European styles of warfare and military uniforms posed by serial conflicts in the new world colonies. Britain, for example, experienced ninety years of conflicts in Canada, Afghanistan, New Zealand, Burma, India, South Africa and India (Barthorp 1978). The harsh terrain and extreme climatic differences coupled with unorthodox means of fighting exacerbated the impact of battle.

The stylish and colourful uniforms did not help. They were impractical, climatically unsuited to extreme heat and cold, and made the soldiers easy targets. Uniform modifications inevitably occurred but in a much more piecemeal and individualistic way than might have been expected. Many soldiers chose to wear their barracks or "undress" uniform for fighting rather than active service uniform because they were more comfortable. Bright colours were eschewed. Headwear was modified – some soldiers would purposefully lose their helmets and replace them with khaki fabric over a forage cap – or wet towels wrapped as a turban (Barthorp 1978: 145).[6] Loose fitting tunics worn over trousers or pantaloons proved more comfortable in hot climates – especially if they were dyed a "khaki" or sandy colour in local bazaars. Before the development of colourfast khaki dye, a range of "dyes" were used including mud, tea leaves, coffee and inks producing a range of colours – browns, greys, lavender and off-white (Barthorp 1978: 146).

Figure 11
Police in Shanghai, 1920.

These ingenious ad hoc solutions meant that imperial forces were not as uniform or as glamorous as often depicted. But nor did it instantly lead to the formal modification of uniforms. Although khaki was widely used during the Indian Mutiny of 1857–9, there was no subsequent attempt to introduce a khaki uniform for active service until 1896 (Barthorp 1978: 145, 147, 155). It was then only in the twentieth century in the lead-up to the First World War that uniforms were modified into less formal garments made of khaki serge with slouch hats or peaked khaki caps,[7] making "the British soldier . . . the most sensibly dressed and accoutred fighting man in Europe" at the outbreak of war (Barthorp 1978: 156).

Not all armies followed this example. The French retained their distinctive colourful uniforms even after their defeat in the Franco-Prussian war of 1870–1, and during subsequent political turmoil. Even in the first world war, the French army favoured style over the utilitarian uniforms (camouflage, khaki, grey, protective headgear, waterproof boots) adopted by the German and allied armies alike until the realities of bitter conditions forced modifications: "The ornaments that had been the French army's glory finally disappeared in the mud of trench warfare" (David 2003: 33). Over time, all the mass armies fighting the war adopted similar kinds of uniforms with more of an eye to practicality, cost and serviceability than previously (Rosignoli 1978a, 1978b).

As we have seen, military uniforms convey symbols of authority, status and power by constructing clean lines and a handsome silhouette. Totalitarian regimes worldwide quickly recognized the value of the discipline of uniforms to transform thugs and riff-raff into disciplined and obedient teams. But uniforms also sometimes result in excess and licentious behaviour, resulting for example in unjustified use of force, interrogation techniques, torture, rape and massacres. As well as legitimizing the exercise of excessive behaviour, military uniforms may invite symbols of eroticism and fetishism. And it is this hidden dimension that explains their pervasive appeal and appropriation in popular culture and particularly in fashion. This is discussed further in Chapters 8 and 9.

When Hitler came to power in 1933, the design of military uniforms became a key symbol of totalitarian power in Germany. Immense effort and cost went into designing distinctive outfits that created strong bonds of allegiance. Uniforms were not confined to the military. Hitler had established the Hitler Jugend (Hitler Youth) in 1923, a movement to train young German boys and girls "in the spirit of National Socialism" and Nazi propaganda of racial and national superiority in order to produce a generation of "victorious active, daring youth, immune to pain". Initially a voluntary organization, Hitler Youth became compulsory for German young people in 1933. Membership grew from 1,000 in 1923 to 8 million in 1939 at the outbreak of the Second World War. For boys, rigorous physical training, drill and an introduction to military procedures (marching, camping, scouting, games, civil service) were undertaken. The uniform was a key component of the training. Borrowing from English scouting, which in turn drew on military uniforms, the uniform consisted of a black peaked cap worn with "a brown shirt and arm band, black shorts, and white kneesocks. There were great variations. Some were seasonal variations and others were modifications in the uniform over time" (Wagner 2002b).

Nazis in uniforms looked highly desirable with streamlined silhouettes in their tight jackets with high collars, peak caps, jodhpurs and black leather boots, symbolizing the power and authority of the regime. A number of leading Nazis were camp and engaged in transgressive sexual practices. As Garber (1992) speculates, there was a constellation of factors that eroticized uniforms:

> Whatever the specific semiotic relationship between military uniforms and erotic fantasies of sartorial gender, the history of cross-dressing within the armed services attests to a complicated interplay of forces, including male bonding, acknowledged and unacknowledged homosexual identity,

carnivalised power relations, the erotics of same-sex com-
munities, and the apparent safety afforded by theatrical
representation. (Garber 1992: 55–6)

Despite the best efforts of the regime, Nazi uniforms became
fetishized and a staple feature of cabaret, film, pornography,
fashion design and sexual perversion.[8] A uniform designed to
mould a new nation and "pure race" became a symbol of impurity,
threat, perversion and cruelty within popular culture.

The line between presenting a desirable image in uniform and
desiring the uniformed body was widespread. The English author,
Quentin Crisp,[9] recalled his desire for "something in a uniform"
(Garber 1992: 57):

> He especially liked sailors, whose profligacy with money was
> an irresistible lure – especially when combined with the
> tightness of their uniforms, whose crowning aphrodisiac
> feature was the fly-front of their trousers. More than one of
> my friends has swayed about in ecstasy describing the pleas-
> ure of undoing this quaint sartorial device. (Garber 1992: 57)

Uniforms were effective tools to arouse sexual interest. As Bell
(1976: 43) put it: "There is a good deal of evidence to show that
a handsome uniform exerts a devastating effect upon the opposite
sex." And because of the importance of military activity in nation-
building, Bell argued that "at different moments in the history of
modern Europe, the costume of a gentleman has, with very little
modification, been that of an officer or a huntsman."

There is also a growing literature charting the role of uniforms
in explicit and covert dress codes in colonial and postcolonial
contexts. Very often, colonists imposed dress codes that combined
aspects of the officials' naval or military uniforms with elements
of local dress. Sometimes, indigenous rulers chose to wear European uniforms. For example, in the 1860s, Cambodia's King
Norodom I was photographed in a French field marshal's uniform.
Ten years later, he wore a French general's cap and jacket with a
sampot (Edwards 2001). Still later, administrators adopted the
colonial suit as their uniform. In some cases, locals used the
adoption of westernized dress codes in order to curry favour with
the colonists. Equally, dress codes were a means of social control
by colonists over the colonized. Dress codes were also resorted to

Figure 12
Major McKenzie in India,
1944.

as a means of expressing nationalistic and indigenous claims (Bean 1989; Callaway 1997; Schulte Nordholt 1997b; Edwards 2001).

Cohn (1989: 304) has traced the role of clothing in Britain's colonization of India, arguing that the dispute about the Sikh's turban was emblematic of clothing skirmishes in colonial India that eventually led to "the creation of a uniform of rebellion by the Indians in the twentieth century". At first, the British chose to dress distinctively in order to emphasise their difference from the locals, but soon, the exchange of clothing and cloth was recognized as a means to negotiate power:

> Clothes are not just body coverings and adornments, nor can they be understood only as metaphors of power and authority, nor as symbols; in many cases, clothes literally *are* authority . . . Authority is literally part of the body of those who possess it. It can be transferred from person to person through acts of incorporation, which not only create followers or subordinates, but a body of companions of the ruler

who have shared some of his substance. (Cohn 1989: 312–
13; cf. Schulte Nordholt 1997a: 9)

In establishing their colonial power, British rulers modified English
modes of ceremonial dress to bestow on "deserving" Indians while
they borrowed some aspects of Indian dress for modified forms of
ruling dress. But when Indian princes visited Queen Victoria at
Windsor, they "were required . . . to appear in their 'traditional'
Indian royal dress rather than Western clothes" (Cohn 1989: 321).
This two-way exchange of sartorial signs also occurred in the
military with British troops adopting some "Indian" affectations
(e.g. cummerbunds and *puggrees* – linen covers wrapped around
their wicker helmets or cloth caps and hats" and even turbans and
scimitars (Cohn 1989: 324), while Indian troops were dressed in
plain British military uniforms or as British fantasies of how exotic
people should look. Not surprisingly, when the push for Indian
independence came, part of the struggle was a sartorial one with
distinctive dress ("a *khadi* 'uniform' – a white handspun cotton
dhoti, *sari* or *pajama*, *kurta* and a small white cap" (Cohn 1989:
343)) singling out activists and eventually, Gandhi introducing "the
uniform of the Indian National Congress" (Cohn 1989: 344). By
manipulating the meaning of cloth and clothing, Bean (1989: 373)
suggests that "*khadi* had become, in Nehru's words, 'the livery of
freedom'."

In these processes, codes of civil dress and "uniform fever" were
an essential tool in the transformation of far-flung outposts. Some
genres, such as the safari suit and the sarong, have become perma-
nent legacies of this era (Frederick 1997; Sekimoto 1997; van Dijk
1997). While men were more likely to be subject to explicit codes
or uniforms, dress codes were also applied informally though often
ruthlessly among women (Callaway 1997; Locher-Scholten 1997;
Taylor 1997). Among girls, as Chapter 3 argues, the imposition of
school uniforms proved an effective technique for instilling westernized attitudes – especially about gendered identities and codes
of conduct that were being instilled by the colonial administrations.

The role of military uniforms in contemporary culture persists.
There have been two main preoccupations. As guerrilla tactics has
once again transformed warfare, electronic tracking and weapons
of mass destruction, the need for camouflage has become supreme
(Rosignoli 1978c; Newark et al. 1998). In the first world war,
camouflage was trialled only by painting disruptive patterns on

equipment and transport – apart from German Storm Troopers who hand-painted their helmets in bright colours and geometric designs for purposes of disguise (Newark et al. 1998: 15–16). It was not until the 1930s that the German Waffen SS experimented with different types of camouflage design with the plane-tree pattern and the oak-leaf pattern being the first. Once tests proved the decline of casualties could be attributed to camouflage uniforms, other designs were developed, including the tiger stripe, the ringed oak-leaf pattern, the palm-tree pattern and the frog pattern.

Different patterns and different colour combinations were selected for different war fronts. Camouflage really took off during the Cold War and refined during the Vietnam War (e.g. tiger stripe, duck hunter and woodland-style leaf pattern) with all armies devising unique designs. After the formation of NATO and the end of the Cold War, urban camouflage and desert camouflage were also developed and refined during the Gulf Wars (1990 and 2003) and Kosovo crisis. By the late 1990s, over 350 camouflage patterns existed worldwide with different armies specializing in particular designs (Newark et al. 1998: 36). Camouflage military uniforms have now become standard provision alongside a proliferation of uniform for dress, barracks and other special circumstances. The current issues for the design of military uniforms relates more to fabrics that can repel thermal imaging and environmentally adjusting fabrics that can automatically respond to changes in the surrounds (cf. contemporary advances on sportswear as discussed in Chapter 6).

While camouflage has preoccupied contemporary armies, the stylish nature of traditional uniforms has preoccupied many regimes in the quest to assert or maintain power. In Europe, traditional uniforms are often retained for ceremonial purposes as a symbol of history, pomp and tradition (as well as political power). Examples include the troops and guards of royalty – such as Britain's Guardsmen (in bearskin hats and elaborate red jackets with gold braid and black trousers), and accompanying contingents of Blues and Royals on horseback wearing brass helmets with plumes, breeches, over-the-knee boots, and fancy jackets and sash. While these displays of past (now reinvented) traditions have become tourist attractions as much as serving royal protocol, the impracticality of such dress should the troops be attacked or thrown from a horse has not swayed the retention of these uniforms.[10] In a similar display of maintaining the symbol of power

Figure 13
Indonesian police.

and tradition, the Vatican is protected by the pontifical *halberdiers* of the Swiss Guard who are dressed in silver helmets with red plumes, silver armour with white neck ruff worn over blue and yellow striped tunics, pantaloons and stockings, worn with white gloves and holding a spear.[11] Examples such as these confirm the abiding allure of uniforms however esoteric and impractical as important markers of status, authority and tradition.

Military Uniforms and Civil Life

So we can see that military uniforms still hold a central place in contemporary sartorial, ritualistic and communicative arrangements as a means of conveying power relations, status, authority and role. These symbols have extended into many aspects of civil life. For example, the Salvation Army – itself an interesting choice of nomenclature – dispenses welfare and raises money with "officers" dressed in traditional militaristic uniforms. Developed out of the Christian Mission, the organization adopted its name in 1878 along with its "quasi-military style and outlook". Formed by

William Booth, its first general, the Salvation Army has retained its military look and structure, with members adopting military ranks (e.g. major, captain, commissioner, territorial commander) along with its military uniforms.[12] Men wore a navy-blue serge tunic with a stiff collar over a scarlet jersey (with a military cap with a red band and Salvation Army insignia in gold). Women wore long navy skirts, close-fitting high-neck tunics with white lace collars, and black straw bonnets with a red band and huge ribbon bow. In many countries the Army established a specialist-tailoring department to ensure standardization of dress.

As "onward Christian soldiers marching off to war", adherents saw themselves as civilian equivalents to fighters for moral and spiritual upliftment and saviours of lost and troubled souls – "overcoming and banishing wickedness". Although the organization is now primarily a major service and charity provider worldwide, it has retained many of the aspects of its early uniforms. Uniforms are now diverse (including white, grey, beige and safari jackets and shorts or saris) – indeed, some wear no uniform – but many still cling to modified versions of the original uniform. Arguably early the adoption and retention of a military-influenced uniform has lent credibility and authority to a civilian welfare organization.[13]

An example mentioned previously was the scouting movement. Formed by a former member of the English 13th Hussars – and resplendent in Hussar ceremonial uniform[14] – Lord Robert Baden-Powell became synonymous with the organization he established. Baden-Powell had a distinguished war record and became something of a war hero with his "aptitude for and enjoyment of irregular warfare" against the Boers during the siege of Mafeking.[15] He wrote a booklet called *Aids to Scouting* detailing his methods and was surprised to find that it became popular among young boys who formed small groups to practise his techniques. Drawing on similar organizations (the Boys' Brigade, Woodcraft Indians, Sons of Daniel), Baden-Powell formally set up the Boy Scouts in 1907 and published a handbook, *Scouting for Boys*, the following year. This programme of camping, outdoor activities, bush-craft, signalling, tracking and story-telling spread like wild fire and within a year there were scouting groups in Ireland, Australia, Canada, New Zealand and South Africa. In 1909, 11,000 British scouts rallied at Crystal Palace resulting in a knighthood for Baden-Powell and immortality (Wagner 2003a). Later scouting spread to many non-Anglo-Saxon countries creating something of an issue for the colonialist ideology of scouting.

The emergence of this specific idea of masculinity hinged on the conjunction between uniform discipline and physical training. Central to scouting was the quasi-militaristic training and uniforms for Baden-Powell thought that British youth were degenerating into "physically and morally weakened" characters with growing urbanization – and the difficulties British troops were having meeting the challenges of new styles and conditions of warfare (Wagner 2003j). Baden-Powell was concerned about the so-called "boy problem" and the need for "character training" to instil appropriate attributes of "manliness" (Warren 1987: 200-1). He sought to create a "manly character" in scouts as latter day "young knights" by instilling "individual self-discipline and improvement" by acquiring "an easy self-confident gait" as he strode "purpose-fully towards adult life" (Warren 1987: 217, 201). He emphasised the following attributes: training in the outdoors; practical skills and learning; personal health and fitness; individualistic basis of pursuits, sport and games; and good citizenship (Warren 1987: 201–2).

The first scout uniforms followed the drab khaki look (military-style khaki shirts and shorts) of the English army though soon added the now trademark coloured kerchief and toggle. Rigorous maintenance and inspection of uniforms became one of the defining features of scouting, so again we see the replication of militarism in organizational practices and dress. As scouting spread across the world, uniforms began to diverge to suit local priorities and conditions however some features recur: the kerchief and toggle, headwear (cap, beret, slouch hat), epaulettes, button-down pockets, badges, insignia, khaki or similar hues, leather belts, etc.[16] On the other hand, scouts wore boyish long socks (also worn by colonial administrators)[17] and lace-up shoes (like school shoes) which, with their boyish shorts, underlined their transitional status from boys to men.

Scouting manuals emphasised the correct way to wear the uniform. Good practice was maintained via regular inspections, sanctions and punishments for incorrect or sloppy appearance and an extreme emphasis on correct ironing of pleated garments and enthusiastic polishing of shoes, brass buckles and badges. The long-term success of scouting and its extension to older boys (rovers) and girls suggests the central place of uniforms – and rules of

Figure 14
Ambulance Service
Commissioner.

wearing them – in gender training in Anglo-Saxon and European-style modernity. Militarism thus influenced the formation of scouting as a means to cope with the pressures of modernity and in the longer term, scouting's military motifs influenced youth culture and youth fashion, especially the preference for short pants which was "to dominate boys' clothing in Europe for five decades" (Wagner 2003a).

While scouts and similar self-improvement organizations based on military principles may have gone out of fashion, there are still many examples of military influence in civilian life and new types of organizations and activities. Thus, we see the adoption of military-styled uniforms by civil security forces, prison officers, park rangers, zookeepers, parking inspectors and immigration and customs officers as occupational dress (discussed in Chapter 7). Even environmental restoration volunteers, such as the Green Corps, a federally funded programme in Australia to train young people in conservation techniques, wear khaki military-style shirts with Green Corps insignia, khaki trousers and slouch hat – virtually indistinguishable from military issue, suggesting an overlap in ideas of military influence over conservation techniques or the "quest" together to redress environmental degradation.[18]

Some of the most curious uptakes of European military uniforms has been outside Europe, for example, the adoption of severe quasi-military dress by peasants in the Maoist Chinese revolution (discussed in Chapter 8). In countries in Africa, the Middle East, Asia and South America, "instant" military traditions have been erected on the visible face of elaborate uniforms that like especially to draw on Napoleonic and Hussar stylistic flourishes. Many such uniforms are overtly "over-the-top" as well as being decorated with countless (usually self-awarded) medals and other decorations (for example, Argentina, Libya, North Korea, Philippines and Russia). Often, the regimes involved balance the wearing of European-style military uniforms with the adoption of "traditional" tribal, ethnic or chieftain dress – with the appropriate look chosen strategically for each occasion (cf. Maynard 2004: 54–8 and her discussion of the dress of politicians such as South Africa's Nelson Mandela, Palestine's Yasser Arafat, Indonesia's Abdurrahman Wahid and the ceremonial "traditional ethnic" jackets at international meetings). To meet competing agendas, leaders such as Libya's Colonel Gaddafi sometimes elect to wear a military uniform under their customary robes.

Finally, the military look has had a profound influence on fashion, particularly for men. Of all the uniform "looks", the military one remains the most desirable perhaps because of the heroism associated with war and the acts of soldiers. But, the question remains, has civilian dress influence military uniforms or vice versa? According to commentators, the influence of military uniforms on civilian fashion has been "back and forth" (Wagner 2000). Many enduring influences occurred during conflicts or immediately after. Some influences have long resonances, for example, the sailor suit which has not only persisted in naval uniforms but also been a mainstay of civilian fashion, school uniforms and theatrical dress. Generally, we can say that many of what we regard as the canonical features of military uniforms have entered the features and language of fashion and everyday dress. And yet historians of military dress consistently cite civilian fashion as inflecting particular uniforms and codes of dress (e.g. Wagner 2000).

Push and pull factors have shaped the development of uniforms. In early military uniforms, the need to create a uniform identity (or at least one where the contending sides could be identified) was the overriding impetus. Such uniforms drew heavily on idealized or adapted civilian fashions, perhaps because the uniforms were cherished items that could also be worn in civilian life. According to Wagner (2000), during the American Civil War, the uniforms on the Union side changed with civilian fashion except for the Zouave uniforms that had a French North African influence (due presumably to colonial occupation of the region). On the other side, the Confederates typically wore everyday dress, although in the latter stages, even they adopted elaborate uniforms, such as that parodied by black American rock guitarist Jimi Hendrix (discussed in Chapter 8).

By the first world war, the fashion system and industry was palpable. Inevitably, it was civilian fashion that influenced military uniforms although these retained the essential feature of the late nineteenth century. One particularly notable innovation was the split between utility and dress uniforms as standard issue. By the Second World War, utility was more important than fashion in shaping uniform codes, though even here, civilian influences – and subversions reflected fashion priorities. After the Second World War, a much more systematic approach to military uniforms could be seen, but even so, retrospectively, links with fashion moments are to the fore. This is especially so when considering the increasing divergence between utility and dress uniforms. Whereas the former are happily guided by utilitarian and practical concerns, the latter are typically a reinvention of past military traditions.

Uniforms of the US military have undergone recent changes, the first since 1981. Led by the marines in 2001, the army introduced a new combat uniform in 2004 (Ackerman 2004; Burgess 2004; The Straits Times 2004; USAREUR 2004; USA Today 2004). The new uniform introduces a digitally devised camouflage ("digi-cammies") uniform (in light green, tan and grey) for all troops in any theatre of engagement. The "computerized digital printout of pixels . . . blends better into the environment than the traditional large splotches" (Burgess 2004). Many of the features of the traditional uniform have gone by the wayside, The new uniform is "wash-and-wear, rip-stop cotton-and-polyester blend fabric" (Burgess 2004). Jackets have a mandarin collar that can be turned up or down, zip-up front, slanted pockets and patches and tabs fastened with Velcro. Underneath is worn a moisture-wicking desert tan T-shirt. Trousers are cargo-style with below-calf, tilted pockets, drawstring waist and elasticized ankles. Suede boots (lined with goretex for cold climates) replace the usual black shiny boots. A beret (patrol cap) replaces the giggle hat. The changes are designed for soldiers who are "bigger and more muscular" and to make the wearing of Interceptor body armour more comfortable. While the new uniform may set a new trend in uniforms in time – and percolate into fashion – some commentators have concluded that "it looks more like a pair of pyjamas" (Ackerman 2004).

Female military personnel still wear uniforms largely shaped by the masculine idea of the military uniform and iconic ideas of masculinity. This remains a field for research and a contentious issue, particularly in the light of the active role that women are playing in armed services worldwide. Overall, however, we can conclude that the influence has mostly been *from* civilian *to* military. When the civilian role (especially in the case of women differs dramatically from that of men), issues of attitude, disposition and conduct may well develop out of the uniformed self of any military personnel.

But whereas the most elegant and ceremonial uniforms once inspired fashion, contemporary influences both *dissect* the components of uniforms – military jackets, trousers, utility belts, vests with pockets and pouches, knapsacks, forage caps, epaulettes, button down pockets, leather accessories and boots, braid, buttons, etc. – other influences have come from the *new style* of camouflage warfare and the uniforms of *less glamorous* war fronts. Aspesi (2000: 151) argues that this pastiche mutes the seriousness and horror of war, renouncing symbols of "heroism, daring, the spirit of sacrifice, but instead pursues and seduces with its hedonistic and sexual lures". Paradoxically, then, literature on wars and military uniforms is not read by

> war-mongering maniacs, but often by fashion designers. There is not an ankle boot, a pocket, a turned-up shirtsleeve, shoulder, bag, belt, beret, overalls, T-shirt, or knapsack – all items that have featured prominently in the mass fashions of the past few years – that wasn't copied from these savage souvenirs of the killing fields, proof once again of how a people at peace can forget the true meaning of war. (Aspesi 2000: 151)

More generally, this is my point entirely.

3

School Uniforms and Docile Bodies

Uniforms and Pedagogy

When will you get it into your heads
That wearing suit and school tie sets
You on the way to social status,
Wealth, career, success?
The school tie focuses the mind
It helps you learn, retain and find
The knowledge for your TEE[1]
To which you are consigned.
So as your years at school pass by
Your sport, your uniform, your tie,
For some office high.

(Poem by Volker Mattar, Australian
Broadcasting Corporation
(ABC) 1996)

This chapter is concerned with the role of school uniforms in shaping the self to create conditions for the habitus of the docile body.[2] Of course, not all schools or school systems have a school uniform, suggesting that school uniforms are part of a particular pedagogic approach to teaching and learning in certain cultural contexts, especially those associated with an Anglo-Saxon heritage, with militaristic or totalitarian regimes or with those that borrowed from this tradition. So, why the school uniform? The concept the school uniform has several connotations including discipline and authority; order and distinctiveness; role models; gender training or performativity; and sensuality and perversion. This might seem like an odd array and one that is strangely anachronistic.

These themes are explored in terms of four questions: first, how and why did school uniforms develop and what role have they played in the formation of modern sensibilities? Second, why do school uniforms replicate themselves? Third, how do such uniforms inscribe gender and with what effects? Fourth, in what ways are school uniforms still relevant to contemporary culture? Such questions relate to the public face of uniforms but this chapter is also concerned with the private face or secret life of uniforms as loci of sexuality, sexual desire and sexual transgression. How can these different facets of uniforms be reconciled?

As discussed in Chapter 1, individuals acquire the attributes of the persona by prestigious imitation and the acquisition of a repertoire of body techniques. Clothes and modes of dress are important devices in acquiring specific trainings. School uniforms are an excellent example of how uniforms function as a cultural practice because of the centrality of the rules about what constitutes the components of the uniform plus rules about how uniforms should be worn. School uniforms depend on the disciplined habitus informing codes of wearing how they should be worn. Importantly, the adoption of school uniforms also entails the elaboration of techniques of surveillance and monitoring of uniform behaviour.

People who have worn school uniforms have very mixed reactions to those experiences. While they may be very proud of their visible membership of a particular school, they are often ambivalent about the uniforms themselves. Memories are often about how uncomfortable or impractical they were or chastisement or punishment for not wearing correct uniform or wearing it in the wrong way. In other words, the cultural work of school uniforms goes well beyond the garments but stems from the behavioural codes surrounding the uniform.

Figure 15
Welsh schoolboys.

More curious is the fact that – although based on military dress that strives for an elegant and disciplined look – school uniforms are typically "ugly and ill-fitting", as a colleague recently remarked (personal communication). So, why, if they evoke typically negative comments, are they so pervasive – or, at a minimum, not more aesthetically designed? Or is there something about their undesirability that is an essential part of the school uniform?

We have already discussed some examples of school uniform regulations. Here is another example: in a new planned "lifestyle" community in Australia, a Uniting Church private college prides itself on:

> Its very high dress standard and appearance standard which is maintained stringently. Students are encouraged to take pride in their uniform and in their appearance, and to strive for high standards of grooming and presentation. (Forest Lake College 2004: 3)

In a twenty page booklet, the uniform policies are elaborated. Students are required to wear full "yard" or "dress" uniform – or be issued with an "infringement notice". Many of the explanations of the uniform are by way of prohibitions: "no hat, no play", "joggers, shoes with stacked heels, T-bar and Doc Martens are not acceptable", "dress uniforms must be not less than mid calf", "no (girl's) midrift (sic) is to show", "bicycle shorts are not to be worn", "jewellery must not be worn" and so on. Rules about hair illustrate the minutiae of these codes:

> Hair should be neat, tidy and clean at all times. Hair must be one colour only. Extremes of style and/or colour are **not** acceptable. Boys' hair will be no shorter than a blade #3. Tracks, steps or wedges are **not** allowed. Hair length must be above the collar. Boys' hairstyles featuring hair all the same length are **not** permitted. Hairstyles that allow the hair to fall across the face or eyes are **not** permitted.

> Girls whose hair is longer than shoulder-length must wear it up. Ribbons or scrunchies must be in College colours. Very short hairstyles are **not** permitted. Hairstyles must **not** interfere with the appropriate wearing of the College hat.

> The Executive Principal reserves the right to determine whether a hairstyle is acceptable. A student may be asked to refrain from attending the College until his or her hairstyle is deemed acceptable. (Forest Lake College 2004: 10)

What is at stake in these rules? The rules eschew current hair fashions instead deriving from an implicit code of "hair modesty". Boys' hair cannot be cropped too short or shaved (is that because it would be too militaristic or too criminal/prisoner-like?) and it must not show any nods to fashionable cuts, colours or treatments. That it must not fall across the face suggests connotations of long hair and immorality – or slovenliness. The rules for girls are even more extreme. They too cannot have it short (not masculine?) and it must be tied back (in college ribbons) if it is long (controlled modesty?). Shoulder-length hair is preferred and normative – perhaps long hair is associated with the lack of discipline (or worse)? These rules confirm the argument posed here that uniforms are a major technology for not only controlling the body and its behaviour but also actively producing the particular attributes of the self that are deemed desirable by the school. Private schools promote themselves by appealing to the aspirational desires of the

Figure 16
Class photograph at
Breakfast Creek School,
Brisbane.

parents who elect to send their children there, for example, high-lighting their record of high academic achievements, high university entry of graduates, schools of excellence in specific activities (e.g. ballet, sport, language, music), "all round" education, and so on. Students are rigorously persuaded to accept the discipline of the school over that of the parents, conforming to dress codes and seeking not to stand out in the school assembly. So, official items of the uniform are preferred to approximations (e.g. designated school jacket or sweater rather than one of the same colour – and certainly not one that was hand-made or a hand-me-down). Increasingly, it is not just students who are chastised and forced to change their clothes; parents, too, are verbally dressed down for their child's vestimentary infractions. And mothers often complain of being ostracized by other mothers if they do not wear informal consensual codes of "appropriate" wear when picking up children or attending school events.[3] In other words, the school constructs a particular habitus that is formally articulated in the specialist training offered by the school and reinforced by informal codes of conduct.

Other dogmatic or affected rules about school uniforms merely confirm this explanation. Most people can recall idiosyncratic rules and penalties for infractions. Why should the top button under the tie be done up? Why should skirts touch the ground when kneeling? Why should girls wear not one but two pairs of underpants? Why should school hats be worn at a certain angle? Why should hair be above the collar for boys? Why should girls' hair be tied back with no strands visible? Why are ear studs permitted but not earrings or nose studs? Why are clothes with brand logos not permitted? Why are jeans not permitted? Why should socks be either folded down or pulled up? Why should shirts be tucked in?

These examples – and there are countless others – seem very odd when listed in this way. There is an arbitrary code devised for particular uniforms and enforcement becomes an integral part of the management of uniforms.[4] While there are degrees to which rules are imposed and monitored as well as varying codes of do's and don'ts, all uniforms entail as part of the prescription of what constitutes the uniform another set of *prescriptions about what is not permitted* – that is, a set of NOT statements. Arguably, it is this set and the manner of their enforcement that is more important than the elements of the uniform itself.

School uniforms have become an important and effective selling point for private and religious schools as a way of establishing the values of the school: pride, a sense of community, discipline and success. Promotional materials for such schools emphasise their attention to uniforms as an advantage over non-private (government-funded or community) schools and private schools without uniforms. The purported link between the uniform and academic success is explicit and "justified" in terms of statistics on successful students outcomes, extracurricular activities, provision of computing tuition and digital technology, sporting prowess and so on. In other words, the effectiveness of the marketing of schools with strict uniform codes is based on widely held beliefs about the attitudinal and behavioural attributes of uniforms and their occupants. In many countries, the recent growth in enrolments in private schools and declining enrolments in non-private schools confirms that this perception of the efficacy of uniforms is also growing.

Modern Masculinity and the Rise of School Uniforms

Figure 17
British schoolboy in Lucknow, 1943.

Give me the boy and I'll give you the man. (Jesuit proverb)

The codified concept of school uniforms seems to have developed in Europe with the emergence of civil society (Wagner 2003b). The idea of formal schooling was not new with ancient civilizations (such as China) training at least some children in academic, literary, creative, military and religious topics. However, there is little evidence that such children wore a designated uniform – though they may have dressed in similar distinctive ways. During Europe's "Dark Ages", there is a gap in the record though it is unlikely that schooling would have been a high priority. By the Middle Ages, some education was appearing mostly in monasteries and cathedrals and mostly training boys to enter religious orders. The training was on spiritual and religious matters and the clothing – where adopted – was almost certainly ecclesiastical – probably a surplice (like the novitiates they would become).

This religious basis of modern education had a lasting legacy in the form of academic dress worn in early universities, such as Cambridge and Oxford, dating from the 1300s. University gowns – compulsorily worn by lecturers and students until the 1960s – were based on clerical gowns and surplices traditionally in black and offset by coloured bands, clerical dog collars, trimmings (including ermine), satin linings and elaborate medieval-style headwear.

Later on, customs in ecclesiastical and military uniforms set the scene for the emergence of school uniforms. Broadly speaking, we can identify two main types of school uniform – ecclesiastical-influenced smocks originating in France then spreading to other Mediterranean counties (Belgium, Italy, Portugal and Spain) and military-influenced uniforms emerging in England and adopted in neighbouring countries and most colonies (Scotland, Ireland, Australia, New Zealand, South Africa, Kenya, Malawi, Zimbabwe and India). Military influences were also present in schools uniforms in Germany and Austria, later in communist Eastern Europe (Russia, Latvia, the Ukraine) and in totalitarian regimes (Korea, China, Japan, the Philippines, Cuba, for example). Some European counties have tended not to have school uniforms (Scandinavia, Switzerland, Hungary and the Netherlands); nor has the United

States (until recently) and generally not in Canada. This chapter concentrates on countries where school uniforms have been adopted.

Although now mostly associated with elite schools and wealthy or aspirational parents, school uniforms of both ecclesiastical and military types originated with "welfare" motives. In the case of uniforms in England, they were first adopted in charity schools during the sixteenth century and later were codified under the Poor Laws (of 1597 and 1601). The charity schools were essentially workhouses for children and, as they were financed by levies on parish members, were the object of considerable public scrutiny. "Uniform" clothing was provided to the children in order to clothed them as cheaply as possible and to make them distinctive (rather like present-day prison uniforms). Many were not benign institutions – brutality, hunger, deprivation, punishment and Spartan conditions were the norm. Yet, they did augur the emergence of institutionalized schooling for boys (and girls – although the latter were confined to instruction for assuming "domestic" employment).

By contrast, in France, school uniforms were adopted much later (in the 1870s) as part of the reforms of the French Third Republic to "democratize" public education. Uniforms were of a different character, typically a smock worn over everyday clothes (rather like the smocks now worn in art classes). Smocks spread to other European countries (Belgium, Italy, Spain, Portugal, Greece, Morocco, Algeria and Turkey) as well Latin American countries like Argentina and Uruguay), although smocks have gone out of favour since the Second World War (Wagner 2002c, 2003a–i).

The introduction of compulsory school uniforms was entirely in keeping with the role of schools as disciplining institutions to shape young boys into citizens. The first of the English charity (or "Bluecoat") schools to adopt a uniform was Christ's Hospital founded in London in 1552 – and other charitable foundations soon followed.[5] Generally, there was little attention to the children in charity care – "welfare" was meant to contain a perceived social decay (abandoned or orphaned children) with the visible sign of the problem being institutionalized and "hidden" away. The plight of these children was felt to be of their own making ascribed to the "hand of the wicked". A sense of the subordinating intent of charity school "uniforms" was indicated in this comment by critic Isaac Watts in 1728 when he commented:

Figure 18
Indooroopilly State
School photograph.

Their clothes are of the coarsest kind, and of the plainest form, thus they are sufficiently distinguished from the children of the better rank, and they ought to be distinguished. . . There is no ground for charity children to grow vain and proud of their raiment when it is but a sort of livery. (Watts, cited by Ewing 1975: 23)

It seems that the children of Christ's Hospital may have been more serendipitously provided. Derived from clerical dress, the uniforms consisted of ankle-length bluecoats buttoned to the waist with pleated skirts and dolman sleeves, knee breeches, stockings and clerical-style neckbands. Blue was chosen because it was the cheapest dye available. The Christ's Hospital uniform featured silver buttons on the coat, a narrow leather belt, yellow stockings and a loose-fitting collarless shirt. The uniforms were designed to produce students of a certain type and was copied by other bluecoat schools (The School Uniform Galleries 2002). Boys in bluecoats were expected to exhibit humility as well as agility and grace when wearing these cumbersome outfits. And because they were so distinctive, uniforms also functioned as an effective deterrent to misbehaviour – especially in public.

While most of the bluecoat schools have subsequently abandoned the bluecoat uniforms – or reserve them for special occasions – Christ's Hospital (now located in Sussex) – has retained the uniform.[6] Many former pupils recoiled at the memory of the uniform, one describing it as "ridiculous, uncomfortable and unhygienic Tudor ensemble" (Norman Longmate, *How We Lived Then*), and another reflecting "I hated the archaic uniform" (Michael Wilding, filmstar). But other were proud of the curious historic garb – or eventually became "apathetic" about the "funny looks" people gave the pupils. As one said: "it was usually convenient and advantageous to wear the bluecoat and yellow stockings even when at home. It was distinctive and dignified, allowing one to look smart in any surroundings."[7] A more recent reflection observed that:

> The uniform. Well, it is the oldest school uniform in the world. It is different, and you certainly don't get ignored wearing it . . .
>
> When out in public in uniform you sometimes get asked whether you are from a monastery, or by American tourists if you are young vicars or the like. However, I wouldn't have swapped it for a normal uniform . . .
>
> The time I most realised what the uniform can mean to people is when I went to South Africa to play cricket for the school. We met up with a number of expatriate Old Blues [ex-Christ's Hospital pupils] and wore our uniforms to meet them. Some of them had not seen the uniform for thirty years and believe it or not many of them were in tears.[8]

But with industrialization taking off in England, charity schools became the precursive model replicated across the expanding education system. It was not until the nineteenth century that the great public schools (elite, fee-paying) in England borrowed the idea of adopting uniforms. But this was for very different reasons:

> The English public school in the 18th and early 19th century had become anarchic, dangerous places in which boys from aristocrats and wealthy families did as they wished and played voluntary games in whatever worn and battered gear was to and . . . Conditions were so bad that many parents refused to send their boys and instead had them educated at home until they were ready for university. The uniformity of clothing was one of the measures designed to replace chaos with disciplined order. (Wagner 2003b: 2)

Figure 19
Later Indooroopilly State
School photograph.

The reforms were not just superficial. Schools began to supervise behaviour more rigorously, games were organized into formal sports (rugby, football, cricket and baseball), and the curriculum was transformed from an archaic emphasis on the classics to encompass new kinds of knowledge and discoveries. Schooling also adapted to the need to train "administrators for an expanding empire". This new approach to schooling was symbolized by the uniform and the fashion spread to preparatory schools as well as other private and (after 1870) government-sponsored schools. As Britain expanded its empire, school uniforms followed and were instituted – with climatic concessions – in most British colonies and dominions, Canada being one of the few exceptions. The result was that "school uniform was an essential characteristic of the reformed public schools that emerged by the later nineteenth century as some of the most effective and prestigious schools in Europe" (Wagner 2003b: 2).

Perhaps the most generic type of uniform to develop was derived from the so-called Eton suit, the uniform of younger students at Eton College near Windsor. This emerged during the nineteenth century and became popularized in Edwardian times as the "best wear" of young boys – hence its celebrity. The uniform consisted of a short jacket with black waistcoat and striped trousers. The white shirt featured a broad stiff collar worn outside the jacket with a knotted striped tie. All students wore a top hat until the Second World War after which it was replaced by a boater hat. The Eton suit captured the popular imagination and has been used as the outfit for many boys' choirs, often worn with a surplice worn over it, and has also featured prominently in films and recreations about boys and schooling.

Other early school uniforms were adopted by military schools that chose modifications of adult military uniforms. These typically featured jackets with braided toggles, a stiff upright collar and black trousers (Davidson 1990). Other choices included khaki shirts and shorts; jackets and kilts with braided decorations and sashes; and "sailor" suits with cravat. Again many elements of these early uniforms can still be found in present-day school uniforms. Military schools were also important as the first institutions to adopt physical training regimes and exercise as a central part of their curricula. These training methods and sports uniforms were readily adapted to civilian schools as they emerged.

By the early nineteenth century, schools and universities had begun to adopt "house" colours and badges to indicate membership of different groups and gradually this use of colour was extended to caps, ties, socks and scarves. The custom was subsequently adopted by the armed services, who used colours and badges woven into the design to indicate differences between groups and specialization in roles. The production of ties for school, university and military dress became a major part of the business of silk manufacturers (Hart 1998: 61–2). Concomitantly, ties became a shorthand means of indicating class, status, educational pedigree and distinctive body training – qualities embodied in the term the "old school tie".

School uniforms were, then, shaped by ecclesiastical and military influences conjoined with new ideas about masculinity and citizenship. Nowadays, people probably identify the following elements as typical of a traditional Anglo-derived boys' school uniform: boater hat or peaked cap, single-breasted jacket often striped, tie often striped, white, grey or pastel shirt, V-necked jumper, tailored shorts, long socks and black lace-up shoes. These school uniforms have become a taken-for-granted part of the training in masculinity where certain attributes and characteristics are instilled and internalized, that is, they become unremarkable. School rules and curricula rest on uniforms and their rules to constitute a comprehensive training for adult masculinity and the roles boys will be expected to play as men.

Figure 20
Brisbane school
uniforms, 1990s.

This is, however, normative and assumes that graduates from these uniforms will adopt a particular set of norms, goals and aspirations as adults. In this sense, the uniform performs the role of *agent provocateur* for boys who frequently reject normative codes of adult masculinity and favour alternate constructions. In such cases, these boys must also overthrow the uniform and the trainings and attributes embodied within it. Above all, school uniforms are about the acquisition of a particular form of discipline and specific elements thereof: authority, leadership, hierarchy, status and bonding.

School is not just for the duration of one's school days: attendance qualifies the wearer of the old school tie to life membership of an exclusive and distinctive club. Thus, years later, former pupils will wear their old school tie for certain functions in order to signify their membership and identify themselves as alumni to others from similar institutions. Equally, the camaraderie associated with wearers of the same tie excludes those who were educated elsewhere, creating a hierarchy of "in" groups and "out" groups. School ties and insignia are often worn by members long after leaving school (or at certain events or public occasions).[9] Which school one went to is often an initial question in interviews for employment in business and public administration.

The stereotypical school uniform has often influenced post-colonial dress or uniforms at work. These resonances may perform the same function. Hence, in business, the professions, the police force, the armed forces, medical careers and so on, each profession has adopted versions of a uniform as a way of distinguishing its members and excluding others. Most male uniforms still retain elements from school uniforms: tie, coat/blazer, shirt with collar, tailored trousers and lace-up shoes.

As noted earlier, teachers and academics (those closest to schools) have retained or developed a formal or ceremonial codes of dress based on ecclesiastical dress, once worn when teaching but now mostly reserved for ceremonial occasions. The adoption of specialist dress to denote the profession of teaching (and research) not only distinguishes the wearer as a specialist but also conveys to the wearer a confirmation of their specialist skills and member-ship of a professional community. As a senior academic remarked about wearing academic gown for graduation ceremonies:

> But you do feel different when you put it on. There is a sense when you're processing . . . with a lot of other people in academic gown, there is a sense of academic occasion and a sense of tradition that's associated with the gown . . . you do feel a bit of pride because it represents . . . that you're part of a community of scholars and that's a tradition that goes back quite a long way. (Alan Robson, interviewed by Jane Figgis, ABC 1996)

As this overview suggests, school uniforms have played a dominant role in defining modes of masculinity and as an apparatus for training the body and refining particular techniques. But do school uniforms provide a similar normative training in techniques of femininity for girls?

One of the Boys? Uniform Codes and Feminine Persona

Girls' school uniforms not only play a similar role to boys' uniforms in some respects but also perform very different and highly problematic roles. While girls' uniforms function as a coda of discipline and other attributes of the *ideal female pupil*, the role of the uniform in relation to acquiring codes of sexuality is radically aberrant. Further, the sexual and sensual connotations associated with uniforms suggest that some deep-seated issues concerning the formation of sexed identities and gendered persona are associated with and inscribed in the nature of uniforms and how they are worn. Indeed, as we will see in Chapter 8, uniforms are an integral prop in subcultures of licentiousness and sexual perversion.

Figure 21
Nun, matron and schoolgirl.

Some light on the interpretation of girls and women's uniforms can be found in a chapter by Judith Okely (1993) on uniforms in English girls' boarding schools in the 1950s. Okely speculated on the disjunction between girls' training in schools and female adult attributes of gender. She contrasted the habits acquired in school with the very different ones expected on graduation. In particular, she related the role of uniforms – and minute details of how they should be worn – with other training about the highly refined control of the bodies, minds and even the language of girls. Okely traced the contradictions and ambiguities between two kinds of training that were offered simultaneously to schoolgirls. In part, much of school training was directed towards the acquisition of a second rank array of attributes of *masculinity* – discipline, achieve-ment, leadership, conformity. But, additionally, girls' training was also directed towards the acquisition of attributes of self-control and self-negation. Okely wrote:

> We did not merely unconsciously imitate movements and gestures, we were consciously made to sit, stand and move in uniform ways. We were drilled and schooled . . . by those who had power over us. Our flesh was unscarred, yet our gestures bore their marks . . . Our minds and understanding of the world were to reflect our custodians. With no private space, we could not even hide in our bodies, which also had to move in unison with their thoughts. (Okely 1993: 112)

In the finished product – the "finished" young woman – those latter attributes were intended to prevail since many of the former became irrelevant on graduation.[10] This contradiction between the rhetoric and the reality was perhaps the reason for adopting a very different approach to enforcement and sanctioning of uniform and other behavioural rules in girls' schools. Instead of relying on corporal

punishment as in boys' schools, girls' schools used psychological
and physical forms of enforcement and punishment (including
techniques to shape emotion, language, gesture and deportment).
Although ostensibly less brutal, it was a more pervasive strategy
that effectively retooled the very ways of apprehending and communicating with one's surroundings. Consequently, the nature of
girls' training was arguably more effective as a means to training
the body as a whole. As Okely put it: "power may be exercised
more completely over girls precisely because it is not visible as
physical force" (Okely 1993: 119). School uniforms and school
discipline imbued the body with specific techniques that were
building blocks of modes of personal conduct. In a rather puzzling
process:

> The girls' schools demand[ed] the opposite to the notion of
> sexuality in the world outside. Our appearance was neutered.
> Our hair could not touch the backs of our shirt collars; in
> effect we were given the male "short back and sides". (Okely
> 1993: 114)

According to Okely (1993: 113, 114), the uniforms were composed
of "strange male traits": tunics (pleated or unpleated – reminiscent
of Roman gladiators), thick black or brown stockings, two pairs
of knickers ("white 'linings' and thick navy baggy knickers complete with pocket"), regulation knee-length skirts (for modesty),
as well as "lace-up shoes, striped shirts, blazers, ties and tie pins":

> Unlike some of the boys' uniforms, ours was discontinuous
> with the clothes we would wear in adulthood. To us the old
> school tie had no significance for membership of an "old boy
> network". We were caught between a male and female image
> long after puberty, and denied an identity which asserted the
> dangerous consciousness of sexuality.

Indeed, on completing school, girls were expected to consciously
discard many of the "masculine" attributes acquired at school and
acquire a new set of attributes appropriate to adult feminine conduct:

> Immediately we left school, we had to drop all masculine
> traits, since a very different appearance was required for
> marriageability. Sexual ripeness, if only expressed in clothes,

Figure 22
Girls' school photograph.

burst forth. The hated tunics and lace-ups were torn, cut, burnt or flung into the sea. Old girls would return on parade, keen to demonstrate their transformation from androgeny to womanhood. To be wearing the diamond engagement ring was the ultimate achievement. There was no link between our past and our future. In such certainty our confidence was surely broke. (Okely 1993: 114)

In effect, a radically different triple viewpoint or gendered uniform replaced the girls' school uniform. This contrasts with the experience of boys who merely swapped one uniform for a similar and related one. It was not just a question of clothes. Okely (1993: 116) emphasises how precisely and highly prescriptive modes of conduct were conveyed through trainings in correct deportment, gesture, use of language and tone of voice. These were annexed to the "work" of uniforms and the system of sanctions for transgressions. Even on the sporting field, girls were expected to match "a certain aggressive muscularity" with a "chaste and feminine" demeanour as well as being expected to abandon these sporting behaviours as "unfeminine" off the field and when they left school:

> That straight-shouldered gait with swinging arms and regular footwork would have to be discarded, indeed unlearnt, as feminine step took over. We would only need it for country

walks and following the hounds. Just as hockey hinted at
impotence, so did the mode of marching. Instead of thumping
our heels first on the ground, we had to point our toes: the
feminized fall of the foot. (Okely 1993: 118)

Here then we can see that the question of clothing girls in uniforms
is a highly vexed one because, in its aim of restraining and disciplining the body and mind, it actually incites unrestrained and transgressive conduct that has at its heart a gendered subject that is
normatively male and transgressively feminine. And while it could
be argued that the English girls' boarding school was an extreme
example, there are many parallels with other uniforms and an
overwhelming consensus by girls about their experiences wearing
military-styled uniforms during their school days.[11] This is a theme
developed in Chapter 4.

Modifying School Uniforms amid Youth Culture

Although school uniforms were well entrenched across many
countries by the twentieth century, the situation was about to
change. After the Second World War, school uniforms were partly
allied to other strategies of rebuilding nations but as youth culture
began to emerge as a distinctive entity, the traditional genre of
school uniforms became an obvious target. Already, some of the
traditional features – "more expensive or ludicrous uniform items"
– had gone by the wayside, but the "social revolution of the 1960s
ended much of the English obsession with school uniforms"
(Wagner 2003b: 3).

Uniforms became more informal, reflecting trends in "leisure"
wear – such as polo or T shirts, shorts, casual slacks, no hat, no
tie, trousers for girls, and the like. Smocks disappeared and were
not replaced – everyday dress became the norm for school in those
countries. This change in uniforms enabled schools in former
colonies to devise uniforms that were better suited to the climate
than before as well as distinctly different summer ("sun-smart" hats
with wide brims or legionnaire style, lightweight shorts or skirts,
T-shirts, bike pants, sleeveless dresses, etc.) and winter uniforms
(long trousers, sweaters, tracksuits, etc.).

Many schools make regular updates to uniforms to adapt to
current trends in everyday dress and deal with the most intransigent

Figure 23
Macgregor High School photograph.

uniform infractions. The advent of the *designer uniform* has also been a feature of the post-1960s period. Not content with the designs of traditional uniform suppliers, schools have increasingly commissioned uniforms from popular designers, thus hoping to creature a uniform that is more wearable, more aesthetically pleasing and more acceptable to students.

Even where uniforms have not been enforced, students impose their own dress codes, which are equally repressive, and normative and arguably even more draconian in at least superficially creating body techniques and shaping habits. An American author recalled her school days when she did not have to wear uniforms but "did have a rather rigid dress code" – a white shirt and "a snappy-looking clip-on bowtie" (Poncet 2000: 58). Even in the 1960s, although the code loosened up, it was still in force:

> In school, the dress code, like society, was breaking down into several factions. There were the greasers (we called them "jives"), the preppies and jocks (we called them "conservatives"), the roods and hippies . . . and the rest of the student body: the twerps, geeks, dweebs, nerds, goons; the mama's boys, the braniacs, the suck-ups, the dimwitted, the friendless, the future-psycho loners, the lonely and every other sorry loser who obviously lived in a house without mirrors or television.
>
> I became one of the roods and hippies. I had finally found my niche.

> But first, see how I casually labelled all the kids by the way
> they dressed? Social order was dictated by clothing. You
> could not escape your wardrobe. (Poncet 2000: 59)

In a very short space of time, the ideas associated with school
uniforms were modified significantly with major changes in design
and less stringent enforcement. But did that mean that uniforms
were an anachronism and would become extinct?

The School Uniform Debate Today

Despite the greater informality, and more relaxed policing of
uniforms, school uniforms are still a major issue in school debates.
There seem to be a number of reasons for this: concerns about
discipline and an appropriate attitude to learning; cost and inequal-
ity; the tyranny of fashion; fear of gangs and violence; concerns
about comfort in extreme climates an seasons; and the differenti-
ation of schools into lower and upper primary, secondary schools
and colleges.

At stake is a tension between the original rationale behind
uniforms and the contemporary rationale. Uniforms were designed
to produce disciplined citizens by adopting military and ecclesiastical motifs and modes of clothing and reworking them as
elements of uniforms. Uniforms were compulsory and as well as
including specified items of clothing, uniforms required precise
codes of how they should be worn. Thus much of the habit surrounding uniforms concerns the surveillance of transgressions and
sanctions for such deviations. In short, a highly trained body is
produced through the uniform bringing attention not only to the
surface of the body (which school the person belongs to) but also
to detailed knowledge of how to wear the uniform. But is such a
rationale still relevant?

In place of conformity, discipline and acceptance of rules and
authority – no matter how arbitrary and bizarre – it can be argued
that the cult of individualism currently pervades contemporary
culture and is epitomized in educational curricula. This creates a
set of oppositions or perhaps bipolar statements that are embodied
in the discourse and rhetoric surrounding uniforms as well as in
the outfits themselves. These are: discipline versus spontaneity;
group identity versus individual expression; formality versus

Figure 24
School students and
clinical nurse.

informality; compulsion versus choice; and a tension between asexuality, sexual immaturity and sexual titillation.

In the United States, debate about school uniforms was sparked by President Bill Clinton's 1996 and 1997 State of the Union addresses in which he encouraged the adoption of school uniforms as a way to improve school safety and discipline (Starr 1998). Clinton said:

> If it means that the school rooms will be more orderly and more disciplined, and that our young people will learn to evaluate themselves by what they are on the inside, instead of what they're wearing on the outside, then our public schools should be able to require their students to wear uniforms. (Clinton 1996)

To this end, a *Manual on School Uniforms* was issued by the US Department of Education and the US Department of Justice (1996). The manual advocated that "school uniforms [are] one positive and creative way to reduce discipline problems and increase school safety" as well as enhancing the learning environment. Various case studies were cited in the manual to illustrate the benefits of adopting uniforms. One frequently used example was that of Long Beach, California, where the introduction of uniforms in all elementary and middle schools was correlated with significant decreases in school crime (fights, sex offences, weapons offences, assault and battery offences and vandalism). As one district official put it: "We can't attribute the improvement exclusively to school uniforms, but we think it's more than coincidental" (http://www.ed.gov/updates/uniforms.html) while a police chief provided this evidence:

> Schools have fewer reasons to call the police. There's less conflict among students. Students concentrate more on education, not on who's wearing $100 shoes or gang attire. (http://www.ed.gov/updates/uniforms.html)

Much of the debate about school uniforms arose because some urban schools were becoming out of control. According to Jim Lehrer's *Online NewsHour Extra: News for Students* (Online NewsHour 1996, wysiwyg://9/http://www.pbs.org/newshour/infocus/fashion/school.html) at Farragut High School in Chicago in 1994, it was "a riot zone"; gangs ran the school and conducted "daily mob action fights in the halls". Police and security patrolled the corridors. Amid other (expensive) changes, the cheapest option – the introduction of school uniforms – proved "the most effective". The enforcement of the uniform code – white T-shirt and black bottoms – eliminated gang behaviour and graffiti, increased attendance and performance scores, and reduced dropout rates. Uniforms showed people cared. Similar findings were reported in other schools as well as other more subtle changes (http://www.ed.gov/updates/uniforms.html):

> The children feel good about themselves as school uniforms build a sense of pride. It forces adults to know a child. (Principal of Carver elementary school, Kansas City, Missouri)
>
> The tone of the school is different. There's not the competitiveness . . . about who's wearing what. (Guidance Counsellor at Douglas elementary school, Memphis, Tennessee)
>
> [The uniform policy] has enhanced the tone and climate of our building. It brings a sense of seriousness about work. (Assistant Principal, Mt. Royal elementary/middle school, Baltimore, Maryland)
>
> The main result is an overall improvement in the school climate and a greater focus on positive behaviour. A big portion of that is from uniforms. (Principal, Phoenix Preparatory Academy, Phoenix, Arizona)

Comments such as these are positing uniforms as a technique of transforming behavioural and psychological habits to construct new *personae* better equipped to perform scholastic and pro-social activities. Federal pressure to impose uniforms throughout US schools led to considerable debate about whether such far-reaching effects could be attributed solely to uniforms. For example, a study of 5,000 students suggested that there was no statistical basis for the claims concerning discipline and security; in fact, students in uniforms scored slightly lower on standardized achievement tests than a comparable group of non-uniformed students (Brunsma and Rockquemore 1998). Nonetheless, the introduction of uniforms convinced many sceptics, as shown in this example of a teacher at Northshore High School in Louisiana:

> I've never been concerned with what my students wear. Supervising uniforms and dress codes only lengthens the long list of parental jobs that educators have taken over in recent years. Uniforms, which are economical and easy for parents, are sometimes looked on as a solution to the atmosphere of impending danger that has settled on schools nationwide.
>
> However, after seeing our students in uniforms for the last two weeks, I see an almost magical change in the student body. My seniors talk of the ease with which they dress in the morning, and all the kids seem calmer and more mild-mannered. Almost all the students were wearing the uniforms although the deadline for wearing them was weeks away. Maybe there's something to them. Perhaps they draw us all into a sense of false security and well-being that only conformity can give. (quoted by Chaika 1999)

Reactions such as this illustrate the power of codes of dress and clothing discipline over bodily attributes. But, as one might expect, most of the debate about uniforms in the United States has centred on whether uniforms act as an oppressive force against individual rights and freedom of expression (Cocks 1988; Siegel 1996; Roufos 1997; Brunsma and Rockquemore 1998; National Association of Elementary School Principals (NAESP) 1998; Starr 1998; Chaika 1999; Poncet 2000; Williams n.d.). One mother complained that her daughter hated uniforms because she likes to be an individual, to wear what she wants. She doesn't want to have to wear what everyone else is wearing. It doesn't make her feel good about herself; it doesn't make her feel special. (quoted by Chaika 1999)

Numerous websites invite comments from students concerning what they think about uniforms.[12] These invite personal reactions to uniforms based on comments about individuality, freedom of expression, suppression of personality, choice and so on. While the election of the Bush administration led to the abandonment of the president's school uniform policy, the issue has remained contentious.

In Australia, the debate about school uniforms is far less polarized. For a start, uniforms have been a more readily accepted part of school life than in the United States and have signified being a school pupil in general rather than class and status as in the United Kingdom. Most of the attention has focused on whether traditional uniforms are appropriate for present-day lifestyles or whether they are an anachronism. Many schools have moved towards more informal and less structured uniforms often with alternative options so that students can "mix and match" different garments to suit their personal taste or needs (often prescribed). There is a much closer relationship between modern uniforms and everyday "leisure" clothes such as sweatshirts, polo-necked shirts, track suits, loose shorts and trousers, etc. (Nicklin 1993). Contemporary fabrics include fleecy fabrics and jersey knits.

In some places, private schools have retained traditional or modified uniforms while state schools have adopted "easy wear" uniforms or abandoned them. Some schools abandoned uniforms only to reinstate them as opinions within the school community shifted. Generally, there are stricter uniform codes within private schools – unless the school positions itself as an "alternative" school. Thus, the presence of a uniform is often now used by private schools as a selling point – as the marker of distinction, exclusiveness, discipline and future success.

Uniforms in schools are not confined to the students. Many schools once had rigid dress codes for teachers and most still have an informal or tacit set of guidelines, for example, not to wear jeans, leggings, low necklines, transparent fabrics or very short skirts. Again this set of "not statements" constructs a defined boundary of acceptable modes of conduct and intercommunication. Often the effect of such guidelines is illustrated by extreme examples, such as the following memory of one teacher who had adopted her own uniform code to signify her occupation and underscore her professionalism:

> The teacher I remember was in fact the first teacher that I can recall who made it clear that intellectual capacity was more important than presentation. She was tall and craggy, she had wild, greying hair, and she was the only teacher that I ever came across who wore her academic gown into class, in fact all around the school. It was liberally dusted with chalk-dust and she used to sweep into the classroom and there would be this aura about her, because she was so black and powerful. And we just saw her as this wonderful figure, who stood out because she was so different from the others. All the others were dressed in pastel-coloured suits, and had bobbed hair and wore make-up. But she didn't. (Interviewee on the dress sense of teachers, interviewed by Jane Figgis, ABC 1996)

A well-known Australian fashion designer, Liz Davenport, was formerly a teacher. Asked how she would "deck out" herself to teach some "grotty Year 9 students, 14-year-olds", she gave this response:

> I would go for [a] smart skirt, no shorter than on the knee, longer if you wish, but no shorter than. Because it's a distraction, and you can't move around and be active and be bending for this and reaching for that . . . [or alternatively] very smart slacks. And I stress very smart slacks, not jeans, not that very casual, tracky kind of feel; [and] a smart shirt. Having an image which people look at and respect from every aspect – a little bit of fashion content, a little bit of authority, and if I went back into the teaching world today, I would be packing every bit of authority into the way I dress that I possibly could, because it's authority that gives control, and it's a controlled classroom, not being Hitleristic, but it's a control, an authority, that gains you the learning situation – you can get the students to actually listen to you. (Liz Davenport, interviewed by Jane Figgis, ABC 1996)

In other words, a dress code is implicitly invoked when we think about appropriate and effective learning environments. Indeed, in a debate about declining literacy rates, the dress standards of teachers were blamed by a caller to a talk back radio show who pronounced: "I know why students don't learn to read. Have you ever seen the way teachers dress? In jeans and sloppy T-shirts!" (quoted by Jane Figgis, ABC 1996). This has led some schools to adopt a compulsory "corporate wardrobe" for administrators and teachers. The school uniform wheel appears to have turned full circle.

Uniform Techniques despite Fashion Changes

While there has been considerable debate about the efficacy of uniforms, the majority of schools still enforce at least minimal uniform or dress codes. However, arguably, there is a greater range of ways of reading how school uniforms "work" as clothing statements and in constructing personae in Australia depending on the choice of uniform and nature of the curricula. And, as we have seen, school uniforms are regaining popularity in many educational contexts. Accordingly, there ahas been a proliferation of specialist providers of uniforms and the involvement of well-known designers in the styling of contemporary uniforms (Nicklin 1993; Carlsen 1996; Sebring and Coleman 1996; Kanter 1997; Reiss and McNatt 1998).

As this chapter has argued, uniforms have played a dominant role in defining modes of masculinity (for both men and women) and as an apparatus for training the body and refining particular techniques. In particular, it entailed a discipline of being looked at, of looking and of performing as particular types of person. The emphasis on disciplined dress codes produced an aesthetic as well as disciplinary and regimes of spectacle – as evidenced by drill and school parades – that informed a specific sense of aesthetics in which looking, being looked at and performativity were united.

While the early school uniform was adopted mainly in private schools and training organizations for boys-at-risk, school uniforms were widely adopted over time, especially in Anglo-Saxon and European contexts (School Uniform 2002). The English school uniform was adopted in former colonies such as Australia and South Africa, military styles in Russia, Japan, Korea and Germany;

and smocks in romance language countries such as France, Italy, Argentina and Uruguay. Cuba stands out as distinctive choosing red trousers or skirt with blue and red kerchief (symbolizing involvement in revolutionary activities). Perhaps more bizarrely, European-style uniforms also became popular in former colonies and developing countries where they were regarded as instilling western values and codes of conduct that would enhance success.

Versions of the traditional school uniform are still widely found in some Anglo-Saxon and developing countries although many education systems have modified uniforms (e.g. Australia, Chile) or abandoned them altogether (Germany, France, Italy). However, as noted earlier, the debate about school uniforms remains lively, leading some schools to reintroduce them while commercial private schools increasingly promote their distinctiveness by reference to their policies about good uniform discipline.

Despite some recent casualization (and also countervailing reactions) school uniforms remain an integral technique of school-ing the body and shaping the citizen. If the desire of discipline is the most publicly voiced issue in relation to the role of uniforms, this chapter has argued that creating gendered subjectivity is an intrinsic effect of uniforms. While attributes of masculinity may be normatively inscribed through the work of boys' school uni-forms, the construction of female sexual identities is marked by contradictions, ambiguity and erotic desire. School uniforms can play a part in this.

Female popular singers have frequently worn school uniforms to titillate their audience. Even in Russia, the singing duet, Tatu, consisting of two teenage girls dressed in "skimpy school uniforms kissing and caressing", became a worldwide hit phenomenon. Despite the attention and fascination the singers drew, the director of a child-protection charity denounced the ploy: "It's pandering to dirty old men's images of young girls in school uniform being sexual. It's very irresponsible" (quoted by Porter 2003). Equally, the sexual potentialities of Japanese schoolgirls in their uniforms – to be discussed in Chapters 4 and 9 – highlights the mismatch between girls' school uniforms and the constructs of femininity.

Together, then, school uniforms construct a secret life – an arena of perverse potentialities and multiple sexual sensibilities.

4

Uniforms for Women

Modern Identities for Plucky Heroines

In an English history school textbook, *A Pageant of History* (Collins Pageant of Knowledge Series 1966: 18), an account of the first world war includes eight photographs of women's war contributions as bus conductors ("for the first time ever"); land girls ("to help food production"); ambulance officers ("marched smartly by to do their bit"); "there were even women in the Fire Brigade" saluting at dismissal; "factories, too, were 'manned' by women"; and "when it was all over, the women cheered as loudly as the men." The photographs show women proudly wearing their respective uniforms, all based on feminized versions of male military uniforms, albeit with long skirts and tightly belted waists that accentuate the "lumpy" fit of the uniforms.

On the facing page is another photograph of a louche woman with attitude, standing legs astride and arms behind her back (a "male" pose), wearing a bandana, smoking a cigarette and wearing a flowing silk scarf over a tight bodice and silk "harem-like" trousers with the caption: "Women's new-found freedom caused some odd reactions as in this 'smoking-suit' of 1922." These photographs – and rather more the captions – epitomize the ambivalence surrounding women in uniform. While women have been willing to contribute and serve in times of need, they do so in somewhat compromised situations that are structured by male ideas of their role, their uniform and their "proper" place. The smoking suit photo is as much a renunciation of the new public face of women in the war as it is a commentary on post-war femininity and opportunities for women.

The theme of the misfit between women and uniforms has been raised already. This chapter explores the issue in detail. As we have noted, whereas uniforms reveal continuities between vestimentary and masculine training, girls and women in uniforms challenge normative training in femininity (Ewing 1975; Steele 1989; Adie 2003). Uniforms for women are of two main types: *quasi-masculine uniforms* associated with instilling discipline, confidence and particular skills to operate in the public sphere derived from ecclesiastical dress (robes, headdress) or military tailoring (as in the examples cited above); and *feminized uniforms* that promote physical and emotional training in attributes of nurturing and helpmate derived from service and servile occupations. Although female uniforms function as a coda of discipline and some attributes of an idealized femininity, the role of the uniform in relation to acquiring codes of sexuality is radically aberrant. Further, the sexual and sensual connotations associated with uniforms suggest that some deep-seated issues concerning the formation of sexed identities and gendered persona are associated with and inscribed in the nature of uniforms and how they are worn.

So, when did women start wearing uniforms? According to Ewing (1975: 11), in the only dedicated analysis of the subject, "the history of women in uniform is closely bound up with their position in the community," in particular, "their movement into the community". In this process, uniforms were a key element of this process of negotiating new forms of femininity. As we have already seen in Chapter 1, clothes – and rules about who can and cannot wear certain items – have been common throughout history. Indeed, in some ancient societies, the right to wear clothes at all indicated status. Where low-status people did wear clothes, they were frequently restricted to undyed cloth or coarse fabrics.

One curious exception to this was the dress of prostitutes who have, in many cultures, been made to wear distinctive items of dress. For example, permission to wear jewellery has often been restricted to women of "ill repute" even though in contemporary society it is highly valued by all women. Ewing (1975: 12) cites the following examples of the indicated status of prostitutes over the ages: permission to wear a toga, a freedom denied to "respectable women" (Ancient Rome); to wear elaborate sandals (Ancient Greece); masks (Venice); yellow veil (Florence); red shoes (Italy); or tight-fitting boots (Victorian England). Hunt (1996: 246–8) describes these as "marks of infamy" as a "shaming" strategy to identify the miscreants and by contrast to display morally conforming citizens. It also functioned as a "trade" advertisement. Hunt traces a long history of imposing marks of infamy from antiquity through to modernity. Often these involved wearing an item of red or yellow (akin to the Nazi-imposed star of David armbands for Jews).[1]

This vestimentary marker functioned, at one level, as a kind of "immorality" warning yet the attention to elaborate details of dress suggests that at least a few (wealthy) prostitutes were also revered by some – in particular their elite, high-status clients. Despite the passage of successive laws in many states and cities, it would appear that constant transgressions were the reason for revising legislation – and not just by the prostitutes themselves. The regulations implied some toleration of prostitution and even respectable women would show "daring" by wearing a mark of infamy (Hunt 1996: 247). And, over time, the dress that set prostitutes apart became coveted by other women and eventually became high fashion. We could speculate that just as prostitution is often said to be the oldest profession, the dress codes of prostitutes may constitute one of the earliest kinds of "uniforms" for women. On this question, Hunt (1996: 394-5) argues that sumptuary laws governing the appearance of women were inspired by the imperative to distinguish respectable women from prostitutes in the establishment of "the political economy of marriage". Usually, however, it is the "plain, severe habits enjoined for wear by monks and nuns dedicated to a life of prayer, charitable work and renunciation of the world [that] are the [regarded as the] first established uniforms of our epoch" (Ewing 1975: 13).

Surprisingly, deaconesses were common in the early era of Christianity, their robes and headdress (veil or wimple) denoting "their renunciation of the sensual world", although some orders wore more elaborate dress that perpetuated elements of medieval fashion (Ewing 1975: 13). The status enjoyed by religious women declined from the eighth century in the lead up to the Reformation including the use of secluded nunneries as the institution for the education of girls. This passed to court society. The world of religieuses was in question. As nuns sought more earthly pleasures and relaxed dress, a series of regulations about appropriate religious dress were passed between 1200 and 1500 – a precisely targeted form of sumptuary law. Nunneries became associated with hospitals and charities and gradually the link between ecclesiastical dress and nurses' uniforms was set in train. However, the Reformation (sixteenth century) resulted *inter alia* in the secularization of nursing and – perhaps inevitably – the loss of structure, discipline and strict dress codes lead to the decline of nursing standards and the behaviours of nurses. This situation was not addressed until the nineteenth century when reforms to nursing hinged on the reimposition of uniforms (Ewing 1975: 18–19).

In the mean time, questions of appropriate dress for women in particular occupations became an issue elsewhere. For example while domestic staff did not (contrary to belief) wear uniforms as such, they established a quasi-uniform in the form of a white apron or pinafore and cap over their everyday dress. It was not until the mid-nineteenth century that a standard maid's uniform was formalized as a black dress or shirt and skirt under an apron. It was this outfit that was the immediate precursor to nurses' uniforms.

On another front, the "problem" of destitute children was addressed by charity "hospitals" – a forerunner of boarding schools – that looked after boys and girls from the mid-sixteenth century. As we noted in Chapter 3, pupils were outfitted in distinctive clothes – perhaps the first uniform in the modern sense – although these clothes were cheap and of poor quality, designed to remind the children of their culpability. At Christ's Hospital, girls wore the same uniform from its opening in 1553 until 1875, consisting of a blue dress; white, green or blue apron depending on their age; white coif and peak (cap); and yellow stockings (Ewing 1975: 22). Ewing claims that this is "the oldest non-religious women's uniform in the world" (Ewing 1975: 22). Minus the apron and cap, the modern girls' uniform retains the navy dress and yellow stockings.

The Bluecoat pupils (boys and girls) were distinctive then and seemingly better dressed than their compatriots in other charity

Figure 25
Hospital matron.

schools. While the aim was to hide these children away from the public gaze, their distinctive uniforms and the fact that they were supported by parish largesse meant that their benefactors were not averse to seeing the products of their charity. Accordingly, charity school children were trotted out to church and on other public occasions sometimes even entertaining the crowd with special recitals. These were not celebratory performances. She cites the observations of one Bishop Butler in this regard:

> The various coloured coats and kirtles of the "Clothed children," garments which by making the wearers public objects of charity did nothing to encourage vanity and reminded them continually of their servile rank. (cited by Ewing 1975: 23)

By the eighteenth century, charity schools proliferated and – as we have seen – were the model for the later establishment of fee-paying schools for the wealthy. So, although education for girls was uncommon, the Bluecoat girls were path-breakers in both gaining some education ("in all such work as becomes their sex": Ewing 1975: 22) and wearing "uniforms" despite the ambivalence surrounding them. Other groups that experimented with "uniforms" were the Quakers in their dour, modest dresses and bonnets and the Blue Stockings (groups of independently minded literary and cultural women) – though they did not actually wear blue stockings (Ewing 1975: 27). Even so, the term "blue stocking" has remained a common epithet for strait-laced, bookish women.

In a history full of surprises – and perhaps contributing to the ambivalence surrounding women in uniforms – the seventeenth and eighteenth centuries saw numbers of women masquerading as men in armies and navies and performing as valiant soldiers and sailors. While it seems that their intentions were motivated by romantic reasons (to follow a lover or husband) there are many accounts of heroic fighting capacities of these women, whose disguises were often discovered only on death or injury. These "women in drag" seemed to become iconic figures – revered as much as denounced. They were not the only women on the battlefield: vivandieres and cantinieres (camp followers selling provisions or canteen ladies) also accompanied the armed forces – a taste of the official provisioning of armies of the future.

The figure most commonly cited as putting women in uniform is Florence Nightingale who, from the Crimean War of the mid-nineteenth century, spearheaded reforms in nursing on an unprecedented scale. First sought out to staff the field hospital for British soldiers fighting in Crimea, Nightingale identified a formal uniform as the key to disciplined training and performance of nursing. After various attempts to instigate an appropriate uniform, a combination of dress and pinafore, plus cap covering the hair and a cape for streetwear became the standard theme of nurse uniforms for over a century. Further techniques followed including the establishment of training schools and reforming hospitals to inculcate a disciplined workforce of nurses and doctors – all appropriately dressed. It was a cultural hegemony of lasting significance. Not only was there a demand for the services of nurses in other colonial conflicts but also the allure of nursing grew and it became a desirable occupation for women – not only in England, but also in the United States, Canada, Australia, New Zealand and South Africa.

A subsequent phase in the history of women in uniforms occurred on the domestic front with modified versions of nurses' uniforms (which had derived from servants' wear) being reworked into formal uniforms for domestic staff – nannies, parlourmaids, kitchen hands, cooks, housekeepers and "nippies" (waitresses) – identifiable in their demure black dresses (or shirts and skirts), white coveralls and white caps/hats. Other female uniforms to emerge in the nineteenth century included Salvation Army women in their distinctive "hallelujah" bonnet (Salvation Army 2003b) and military-inspired severe, high-collared black shirt and skirt. Royal women were also influenced by rather more dashing military uniforms and enthusiastically embraced feminized versions of military uniforms for regimental ceremonies (Ewing 1975: 62–4). The ecclesiastical legacy of robes and headdress was noticeable among the garb of recently revived orders of deaconesses – and the belated admission of women into universities and law.

The greatest impetus to the popularization of uniforms in civil life, as we have argued in Chapter 3, undoubtedly occurred in schools. For women, this was a double-edged sword. Despite the experiments of the charity schools in devising uniforms for girls, it was not until the rise of the movement in the 1870s to promote active games and physical education for women that school uniforms were both introduced on a wide scale and reformed. Illustrations exist of girls whirling around exercise equipment in comparatively loose sailor shirts, full skirts, waist sashes and soft slippers – a far cry from the corseted static images from earlier decades. One after another, girls' schools introduced uniforms – initially for sport. The first women's college at a university, Girton College at Cambridge, also introduced sports uniforms as part of its bid for respectability and distinction. By the 1890s, the gym tunic worn with leg-of-mutton sleeved blouse had become the norm and remained so for over half a century. Sailor suits too were popular for girls – or at least the top blouse with sailor suit collar edged in braid.

The Girl Guides, established in 1909 to complement the scouts (despite Baden-Powell's reluctance to include girls), also adopted an obviously militaristic uniform. Although a uniform was pre-scribed, there were in practice a wide variety of uniforms until standardization in the mid-1930s. This was essentially a khaki military-style shirt, tailored skirt, tie, epaulettes, leather belt, lanyard, and long brown socks. At one time the "biggest female organization in the world" (Ewing 1975: 80), Guides had a major impact on the popularization of girls' uniforms, the aims of scout-ing and the introduction of military dress into everyday fashion.

At school, girls' uniforms in the twentieth century increasingly combined the gym tunic with the military uniform. I have already mentioned the ambivalent role of uniforms in girls' boarding schools in 1950s England (Okely 1993) in Chapter 3. Okely (1993) traced the contradictions and ambiguities between two kinds of trainings that were offered simultaneously to schoolgirls. On the one hand, some aspects of school training were directed towards the acquisition of a second-rank array of attributes of masculinity – discipline, achievement, leadership and conformity. On the other hand, schools were equally concerned that the girls acquire attributes of self-control and self-negation. The latter entailed a set of psychological and emotional techniques rather than physical ones. Arguably, these were the more valorized attributes because the girls – on leaving school – were actively exhorted to abandon many of the "masculine" attributes acquired at school and acquire a new set of attributes appropriate to adult feminine conduct: being attractive, socially passive and in search of a husband.

Policing Femininity

A noteworthy study of the development of women's uniforms concerned successive designs for English policewomen. At stake was what constituted an appropriate uniform for women pursuing this traditionally male occupation. Young (1997: 282) observed that "an almost religious zeal and fervour in the use of metaphors of 'social chaos' [was] posed in the symbols of female dress, deportment, and modes of address." Arguably this was not coincidental but related to the ecclesiastical basis of ideas about social order and normative male and female roles.

Women were first admitted to the police in 1907 in England, but a uniform was not implemented until the first world war.[2] There was a military derivation in early policewomen's uniforms. They were dark blue (others were black) and consisted of "a topee-style pith helmet, a long-line belted tunic with brass buttons from neck to waist, over an ankle-length skirt hiding lace-up knee-length leather boots" (Young 1997: 269; cf. Ewing 1975: 98). As one 1950s policewoman recalled:

> The uniform was unspeakable . . . designed surely by men
> who had a spite against us . . . When, at last, I stood before

a mirror clad from head to feet in police provided clothing, I shuddered, and for the first time regretted my choice of career. (Lilian Wyles, quoted by Young 1997: 266)

Young identified an ambivalent depiction of policewomen as possessing both "a natural animality and sensual helplessness which has to be guarded against" (Young 1997: 267). They were regularly described as either butch "burglars' dogs" or small weaklings; "icy virgins" or "scarlet women", "singularly unattractive spinsters" or "shapely sex bombs" (Young 1997: 270, 271, 280). Policewomen were reviled as

a danger simply because of their propensity to "fall from grace" and [their] need [for] masculine protection, yet at the same time they will be guilty of distracting the policemen by their Medusan charms. (Young 1997: 281)

Consequently, policewomen's uniforms tried to neuter the women typically by advocating a military-style outfit featuring buttoned-up jackets, black stockings, heavy skirts, short back and sides hair "with no strands visible", male-style hats, flat lace-up shoes, and so on. Throughout the twentieth century, the debate about policewomen's uniforms simmered in police force after police force. But attempts to neutralize the ugliness/threat of the uniform seemed only to provoke other connotations of sex and sensuality – hence the ongoing contemporary concern about make-up, jewellery and visible or sexy underwear.

Subsequent efforts to make policewomen's uniforms more fashionable – typically adopting modifications of air stewards' uniforms (e.g. court shoes, short skirts, tunics and shoulder bags) – unintentionally exacerbated the ambiguous sexual denotation of female police. As Sir Robert Marks wrote in his biography about changes to the British policewoman's uniform in the 1960s: "The effect was electric, our recruitment rocketed. So, alas, did our matrimonial rate of wastage" (quoted by Young 1997: 275).

To counteract this, some policewomen suggested that culottes be adopted. Culottes were deemed to be more practical – like trousers because women could move easily, yet not run the risk of revealing their knickers. At the same time, culottes were purported to be more fashionable than regulation skirts and more flattering than trousers. In fact, culottes meet these specifications only if they

Figure 26
Nurse and baby.

are extremely well cut and tailored to the individual body, otherwise they tend to pull or bunch and can be quite uncomfortable and impractical. The chance that police uniforms would be customized to fit well seems unlikely. In any case, the solution is very much a non-resolution in that it is inscribing a perpetual sexual ambiguity into policewomen's uniforms as neither male (not quite trousers) nor female (not quite a skirt).

The suggested reform captured perhaps unexpected attention when the cover of the police journal, *Police Review*, depicted a policewoman in the recommended culottes (Young 1997: 274–5). She wore a tunic/jacket buttoned to the neck, a police issue hat (white soft-topped air-hostess cap), black stockings and flat lace-up shoes. In addition to this odd combination of garments, the policewoman was posed with legs wide apart with outstretched arms holding her divided skirt out wide. This pose not only revealed but also emphasised the split between her legs. This had the effect of ridiculing the suggested reform by, at a minimum, turning the reform into a parody, and at a maximum, reinvesting sexual allusions into the culottes. Thus, rather than working to promote the idea and champion the concerns of policewomen, the journal undermined the issue. While this could be regarded primarily as an issue of uniform codes, the implication of "problematic" sexuality and sexual titillation inscribed in this hybrid uniform was also present. Indicatively, it was this image that was used on the cover of the volume, *Dress and Gender* (Barnes and Eicher 1997) in which Young's chapter was published. This choice seemed to confirm the argument that the image was deeply ambiguous and redolent of inappropriate sexuality.

Similar struggles to come to terms with women in the police have occurred elsewhere. In all cases, the battle over uniforms alludes to other deep-seated tensions and contradictions. Valerie Steele (1989) traced the emergence of uniforms for women police in the United States. When they were first admitted, policewomen wore long skirts, bodices with buttons, decorated with a police badge, and carried a gun in a handbag. This outfit rather circumscribed the kinds of duties a policewoman could easily perform and they were typically found doing the duties that did not require physical exertion: welfare, domestic incidents, public relations and clerical work. The campaign to wear uniforms that were better suited to physical tasks was mirrored by a rhetorical battle as to whether it was appropriate for women to undertake such roles. It was not until the 1980s that trousers became an option for policewomen. Even now, uniform designs offer basically two options: a derivative of the traditional policeman's uniform or a "soft look" uniform of blazer and slacks (Steele 1989: 72).

Contemporary uniforms for policewomen retain the tension between versions of male uniforms – tailored shirts and slacks with epaulettes, necktie, leather belt, neat hair (tied up if long), heavy lace-up shoes and modified airman's cap – and feminine embellishments, such as ear studs, flesh-coloured stockings, hair bows and dress watches. While uniforms vary between jurisdictions, some have even opted for a quasi-military khaki look more like a park ranger than a law enforcer. They are not policemen – but they are marked out from non-uniformed attributes of femininity.

Fighting Women

As with the police, women in military forces have often had ill-fitting and unflattering uniforms. In England, the first women attached to the military – in support activities – were kitted out in a range of uniforms from the dark severe "feminized" masculine uniforms ("ankle-length skirts and navy service-type jackets") to khaki overalls for munition workers in factories (Ewing 1975: 94–5). After the war, many of the war-related occupations reverted to male domains and women were encouraged to return to nurturing roles or take advantage of other expanding public opportunities for women (as secretaries, clerks, sales assistants, etc.). According to Ewing:

> the story of women's uniforms was somewhat disjointed, typical of an era of spasmodic efforts, of high hopes and anxious fears, progress and failure, false starts and brave endeavours, all overtaken by the holocaust of World War Two. (Ewing 1975: 102)

There were particular challenges facing women in uniforms. They had to be accepted by male colleagues, other women and the community in general. To achieve this, women quickly realized that they were more likely to be taken seriously if they wore a uniform. So, as more women entered previously male occupations, the number of specialist occupational uniforms for women also grew.

In other aspects of public life, women also adopted uniforms or distinctive forms of dress, such as women lawyers, school and university students, girl guides, members of the Women's League of Health and Beauty, and – of course – school uniforms for girls. During this time, women were formally recruited into peacetime military corps and support services. The design of uniforms remained a live issue though arguably uniforms of this period were becoming more stylish and emulating some elements of fashion and incorporating feminine touches. The uniforms of military corps were more tailored than policewomen's uniforms but still retained their masculine origins.

Marjorie Garber (1992: 21–5) described a similar dilemma within the US military about the design of uniforms for female cadets that were neither too "masculine" (trousers and short hair) nor too "feminine" (softer lines that revealed female contours). The result was a uniform that feminized masculine elements and introduced feminized ones. Tailored slacks (not trousers) or skirts (pleated not gathered) were worn with a plain shirt (not too severe nor too much like a blouse) and decorated with military insignia.

In a discussion of the centrality of military motifs in Hollywood musicals, Wills (2000) argued that the use of women in uniforms and military-influenced female fashions enabled musicals to address issues about emerging identities for American women. Film became a medium to realign ideas about femininity with new ideas about national identity and to deal with a turbulent period. The use of women in uniforms served simultaneous functions – it was humorous (due to its origin in burlesque and carnival) and it was erotic (evoking all the tensions about women in uniforms and displaying attributes of power and authority). This combination "made this potentially provocative image . . . innocuous" (Wills 2000: 318).

In the 1920s and 1930s women's uniforms took on additional connotations of changing gender roles and gender confusion. Military uniforms were incorporated in fashion, but in film the preferred uniform was a sailor suit "which connoted a strangely sexual innocence derived from children's fashions and girls' school uniforms" (Wills 2000: 319). The so-called sailor suit had been introduced to the Royal Navy in 1628 but it was its adoption by the Prince of Wales (later King Edward VII) that popularized it as a fashion in the mid-nineteenth century and again after 1910. Entrenched as a periodic fashion, the sailor suit also became common as a school uniform, especially in Japan. Perhaps because of this odd association of the sailor suit with children, the suit has also become a prop of fetish behaviour including the lucrative Japanese schoolgirl pornography industry, discussed later in this chapter.[3] Hollywood, too, played a part in this transformation. The sailor suit was sexualized and the filmic role of women-in-uniform changed accordingly. The comedic symbolism of military-style fashion and women-in-uniform gave way to sexual connotations and ambivalent images.

By the 1930s, women in uniforms had acquired new meanings. When used as costume, uniforms retained their dramatic and spectacular functions but as fashion, military uniforms conveyed the threats posed by the growing visibility of women in public life. Within musicals, women in uniform came to signal transgressive femininity and sexuality signalling ambiguity and misplaced eroticism. The emphasis on spectacle was thus combined with "an unruly feminine overabundance of unstable female bodies" epitomized by the Busby Berkeley chorus lines (Wills 2000: 323). Indeed, the use of women in uniform provided a cinematic space for the partial rehabilitation of troubled tropes of masculinity (cf. Mrozek 1987). Uniforms as costumes served to give credence to strong notions of masculinity but less favourable notions of femininity. Female characters were portrayed as social "problems" (threats, unstable, ambivalent or weak). Generally, their cinematic predicaments were resolved once the female characters abandoned their uniforms for civvies and exchanged the public sphere for the fantasy of domestic bliss.

Uniforms functioned as a language that bridged screen fantasies with real changes and challenges for women. The expansion of consumer culture, involvement of women in public life and political undercurrents in the lead-up to the Second World War ensured the persistence of military and uniform themes in clothing styles. During the war, the relationship between women and uniforms took centre stage. Women were exhorted to play an active support role in the war effort while accepting wartime rationing that was at odds with the comforting and stylish front they were encouraged to exhibit on the home front.

In Germany, a campaign after the first world war had attempted to persuade women to dress with appropriate decorum and morality, to abandon frippery and individuality, and instead to display uniformity and conformity (Guenther 1997). It was particularly targeted at persuading German women to reject foreign influences, especially Parisian fashion. The campaign accelerated as Aryaniza- tion took hold and only German-made clothing was exhorted as being appropriate for the noble German woman. The campaign recommended clothing that emphasised uniformity, not individu- ality, and eschewed jewellery. The use of cosmetics was also opposed. Accordingly, the uniform of the League of German Girls (*Bund deutscher Madel* or BDM) was a modification of male uniforms (Guenther 1997, 2004), consisting of

> A white short-sleeved blouse that was closed at the neck with a black tie, a navy blue skirt, the length of which was exactly prescribed, short white socks, and brown leather shoes. No embellishments, no individual touches, nothing was allowed that might take away from the symbolic significance of the uniform – *Einheitlichkeit* and *Gleichheit*, uniformity and conformity. When not in uniform, BDM girls were to wear clothing that portrayed simplicity, clarity, naturalness; a practical yet beautiful style. (Guenther 1997: 37)

While uniformed women complied, civilian women flaunted the edicts. Fashionable clothes were still coveted. German officers bought Parisian fashion for their wives and mistresses while silk stockings were a popular frequent gift to lovers from less privileged troops. Despite the efforts of the German authorities to close down the Paris fashion industry, it managed to survive through the Second World War. Although women supporting the war effort wore trousers or overalls to work, they were also "trading bacon for dress goods, eggs for jewellery, butter for silk stockings" (Guenther 1997: 40). Eventually the campaign was acknowledged as a failure with women. Although it destroyed the German textile and clothing industry, some German designers remained in business throughout the war, largely dependent on the custom of wives and lovers of the Nazi elite.

In Britain, too, there was a battle to come to terms with women in uniform during the Second World War as well as their ability to dress fashionably in the face of rationing (Lant 1991). The intro- duction of "utility" clothing – that was specially designed clothes in approved fabric to minimize wastage of raw materials – received mixed reactions. While it seems that hostility towards government- regulated garments receded over time, the campaign undoubtedly

Figure 27
Policewomen's uniforms.

spurred home sewing as restrictions did not apply to such garments (Sladen 1995: 43–54). There were constant references – some comic, some government produced, some in advice columns and magazines – to recast ideas about femininity in order to accommodate both the new look of women and their expanding roles in war support. Lant argues that films were a particularly important means to negotiate and renegotiate the new femininity. There was always an erotic or sexualised dimension to these representations – according to Lant (1991), cross-dressing and lesbianism were targeted as particular concerns:

> It was feared that legislating women's dress, by equipping them with practical uniforms in order to unify them, might have the power to disguise, alter, or even reconstruct their real selves. The connotations of male strength attached to a military uniform might permanently empower a female wearer. The question was, "What would be the effect of the uniform on the 'real' woman underneath?" Would it promote lesbian relations among women? (Lant 1991: 107)

The struggle to come to terms with new look femininity and active women can also be traced through the covers and contents of fashion magazines from the period, such as *Vogue* (Hall 1983,

1984, 1985; Packer 1985; Lloyd 1986; Mulvey and Richards 1998: 114–16; Lehnert 2000: 32–41). While explicit attention to the war was largely confined to copy, the aesthetics of the covers and fashion spreads was consciously and unconsciously shaped by the reality of war and the proliferation of uniforms in military and non-military activities as well as their influence on civilian fashion.

And yet, even magazines like *Vogue* managed to accommodate women in uniforms and in active support roles. Princess Elizabeth became a role model as the honorary Colonel of the Grenadier Guards. She wore a cap with the regiment's grenade and a diamond brooch of the regimental badge, with a simple blouse with Peter Pan collar and single-breasted jacket (Hall 1985: 20–2). Women in uniform became a regular sight – even when off-duty. Lady Edwina Mountbatten (wife of Louis), Chief Superintendent of the St John Ambulance Brigade, "was reported to dine out frequently in her chic uniform" (Hall 1985: 20). Admittedly her uniform was tailored by Saville Row – "just that little bit shorter, and her shoes copied in a tiniest bit more delicate shape" (Mulvey and Richards 1998: 114–15).

Commentators stressed that female recruits to the war could remain "pretty and feminine, as well as well-groomed and well-dressed, and as concerned with complexion, manicure, and hair-dressing as any other woman, in or out of uniform" (quoted by Hall 1985: 23). War propaganda and fashion photography became intertwined. So, Toni Frissell's photograph for *Vogue* – "the WACs are pretty" – "was adopted by the US Government for the cover of the official WAC [Women's Army Corps] recruiting brochure" in 1943 (Hall 1985: 24–5). Photographers like Lee Miller were particularly important in normalizing the image of women in uniform, in active roles, working on machines and facing difficult challenges in harsh environments.

Nonetheless, the number of women in the military declined dramatically after the Second World War and took some time to build up again, especially after ideas about female roles and occupations were revised from the 1960s and as jobs and careers in previously "feminine" fields disappeared. As military forces incorporated tertiary education into their training regimes, the military became an even more attractive option. The use of women in combat roles has been even more recent. This has necessitated adaptations in uniforms as the need for practical garments has taken precedence over attention to "feminine" details or military tradition. Unisex T-shirts and loose-fitting trousers (often in camouflage fabric) are common wear, as worn in the Iraq wars and aftermath. The corollary of women in combat situations has been both an increase in service families where both adults are on active service and on the involvement of women personnel in war atrocities and other non-sanctioned behaviour such as torture and abuse of human rights.[4]

Previous notions of feminine codes of conduct were severely buffeted by the new involvement of women in military engagements. While western states have opted for an ostensible affirmative action approach to accommodating women in the military, Islamic states armed their women recruits with heavy weaponry at the same time as dressing them in modest, full-length uniforms of ill-fitting single-breasted jackets with epaulettes and extra-long cuffed sleeves and ground-length A-line skirts. These were worn with headscarves under berets (Anon. 2001). Changes such as these suggest that the military roles of women in uniform have shifted and yet still pose problems for military protocol and ingrained macho attitudes.

Brides of Christ or Sister Act: Dressing Women Clergy

Because of these ambiguous references, women clergy – where they have been ordained and permitted to practise – have faced considerable vestimentary struggles as to the appropriate mode of dress. Keenan (1999) cites one woman deacon as rejecting

> the "schoolgirl" clothes on offer for female clergy . . . the little-girl image. "It's about submission, it's about subservience: there are a lot of messages going on" . . . she finds second-hand men's clothes and adapts them if necessary . . . she bicycles round the parish in culottes and a big black hat . . . so multi-ethnic is the population of East Ham that some passers-by do not know the meaning of her dog-collar; they think she must be a policewoman or a private detective. (Keenan 1999: 399)

This individual struggle to find a suitable mode of dress articulates the inability of female uniforms to match the attributes required for roles such as being clergy. A clergywoman in a girlish uniform would not be taken seriously (because she was too sexually coded) but the adoption of elements of male clergy's attire – trousers/culottes, big black hat, dog collar and the like – creates the risk that a clergywoman is either treated as a second-rate man (boyish, bicycling) or as sex-less, neutered or not sexually desirable.

In Australia, too, the ordination of women necessitated the creation of special clerical robes. The Anglican church chose red, flowing, yoked surplices featured a broad frontal panel decorated with a design chosen by each woman, an apparent concession to women's frivolous nature perhaps. Other Protestant churches have opted for white surplices, perhaps more in keeping with connotations of female purity.

For non-pulpit duties, female clergy have worn outfits more like corporate wardrobes. In the 1980s, the newspaper, *The Sydney Morning Herald Good Weekend Magazine*, asked three leading female Australian designers to come up with appropriate yet stylish outfits for clergywomen (Craik 1994: 2–3). Their suggestions were very revealing. Adele Palmer recommended a mix-and-match array of trousers, shirt, jacket and coat dress in finely pinstriped black wool. She described this as "a fairly demure outlook with a certain reverent attitude". Jill Fitzsimon proposed a long-line jacket and "modest but fashionable" length skirt in mid-grey teamed with a white "draped neckline blouse" featuring "a delicate random blue cross print – a chic alternative to the dog collar". Linda Jackson chose "an intense blue" wool or linen suit, consisting of a straight skirt and long-line single-breasted jacket buttoned to the neck. A matching white blouse featured a dog-collar neckline. She also designed a cyclamen pink smock for formal occasions.

In each of these designs, there was a tension between male and female dress conventions (trousers versus skirt or coat dress, pinstripes versus checks, black or grey versus "intense" blue or cyclamen pink, shirt (with stiff collar) versus blouse (with draped neck), buttoned through (quasi-military/ecclesiastical) jacket versus soft line, loose jacket, and so on. These dress codes are deeply ingrained and unremarkable. They signify not only gender but also the role of the clergy that has been normatively male. Additional elements overlay these gendered codes to specifically label the attributes of the clerical role: dog collar, cross and (derivatives of) the surplice. The language used to describe these garments is also telling of the attitude adopted by the clerical role: demure, reverent, modest, delicate, intense, and so on. In other words, the clothes must match the gestural, linguistic and psychological attributes of the clergy. This example is fascinating because the designers were obliged to articulate the triple viewpoint of clerical body techniques: matching the practical behavioural requirements with the social ones (gender, conventions) and psychological (demeanour, beliefs, values). This process is very similar to the training in girls' schools discussed in Chapter 3.

Sexualizing Uniforms

These examples suggest that the question of clothing girls and women in uniforms is a highly vexed one because, in its aim of restraining and disciplining the body and mind, it actually incites unrestrained and transgressive conduct that has at its heart a gendered subject that is normatively male and transgressively feminine.

As noted already, uniforms have become an integral prop in licentiousness and sexual perversion. Japanese schoolgirls have found a lucrative way to earn money after school by posing in their sailor suit uniforms for men (see Chapter 9). According to one report:

> As many as 10,000 schoolgirls in Tokyo are making extra money . . . by posing for professional and amateur pornographers, selling their sailor-style school uniforms and underwear to sex shops, or working as telephone sex-operators. (Anon. 1994)

Kinsella's (2002) analysis of the Japanese obsession with the schoolgirl in uniform as a fetishized object of desire in prostitution and popular culture more generally relates to current anxieties about the dissolution of citizenship and absence of new identities in contemporary Japan (cf. McVeigh 2000). Once adopted in order to encourage westernization of Japanese culture and produce citizens that could perform in the transitional state, the widespread enforcement of sailor suits as school uniforms produced an unexpectedly transgressive postmodern subjectivity.

Sexual *frisson* and *jouissance* (Dawson 1997) intrinsically mark the tensions and ambiguities about the very idea of women in

Figure 28
Japanese servant girls.

uniform. There is also an ongoing struggle to try to make female uniforms feminine and fashionable, by modifying the contours and softening the look on the eye. An example concerned girls' school uniforms in Iran. A government edict in 2000 proclaimed that Iranian girls were now permitted to wear brighter coloured uniforms in accordance with the liberalization of the Islamic state. Although still required to wear "manteaus, or loose smocks and headscarves" over their clothes, they could now choose fabrics that were pink, bright green or light blue instead of the dark colours previously prescribed. The directive explained that the permission to adopt bright colours was meant to "create freshness, joy and hope" yet "preserve spiritual health of girls" (Associated Press 2000). Such a change of policy was intended to align codes for uniforms with circulating constructions of femininity as a triple viewpoint of ideal female conduct (cf. Mauss 1973) and to inscribe those attributes into the garments themselves. However, since then a fundamentalist backlash has undermined this uniform reform.

Meanwhile in England, parents have argued for the right for girls to wear trousers at schools that still mandate skirts (MacLeod 1999). Whickham Comprehensive (Gateshead, Tyne and Wear), for instance, argued that the ban on trousers for girls "reflects a well-ordered and high academic, but caring ethos" and rejected arguments that trousers made girls safer from sexual attack, avoided the cost and impracticality of tights and circumvented the perennial issue of the length of skirts. The fact that such bans persist or that culottes are introduced as a halfway measure shows that the question of sexuality and the revelation of female bodily contours especially the contours of the genitals and buttocks is the unstated concern. Girls must be protected from themselves. Just as trousers for schoolgirls have become more acceptable, a counter-move is on. In June 2004, an English secondary school banned girls from wearing skirts because "too many were wearing them indecently short" which was "not suitable" for cycling to school (*Mail on Sunday* 2004). It seems that moral panics about girls revealing too much flesh continue. On the other hand, there have been debates about the right of Muslim schoolgirls to wear the jilbab or hijab (strict Islamic dress) to school in a number of countries (Jones 2004).[5]

The ongoing dilemma surrounding the design of uniforms for girls and women highlights the intrinsically problematic nature of the genre of the uniform (Ewing 1975: 146–55). The problem of how to design uniforms for women – especially when they are in positions of authority, physical exertion or potential danger – is unresolved (cf. McRobbie 1986; Steele 1989; Craik 1994, 2000; Michelman 1998).

The previous discussions suggest that gender dimensions and sexual/sensual dimensions of uniforms are of considerable importance. Although denied, negated or subjugated by the rationale and design of uniforms, this disavowal seems to trigger sexual/sensual reinstatements and subversions of uniforms. The aim of uniforms, to order and control, constantly invokes their social/cultural bases – control of body and minds (souls) through military and ecclesiastical means – hence the insistent borrowing of items of military and ecclesiastical wear in uniforms. While men in uniforms spark particular sets of associations and interests that are consistent with other techniques of masculinity, women in uniforms are inevitably caught up in ambivalent and highly charged concepts of gender, sexuality and sensuality. Their very appearance in uniform is imbued with sexual frisson and erotic possibilities.

Part III

Uniforms for Work and Leisure

Figure 29
Emirates Airline
stewards.

5

Uniforms at Work

Uniforms at Work

This chapter examines the development of uniforms for work in contemporary culture. The adoption of uniforms for work to designate particular occupations is not new. The adoption of specialist clothes to identify particular occupations, skills or roles may be as old as those activities themselves. For example, distinctive modes of dress with precise detail and insignia were found on the Chinese terracotta warriors from the Qin dynasty circa 200 BC distinguishing armoured and unarmoured soldiers, crossbowmen, cavalrymen and officers (Capon 1983). In modern Europe, uniforms have also been commonly used to demarcate trades (bakers, gas fitters, chefs), skills (surgeons, laboratory attendants), professions (ecclesiastical, medical, academic, legal) and specific job functions (bank staff, aircraft crew, shop assistants, beauticians, cleaners).

Valerie Steele (1989) traced the development of work uniforms and related it to the increasing specialization of occupations, normative gender roles and status designation. In particular, she noted that many jobs have been associated with attributes of either masculinity (strong = construction worker; brave = firefighter; aggressive = lawyer; intelligent = doctor) or femininity (kind = nurse; nurturing = teacher; vain = beautician; subservient = assistant; neat = domestic servant: Steele 1989: 65–6). Work clothes for these occupations also embody those gendered attributes whether they be specified uniforms or consensual codes of dress: blue singlet and shorts; fancy protective uniform; conservative suit; smart casual and/or lab coat; maid-style white dress; conservative casual; pastel nurse-type dress; neat conservative; traditional conservative.

Roach and Eicher (1973: 127, 129) distinguish three types of occupational uniform, those that are *functionally mandatory* – necessary to perform their occupational role (e.g. firefighters, bomb disposal squads), *functionally utilitarian* – normative and convenient (e.g. those in service trades and professions including chefs, maids, mechanics, nurses) and *functionally symbolic* – enabling easy identification (e.g. soldiers, police, air stewards, clergy). What is central to these choices is a sliding scale of achieving a fit between the occupational role and the attributes of the occupant relating to efficiency of performing a role. For example, in the case of the immediate expectation of action by a policeman called to an emergency, one would be reassured by the sight of a symbolic uniform; whereas in the case of a lawyer whose legal opinion was sought by a client, the emphasis would be on the quality of the opinion offered rather than what they were wearing. Joseph and Alex (1972) identify four connotations associated with the meaning of uniforms: as a *group emblem*; as a means of *concealing status*; as a means of *conferring legitimacy*; and as a means of *suppressing individuality*.

As occupational roles diversify and occupants do too, the normative assumptions about appropriate dress have to some extent been challenged. Generally, more problems have surrounded women entering previously "masculine" occupations, such as police, military, politics, medicine, law and "blue-collar" jobs. Here they are pressured to perform "asexual femininity" in their dress and demeanour (Garber 1992: 43). A Welsh lawyer recounted that she had a wardrobe of court wear – from a pinstriped feminized suit (with skirt) to black skirts of varying lengths, a suite of ties and scarves, and a range of blouses from men's style shirts to cowl neck silk. She chose which outfit was appropriate depending on the nature of the judge and the crime. Her most important sartorial weapon was her spectacles. Although possessing 20/20 vision, she had a wardrobe of spectacles that she chose for effect. In short, although no uniform was prescribed, she had adapted conventional male lawyers' wear to create a wardrobe of feminized, specialist apparel that evoked conservatism and merely alluded to fashion through the spectacles and neckwear.

In an Australian case in 2003, a leading female lawyer who acted as prosecutor, in a case involving another high-profile female legal colleague, mixed traditional legal garb (legal wig, white collar, black gown) with a contemporary twist (tight-fitting front-buttoning black waistcoat, miniskirt featuring an off-centre split to the thigh and sheer stockings). This outfit was much photographed and discussed in public. The defendant, by contrast, chose a wardrobe of colourful, loosely tailored suits and hand-painted silk scarves. Both choices were the object of considerable media speculation as to the intended attributes and images being purveyed (e.g. Ober-hardt 2003).[1] On her unexpected conviction, the defendant would swap the suit for "the standard [prison issue] blue T-shirt and grey tracksuit pants" on her admission to a correctional centre (Done-man 2003). Discussion of this sartorial shift seemed to reflect the loss of professional and social status more than the merits of the legal judgment. When she was released to a halfway house, the media reported that: "She can now wear her own clothes, cook her own meals and will even be able to leave the centre" (Willis 2003), a signal that her status was being regained.

But some things do not change. Female judges in certain courts in some Anglo-Saxon countries are still expected to wear the traditional horsehair wigs of their male peers. And when women were grudgingly admitted as pilots in Britain – after years of argument about the lack of appropriate toilet facilities on planes – they wore flying suits styled for men's bodies under which those in the Royal Air Force were "supposed to be wearing Y-front long johns" (Fussell 2002: 87), even though these were completely useless. Ewing's (1975) study of women in uniform traces the slow sartorial acknowledgement of adapting military uniforms for female bodies and more fashionable looks. Even current female pilots' uniforms – in the military and civilian airlines – are female versions of traditional captains' suits (black or navy jacket and trousers trimmed with gold buttons and braid, and worn with a white shirt). The highest ranking female in the Australian military was allowed to design her own uniforms because none existed for a woman at that rank (personal communication).

At a prosaic level, work uniforms are ostensibly worn for practical reasons – to protect or assist the functional role; to designate status, competence and hierarchy; and to indicate the roles and attributes of the worker. Yet, occupational uniforms also denote many other things and people are frequently ambivalent about their attitude to and relationship with uniforms. Uniforms are more than just clothing for the body, more than markers of the social division of labour. Rather, uniforms seem to wear the body and to produce certain performances – the body becomes an extension of the uniform.

Over time, working uniforms have shifted from being at extreme ends of the occupational spectrum to becoming a norm across many occupations. Here the naturalization of uniforms in the workplace focusing on five issues is explored: the tension between function versus fashion in work uniforms; trends in types of uniforms; tradition versus innovation in uniforms in different occupations; how shifting ideas of gender are denoted through uniforms; and the emergence of corporate, quasi and informal uniforms in the workplace.

At a time when our culture is saturated with concepts of individuality and a preoccupation with consumer choice, uniforms are more pervasive than ever – especially in the workplace. Why are we so fond of conforming despite our quest for individuality and difference? How can we account for this paradox?

Classic Elements of Work Uniforms

Uniforms for work come in all manner of styles and accoutrements yet there are some constant elements that recur. These stem from the three key sources of uniform design – military uniforms, ecclesiastical garb and the dress of service workers (Craik 2003). Military uniforms provide a number of automatically recognized elements, such as epaulettes, top stitching, prominent buttons (e.g. double rows of gold buttons), tailored jackets, symmetrical breast pockets, necktie, leather belts and boots, and so on. Ecclesiastical dress provides another source of uniform elements – capes and cloaks, distinctive embroidery and braiding, elaborate decoration, surplices, veiled head covering, tunics, dog collar and the like.

Service occupations lent towards another genre of clothes – aprons and coveralls, coats (from top coats and tails to lab coats), caps and hairnets, tailored suits, plain bodices, bibs, etc.

Contemporary uniforms – as can be seen from burgeoning growth of online uniform retailers (e.g. Yahoo! Directory Uniforms > retailers) – liberally borrow from this array.[2] Traditional uniforms that resist change – such as the wigs and gowns worn by lawyers in court or religious regalia – retain distinctive idiosyncratic elements. Even when circumstances challenge the practicality of occupational dress – such as the entry of women into occupations like the law or church – uniform codes change reluctantly and bizarrely. So we find women judges wearing ancient men's wigs and women prosecutors wearing split short skirts under their robes teamed with a feminized necktie and pinstripe jacket. Some women lawyers deploy a wardrobe of spectacles designed to convey specific emotions – empathy, fear, pity, authority, etc.

Women clergy have also struggled to find appropriate wear (Ribeiro 1999: 120–5). Traditional dress, such as the nun's wimple or veil, tunic, habit and scapular, has often been replaced by modest shirts and skirts worn with a nurse-style veil, neck scarf and badge. While some religious orders have abandoned habits and wimples and adopted civilian dress, they denote their occupation by a small brooch depicting a cross. Some head covering, however, is usually still worn reflecting, perhaps, religious sensitivities to the presence of women in churches. Men attend church bareheaded in western religions although Islamic men wear a lacy cap and Jewish men a skullcap while Hasidic Jews wear a sable hat (Lurie 1981: 85–6). As discussed in Chapter 4, where women have been admitted to religious orders, feminized versions of gowns, surplices and cowls are often adopted, albeit in bright colours (like magenta or purple or blue) or virginal white (Craik 1994: 2–3).

When an Australian newspaper ran a competition to design outfits for ordained women, all three designers chose a high collar or high neckline, "modest" (i.e. long-line) skirts and jackets, and incorporated religious insignia – notably a cross – in the jewellery or fabric. One of the designers explicitly acknowledged that her outfit had "a fairly demure outlook with a certain reverent attitude", thereby signalling that female clerical garb had to embody key attributes of the occupational persona "to produce particular practical, social and gestural effects" (quoted by Craik 1994: 2–3). In contrast to, say, the over-the-top regalia of high church wear

Figure 30
Australian legal team.

and the civilian plus dog collar garb of fundamentalists, these outfits were constructing personal and occupational attributes of modesty, decency, moderate authority, auxiliary religious roles and a nod to fashion. In other words, the outfits constructed the modified occupational activities of female clergy at this time.

Female celebrants don similar garb balancing the religious tradition of piety, respect and spirituality, but expressing a modern twist. The celebrant at a recent burial wore a white surplice under a satin stole embroidered with colourful butterflies, presumably some reference to the journey of the soul. This contrasted with the female Protestant minister at the funeral who wore an elaborate white habit and surplice complete with blue satin pallium and elaborate stole, seemingly a bid to have her legitimacy and authority as a cleric established.

In addition to the classical components of occupational dress, other aspects directly related – or ostensibly did so – to more practical requirements. Function and form (protection, specialism, status, membership, authority) have shaped the genre of work uniforms. Protective uniforms include overalls, coveralls, aprons, helmets and lab coats. These serve a practical function yet become a distinctive element in themselves. Specialist uniforms denote a particular occupational skill or role such as the apron of a "master" craftsman or tradesperson (butcher, blacksmith, baker) or specialist

profession (e.g. medical roles such as surgeon, anaesthetist, physio-
therapist or neurologist).

Differing gowns or protective garb – often in different colours
– indicates the specialism, such as thin blue and white striped gowns
for dentists but thick blue and white striped aprons for butchers.
Vets and surgeons often wear green or blue operating gowns, while
physicians and nurses wear white – though many nurses wear a
pastel or discreetly patterned (e.g. gingham check) uniform. The
latter draws on service uniforms of maids and ancillary staff
befitting their status as handmaidens to the higher status doctors
(cf. Steele 1989: 75). Thus we can see that status within and among
occupations determines occupational dress as does membership of
a specialist group and associated rank. Frequently, badges, stripes,
ties and the type of coverall are used to denote precisely qualifications and specialism. Fussell (2002) observes that students at elite
cooking schools

> wear the traditional outfit, but with the white floppy hat
> instead of the as yet unearned noble toque. But there is one
> important status detail hardly noticeable by outsiders, and it
> is a tiny thing. The students have plastic buttons on their
> jackets, while real graduate chefs' jackets fasten with white
> cloth knot buttons. (Fussell 2002: 154)

What is striking about occupational uniforms is how much we take
them and their intended meanings for granted. We naturalize the
most common elements of uniforms in particular occupations
and expect to recognize them on the job. Equally we naturalize
what each component signifies about the occupation and incum-
bent. Thus, a description of a uniform requires minimal explicit
explanation. We "know" what uniforms mean and what can
be expected of particular choices and arrangements of uniform
pieces.

"Flight Refreshments": Dressing Airlines

Flight Refreshments![3]
Attractively served, inviting flight refreshments are free to all
Ansett Airways' passengers. New, easily handled plastic trays
– for your convenience. Nothing is left undone for your

comfort by Ansett – on or off the ground. (McRobbie 1986:
Ansett advertisement 1940s, inside front cover)

The development of uniforms for the crew of commercial airlines
illustrates the arbitrary yet contingent nature of their design.
Coinciding with the onset of the Second World War, the earliest
uniforms worn on commercial airlines not surprisingly adopted a
military look (Lovegrove 2000: 9, 14). For men, this was essentially
a quasi-naval captain's uniform consisting of a dark – often navy
double-breasted suit with rows of gold buttons, decorated with
gold braid (including stripes to designate status) and a captain's
visor hat with gold braid insignia, and worn with a white shirt and
plain dark tie (cf. Fussell 2002: 85–8). Indeed, the pilot (itself a
naval term) was called the captain and a number of other naval
references were adopted – airships, first officer, purser, cabin
attendant, the crew, naval officers' stripes on epaulettes, naval
badges, clippers and even the greeting "welcome aboard".

These nautical references were hardly surprising given that many
of the early aircraft were flying boats and were staffed by former
stewards on ocean liners (McIntosh 2003: 9, 21). In fact, the
programme of steward training was borrowed from the merchant
navy. The naval jargon had another advantage, attaching a sombre,
high-status reference to flying as a highly technical and elite mode
of travel. The uniform gave passengers a sense of security and
confidence in the competence of the crew to reach their destination.

When Qantas began commercial flights in 1938, it adopted a
single-breasted and belted khaki uniform made of gabardine with
brass buttons that had "a very military appearance" and required
intensive upkeep (McIntosh 2003: 19, 126–7). These were replaced
in 1947 by commander-style double-breasted navy suits still with
brass buttons but much more authoritative.

In contrast to the authority conveyed by pilots' uniforms, the
genre of hostess "uniforms" were coded with markers of service,
frivolity and low skill from the outset. According to Fussell (2002:
87), "There was much uncertainty at first about what stewardesses
should wear and what they should be called. At first they were
dressed as domestic maids, nurses, and even chorus girls."

American hostesses were dressed like nurses, wearing "green
suits on the ground but white nurses' attire, with capes and caps,
on board" (Visser 1997: 3). Indeed, they were initially selected on
their ability to nurse and serve food – although increasingly also

for their good looks and careful grooming. Training was as much about cosmetics, hairstyling and etiquette as it was in practical job skills. But not all the early hostesses looked like nurses. Some airlines drew on military apparel. For example, staff serving on Boeing, Swissair and Lufthansa, among the first European airlines to employ hostesses, wore tailored jackets, A-line skirts, military-style hats or caps – and sensible shoes. In Australia, Holyman Airways' first hostesses – who incidentally were allowed to design their own uniforms – wore dark jackets and skirts, featuring brass buttons and gold badges; underneath they wore a white shirt and black tie; on their feet, sensible lace-up shoes and on their heads, a forage cap adorned with a brass star (McRobbie 1986: 15). The forage cap was modelled on that of the US Airforce – and in turn borrowed from the infantry undress cap – and reflected a gradual mingling of naval with airforce motifs in airline uniforms.

In 1948, Qantas employed women and kitted them out with the following:

> Our uniforms consisted of six white cotton dresses for the tropics, a winter navy uniform of skirt and jacket with a white blouse and navy tie, navy lace-up, medium heeled shoes, wartime lisle (seamed) stockings, a navy bag, navy greatcoat, navy forage cap (to be worn over the right eye), two tone summer shoes, and numerous gold Qantas buttons and shanks for our dresses. There were also navy kid gloves. (McIntosh 2001: 129)

Smart though they were in theory, the reality was rather different. As one hostess recalled:

> We thought those uniforms superb, unique, unaware that we would see them reproduced at every airport in the world. Our white linen dresses were for the tropics, destined, when we were working, to wilt and attract dirt like a magnet. For temperate zones we wore a utilitarian navy blue suit with white shirts and navy blue tie. Our suit jackets were adorned with brass buttons embossed with the Qantas emblem. We were expected to keep these buttons polished to a gleaming shine. The outfit resembled a naval officer's uniform and was just as unfeminine. However, we soon learned to tilt our caps at a provocative angle, not regulation, and cover our legs in

sheer rather than heavy-duty stockings, and slip our feet into seductively stylish high heels instead of sensible, lace-ups. We discovered that it was not what you wore, it was how you wore it. (McIntosh 2003: 33–4)

Subsequent uniforms kept the military theme but used softer lighter-coloured fabrics (e.g. white and cream). These looked more like nurses' uniforms. What is clear is that early hostess uniforms embodied a tension between looking caring, nurturing, serving and trustworthy or serious, disciplined and practical. A 1949 advertisement for Australian National Airways featured a pretty blonde with airman's cap (with gold star), white shirt and tailored jacket accompanied by the words: "LADIES AT WORK . . . Your A.N.A. hostess is a trained officer . . . a charming, capable and highly efficient young lady who aids greatly to the pleasures of air travel." Surrounding photos depicted her as "a child psychologist", "dispenser of palate tempting meals", "friend to elderly travellers", "travel expert", "travelling companion for unaccompanied youngsters" and "watcher of your personal comfort" (McRobbie 1986: end page).

By the 1950s, hostess uniforms merged the genres, combining a nurse-like blouse and skirt with the military insignias of brass buttons, epaulettes and gold badges on a tailored jacket and teamed with an airman's cap adorned by a gold star (McRobbie 1986: 38, 58–9). This type of outfit was an attempt to professionalize hostessing as a career by simultaneously emphasizing the care and nurturing role of the hostess with the authority and discipline of a meticulously trained and turned out career woman. Increasingly, hostesses were "the public face of the airline, the embodiment of the corporation" and how they looked became an obsession. Yet the glamorous image coexisted with extreme chauvinism and the association of hostesses with empty-headed "sexpots" took hold through the 1950s and 1960s, a designation reflected in countless films, books and magazines as well as in airline advertisements, such as a 1971 advertisement that announced "I'm Cheryl. Fly me" (Moles and Friedman 1973: 306). More explicitly: "Braniff International 'ended the plain plane' in 1966, offering 'stews' who made several flashy costume changes en route, ending with hot pants" (Visser 1997: 4).

In deference to this characterization of hostesses, extreme body techniques of deportment, dress and grooming were enforced.

There were almost surreal rules about how uniforms should be worn as well as regulations concerning hair, make-up, jewellery and maintenance of "the look". When Qantas updated its uniform in 1953 "to a jacket without lapels, and no tie (much to the relief of the girls), and a straighter skirt" (McIntosh 2003: 129), it necessitated "some restrictions on hairstyles, namely short hair or a wig! While some crew liked the uniform, it was becoming outdated by international standards – with a group of chic New Yorkers remarking about a Qantas crew: 'They gotta be part of the Russian navy'" (McIntosh 2003: 131). In 1959, Qantas abandoned navy for "jungle green":

> The styling was classic – a shirtmaker dress, slim skirt, small shawl collar which enhanced the uncluttered look of the collarless jacket. The gold buttons with Qantas Empire Airways crest were detachable. (McIntosh 2003: 131)

To maintain the glamorous image, uniforms were regularly redesigned to achieve versatility, practicality and chic. Norman Hartnell for BOAC, Hardy Amies for BEA, Pierre Cardin for Air France, Pierre Balmain for TWA and Minori Monta for Japan Airlines were among the early designer uniforms (Lovegrove 2000).

During the 1960s, the image of hostessing was at its zenith, becoming synonymous with freedom, career and a cosmopolitan lifestyle. Uniforms reflected the new hip connotations. The military theme was merged with contemporary fashion statements – Cardin-inspired collarless round or V-necked jackets and coat dresses, knee-length boots, pillbox hats and miniskirts (McRobbie 1986: 63–4). In 1965, Emilio Pucci designed Braniff International's fuschia pink acrylic outfits that still attract attention. Colour was all the rage! In 1964, Qantas opted for an aqua fitted dress and collarless jacket; and in 1969, chose a burnt coral A-line minidress, short jacket and "powder puff" hat reminiscent of Jackie Kennedy (McIntosh 2003: 133). A return to a more sombre look occurred in 1971 with a navy blue dress worn over a white blouse or white ribbed skivvy:

> The matching navy jacket had gold buttons and gold buttons also trimmed the epaulettes. An overcoat accompanied in Tango Red (not Bravo red) and the jaunty navy hat had distinctive red stripes earning this uniform the name "the

Figure 31
Female prosecutor.

red-back spider." White gloves (great in the heat of Bombay) and black handbag and boots (also great in Bombay) completed this uniform. (McIntosh 2003: 133)

This style was short lived and in 1974, Emilio Pucci became the first international designer to update Qantas (Black 2003; Inchley 2003: 120):

The flower power look of the seventies was personified in the floral, polyester [uniform] totally different from its predecessors. Firstly, no hat, but a very wearable scarf (essential in Bahrain!). The shirt-maker dress came with long or short sleeves, but with the Pucci signature of the border print. Many pieces went to make up the outfit – the options were a green skirt and jacket (worn over the dress which then worked as a blouse for this suit) a choice of soft coral skirt and jacket and an overcoat in pure Australian wool in either green or coral. The shoes, handbag and pantihose that went with this uniform were navy blue. This uniform was worn well into the eighties. (McIntosh 2003: 133–34).

The perception of hostesses changed accordingly, to the image of young, decorative, frivolous "dolly birds" of the air or "Puccis Galore" (Lovegrove 2000: 22, 24; Black 2003). Many designers got into the act including Mila Schoen for Alitalia, Pierre Balmain for Singapore Airlines and Hanae Mori for Japan Airlines. Balmain's sarong kebaya, redolent of western perceptions of Asian femininity, was a particular success, with the Singapore girl becoming the epitome of the hostess as acknowledged in her 1993 inclusion at Madame Tussaud's waxworks in London (Lovegrove 2000: 36, 49).

Designer uniforms proliferated throughout the 1970s, with a dazzling array of innovations – hot pants for Southwest Airlines (1973), tiger-skin jackets for National Airlines (1971), the salwar-kameez for Air India (1971), mod wear by Mary Quant for Court Line Aviation (1973), an East-West melange (Balenciaga for Gulf Air) and sporty uniforms by Anna Klein for United Airlines and Bill Blass for American Airlines. Generally, the outfits were more casual and abandoned the severe military details and tailoring. It was during this period that mix-and-match components of uniforms were introduced, a trend that has continued (McRobbie 1986: 66–7, 83, 97). While designers like Armani (Alitalia), Yves Saint Laurent (Qantas), Pierre Cardin (Pakistan International Airways) and Christian Lacroix have emphasised stylishness, the incorporation of national motifs had become increasingly important in giving uniforms and airlines a distinctive identity.

By the 1980s, the mood had shifted back to a more severe look with padded shoulders reinforcing the sense of authority but keeping the choice of blouses, scarves, skirts or dresses alive. Male flight attendants were introduced, a seismic change that rewrote many of the assumptions about flight attendants and their job. The previous emphasis on pretty young things who dressed to please and maintained rigorous attention to their looks, weight, make-up and hair – and were sacked on marrying or becoming pregnant – became a thing of the past. Female flight attendants began to come in all shapes and sizes, all ages and all nationalities. Rules about how uniforms should be worn were relaxed. Flight attendants could even wear tailored pants on some airlines. Qantas reflected this mood with the designs of Yves Saint Laurent in 1985 and George Gross and Harry Who in 1993. Both resorted to navy jackets and skirts (or grey trousers) and blouses made from fabric with a "flying kangaroo" print (McIntosh 2003: 135). The military legacy persists. Steele (1989: 72) recalls that Eastern Airlines decided to "retain its new uniforms for flight attendants, despite fears that the uniforms look 'too military'", a decision justified by the argument that:

> In-flight assaults on attendants had dropped markedly after the uniforms were introduced, apparently because passengers took the military style as more than just appearance. Predominantly female, flight attendants benefited from looking tough. (Steele 1989: 72)

With the introduction of air marshals on flights following the 11 September 2001 air hijackings, airlines face a new uniform dilemma either to make the air marshals look like military personnel or to adopt a low key "soft" uniform approach and dress them in quasi-ranger or sheriff uniforms. Dressing them in civilian clothes runs the risk that they will be mistaken for terrorists should they need to take evasive action.

The quest to update and design appropriate smart but functional uniforms remains. Contemporary uniforms once again have blended tradition with "now-ness". For example, in 2003 a press article announcing the unveiling of the new Qantas airline uniforms described them as:

> corporate, conservative, stretchy and skinny. And almost all are black or charcoal . . . [They replace uniforms that are] boxy, big-shouldered, and sport an army of gold buttons. The new look is narrow, single breasted and discreet. (Lawson 2003)

The adoption of a suit for male flight attendants and pilots (male and female) as part of the new uniforms denotes a more traditional source of authority reinforced by the choice of black and charcoal wool stretch fabric, thereby combining classicism with comfort (Inchley 2003). This resort to tradition was softened by teaming the suits with ties (for men) or scarves (for women) made from fabric depicting a specially commissioned Balarinji Aboriginal design of an abstract boomerang and "dot" print called "Wirriyarra" screenprinted in brown (Rock) for attendants, blue (Opal) for airport and groundstaff or rust (Ochre) for QantasLink flight attendants (Australian Associated Press (AAP, 2003). The design attempted to incorporate the boomerang as "a quintessential Australian symbol [into] a dynamic icon for all Australians to embrace within a common sense of identity" (Balarinji's Ros and John Moriarty, quoted by ASIA Travel Tips 2003).

Female fight attendants have a choice of tailored black trousers, black jacket, print skirt and either a black or print shirtdress. The "service" look of the flight crew contrasts with the more severe look of the pilots in black single-breasted suits and "plain black ties – and hats – symbols of sobriety and authority". The fact that we have internalized the significance of patterned versus plain ties, and so on, indicates how much about occupational dress we have learned and take for granted. Interestingly, the designer of the uniforms, Peter Morrissey, completely overhauled every aspect of the crew's uniforms – including wing pins, belts, shoes, in-flight pyjamas, earrings and luggage – to achieve a uniform look:

> You cannot put my uniform on and make it your own because it is completely dictated to. Everything is neat, classic and easy – what you'd expect from an airline. (quoted by Inchley 2003: 118)

The result aimed to be "chic" as well as "wearable, classic and easy" (Inchley 2003: 118, 121), or, as Morrissey put it: "Form does follow function. It's an easy uniform to put together" (ABC 2003). From a designer point-of-view this may be desirable but it is compulsory to wear the jacket with the skirt or trousers. Gone are the days of mix and match. From the perspective of stewards, the uniform offers little flexibility when loading and unloading in the heat and humidity of the tropics, for example. The only option is to wear the shirtdress which – though feted by international tourists – is disliked by crew because the fabric is an unflattering shade of brown.[4]

The decision to opt for conservatism may relate to international uncertainties at the time, but it contrasts with other airlines who have opted for more fashionable looks, such as Qantas' main domestic competitor Virgin Blue, whose new uniforms include "trendy hipster pants, white shirts with three-quarter-length sleeves and red sweaters" (AAP 2003) or the casual look of Qantas's low-cost (and short-lived) Australian Airlines, whose staff wore khaki zippered jackets with orange shirts (Wood 2003: 26).

Airlines in Asian and Islamic countries have opted for mixing elements of conservative with nods both to fashion and modesty. For example, Gulf Air has classic navy suits and military-style caps with gold braid teamed with women sporting either a modestly draped pale blue head scarf worn under the cap and covering the throat or a gold and navy patterned scarf and uncovered head. Singapore Airlines sport fashionable versions of the traditional batik-patterned collarless jacket and pencil skirt.

As we can see, airline uniforms have retained their early military influence tempered by service uniforms (nurses and waiters) but have – over time – added elements of the fashionable while retaining moral propriety. As "hostessing" became an attractive option for young women wishing to enter a supposedly glamorous career, more emphasis was placed on the design of uniforms with top designers being commissioned to update an airline's look. The use of international designers has persisted with Air Italia choosing Giorgio Armani, Air France using Christian Lacroix and British Airways selecting Julien Macdonald (ABC 2003).

In this competitive climate, airlines compete for designers and designs, forever trying to balance the need for an instantly identifiable smart livery with a look that attracts attention without being too outlandish (e.g. the hot pants worn by Southwest Airlines flight attendants in the United States) and fulfils the requirements of the crew's occupational duties. A contributor to the internet-based Pilots' Rumor Network speculated:

> I suppose that historically uniforms came from the nautical/military connections, but that all seems somewhat distant and irrelevant now. Why not just wear comfortable clothes? Does anyone know of any research which finds passengers are comforted by uniforms, gold bars, caps, etc., or do uniforms say more about pilots' perceptions of themselves? (quoted by Fussell 2002: 87–8)

While more casual uniforms may be more practical – and have been adopted by budget or "no frills" airlines like Virgin and Virgin Blue – most airlines continue to opt for stylish conservatism redolent of trustworthiness and authority. Yet as many airlines have discovered, there is a trade-off between classicism and fashion: the greater the departure from classic design, the sooner the imperative to update a uniform. While classic airline uniform designs may last a decade, faddish ones are replaced within a few years (McRobbie 1986). Above all, airlines recognize the importance of having a striking corporate livery. As a controversial 1970s advertisement for Ansett airlines that featured a naked hostess wrapped in a curtain stated: "If the hostess was out of uniform would you know which airline you were flying with?" (McRobbie 1986: 98–9).

The Work of Occupational Uniforms

We hold widely shared assumptions about what is appropriate from different kinds of uniforms even when – as with airlines – we are talking about a global industry with a range of uniforms reflecting local norms, values and customs. In other words, our ideas about uniforms are normative and naturalized to the point where we make "automatic" judgements about particular uniforms only when they deviate from what we regard as unremarkable, that is, when a uniform dispenses with the classic elements we expect and have internalized as proper gear for the job.

Uniforms convey mutual recognition and identification, status and skills, internalized response to uniforms of authority. In a dated but important study, Bickman (1974) explored the influence of different kinds of outfits on ordinary people's behaviour. In one experiment he found that a person was twice as likely to return "lost" money to someone who was well dressed than to a poorly dressed person. He also investigated whether "uniformed persons acting outside their accustomed roles, still have greater power than nonuniformed persons" Bickman 1974: 50). Dressing volunteers in one of three uniforms – sports jacket and tie, milkman and guard (dressed like a policeman) – he set up three situations and found that people were more likely to obey the guard and equally likely to ignore the civilian and the milkman. In other words, the uniforms were being read in terms of occupational type and status. While the milkman was a specialist his role carried no authority.

A further experiment showed that people were twice as likely to obey the guard as the civilian, even obeying ludicrous requests. Yet when Bickman (1974) asked people to estimate whether uniforms would affect their behaviour, they denied it, indicating that our conscious perceptions of uniforms in the abstract differs from our

Figure 32
Fiji policeman.

internalized unconscious and the taken-for-granted (unremarkable) behavioural responses to uniforms of authority. There are, then, very powerful reasons why rulers in unstable regimes, private security companies, administrators in roles of authority and punishment, parking inspectors – even surf lifesavers – chose to adopt a distinctive uniform that is redolent of their job.

Equally, ordinary people expect that encumbents should "look the part". We would not trust the dentist with grubby overalls and dirty nails; we would be sceptical of a legal defender in a hot pink mini and low-cut top; and we would wonder if the plumber in a polo shirt and chinos could really unblock the drains. Whether a formal uniform is decreed or simply collectively adopted as the norm, citizens encountering works expect workers to look a particular way. We get irritated and put out when workers do not look the part. Paul Fussell, for example, was irate that hospital nurses were out of uniform:

> The nurses appeared not in their traditional uniform (white shoes and hose, white dress, all important starched white cap, and navy blue cape for outdoors), but dressed any old way, including blue jeans, as if they were ashamed of any sign of education or distinction, let alone simple identification . . . I wanted to see a nurse now and then and the only caregivers I could raise looked like charladies. (Fussell 2002: 156)

He admitted that nurses have long been critical of their uniforms, in particular, that the traditional uniform of white dress, cap and blue cape made them look "subordinate, a servant to a higher class, namely, physicians" (Fussell 2002: 157). However, it also allowed them to show off their status as a trained nurse and to be immediately recognized – and trusted by – their patients. According to Fussell, patients "feel cheated when assigned a nurse visibly not qualified" (Fussell 2002: 157). The American trend towards nurses wearing white trousers under a lab coat seems to be reinforcing the scientific basis of nursing over the caring role, perhaps reflecting a shifting status and occupational designation. Fussell clearly preferred nurses in the traditional uniform. Likewise, he found himself confronted by a doctor who was not in uniform: "I was shocked to find him out of uniform, wearing a tweed jacket and khakis. I felt both uncertain of the roles we were playing and a bit annoyed at being cheated" (Fussell 2002: 158).

So the type of uniform is crucial in public perceptions of the skill, trustworthiness and status of the worker. In some occupations, a formal uniform is almost mandatory. So when people were interviewed about photos of police officers dressed in three different kinds of uniforms – traditional navy, sheriff-type khaki and grey slacks with dark blue blazer – they rated the officers in traditional uniforms as having better judgement, and being "more competent, helpful, honest, fast and active compared with the blazer-donned police officers" (Bridgewater 1985: 72).

In the case of Menlo Park, California, police adopted blazers in 1969 but returned to navy in 1977, finding that officer-directed assaults have "been declining significantly since the old uniforms were reinstated" (Bridgewater 1985: 72). This suggests that perceptions of police remain traditionally normative in preferring an obvious uniform of authority that encodes the ideal attributes of policing and community trust. In other professions, there may be a range of formal uniforms, consensual dress and informal norms.

Professions related to the practice of medicine illustrate how occupational uniforms have changed over time (cf. Steele 1989: 73–7). Nurses have traditionally worn white dresses and caps but doctors adopted a white lab coat over street clothes only in the 1890s – long after Lister's concerns about germs and dirt contamination. So medical staff in hospitals wore uniforms, but in community practices and clinics, only nurses and auxiliary staff donned uniforms. Doctors generally wore civilian clothes (smart casual) unless they were doing a surgical procedure.

Nowadays, there is both a multiplication of uniforms for specialist activities and more relaxed uniform codes. The uniforms of nurses have become more casual – abandoning the cap or triangular (described by one nurse as "starched to buggery") veil and "tiara" (rather like that of so-called "brides of Christ" in Catholicism) and adopting less tailored shirts and skirts, shorts or trousers[5]. Instead of front-buttoning shirts or shirtdresses, the tops are loose, have sculpted sides and can be worn over the top of the skirts or trousers. In many hospitals, there is a choice of colours and/or patterns though these are usually pastel shades and modest prints (e.g. checks or stripes). In many Australian hospitals, registered nurses wear white, while enrolled (student) nurses wear a different colour and charge nurses yet another. Some nurses such as theatre nurses wear no uniform, donning surgical gear for theatre work, while some nurses – as Fussell (2002) observed – wear casual clothes. The only indication of specialist function and status is the stripes or stars on the lapel or badge of a nurse, though this is often only understood by other staff not the patients. Within the nursing profession, there is a phenomenon known as "lapel syndrome" where the behaviour of the nurse seems to be triggered by the importance of the insignia on or colour of their lapel. Overnight, reasonable co-workers become despots on their elevation in rank! (personal communication).

Doctors' "uniforms" have also changed. Many doctors simply wear white lab coats over casual dress while specialists may wear coloured gowns. Paramedics and quasi-medical workers (physiotherapists, technicians) usually wear a lab coat, full apron or nurse-type dress. So in this profession, the formal uniforms are now more likely to be worn by the lowest status workers while the informal uniform (coverall of some sort) is worn by the high-status workers.

There is no clear explanation as to why white became the norm. White became the preferred colour before our cultural obsession with cleanliness of bodies and clothes – especially for surgical procedures or interpersonal encounters. A more likely explanation was the discovery of bleach as a cleaning agent. Clothes could be dyed white and bleached back to white, a virtue that has remained a fixture in medical dress. Steele suggests that white has acquired cultural significance as a symbol of "life, purity and power" as well as redolent of innocence and asexuality (desirable attributes of the ideal nurse: Steele 1989: 75). In scientific contexts, white also became synonymous with technical precision and hygiene so by combining these, white has come to signify healing in the medical profession. However, Steele points out that white aprons and caps for nurses were worn several decades before the germ theory of disease and that their origins seem to be the maid's uniform – an apron suitable for cleaning as well as caring for the sick (Steele 1989: 76). Once again, as the nursing profession has been professionalized then deregulated, the variety of uniforms has grown especially now that men have joined the ranks of nursing. While nurses out of uniform are increasingly common, the specialist nature of their occupation suggests that some kind of vestimentary marker will remain.

Academic dress is an example of multiple uniforms and dress codes (cf. the military and police) plus the trend towards coexistence with informal ones. The wearing of specialist academic dress is a longstanding tradition dating in Europe from medieval times that relates to the ecclesiastical basis of early education. Hence academic dress adopted many elements of religious garb – a full-length gown or robe with trimming on the collar, facings, back and sleeves, a cap or mortarboard, a hood and tie. While the gown was typically black, high-status academics such as the chancellor and vice-chancellor often had robes of coloured brocaded silk akin to papal or archbishop's garb (Venables and Clifford 1973: 209–10). Historically, the elaborate garb was reserved for ceremonies while a plainer black gown was worn for teaching and informal occasions.

During the twentieth century, the custom of wearing full academic dress became an exception and increasingly academics wear normal clothes except for graduation ceremonies. Yet, formal dress has diversified with the establishment of new universities on a global scale and new degrees to be awarded. Each university sets a unique code of dress, varying the colour of the gown, the colour and type of trimmings and hood, the type of headwear and various other insignia of status and specialization, for example, different brightly coloured sashes denoting different degrees.

Students, too, have had dress codes applied. At Oxford University, these were known as "subfusc" clothing. For men, this included "a dark suit, dark socks, black boots or shoes, a white shirt, white collar and white bow tie" while for women "a white blouse, black tie, dark skirt, black stockings, black boots or shoes and, if desired, a dark coat" (Venables and Clifford 1974: 211).

Until the 1970s, some American universities banned students from wearing jeans and for women, any trousers. As dress codes have been relaxed, students have evolved their own informal codes with a preference for casual tops, trousers or jeans and trainers creating a remarkably standardized look despite its voluntary adherence.

For academics, gone are the days of wearing a gown for teaching and casual clothes have also become the norm – generally smart casual shirts (perhaps polo) and chinos for men, and casual top and trousers or jeans for women (plus comfortable shoes). Come conference time, academics shift their code up a notch, especially on the first day or when they are giving a paper. On these occasions, male academics may replace the polo with a coloured business shirt and slacks instead of the chinos plus a sports or tweed jacket, while women may don a dress shirt or high fashion top teamed with a skirt rather than trousers. A tailored jacket may also be added. The addition of a scarf, jewellery, high heels and even make-up complete the look and add an individual touch. Academics choose something in between these two codes when delivering lectures, attending important meetings or meeting special colleagues. So while it may seem that it does not "matter if a scholar wears Gucci, gabardine, or grunge" (Alison Schneider, quoted by Kaiser, Chandler and Hammidi 2001: 117), the selection of academic clothing rests on informal yet internalized rules about appropriate garb for specific occasions, roles and external perceptions.

For women academics, this involves "a complex melding of female culture's attention to fashion with the life of the mind" (Kaiser et al. 2001: 117). Women academics chose their clothes on the "not" principle, namely, to avoid "the power suit":

> The power suit seems to represent what many of the academic women regard as the worst of male and female cultures. It represents a kind of uniform professionalism that is viewed as too slick and hierarchical for the world of intellectual ideas, and the hose and heels just add to the discomfort. (Kaiser et al. 2001: 120–1)

In order to determine what is appropriate and comfortable, female academics negotiate "danger zones" of professionalism and self-presentation encountered in the minutiae of academic roles (administration, lecturing, tutoring, writing, negotiating, giving conference papers, sitting in meetings, etc). This involves a balancing act between constructing attractiveness and professionalism, while marking a look with a personal sense of style.

Women professors in particular practise the careful selection of appropriate clothing. Green (2001) found that women felt pressured to revise their dress codes on their elevation to a chair. This often involved buying new clothes – more upmarket, more expensive and more formal. Tailored suits and jackets were frequently mentioned as the "necessary" garb of a female professor:

> I thought suits . . . but not necessarily uniform style suits . . . I wanted something which would be more individualistic than that . . . On the one hand playing safe through suits but . . . wanting to say . . . I'm not a normal suit . . . look at the fabric, look at the colour. (Sheila, quoted by Green 2001: 104)

These special clothes "acted as a kind of armour or protection" (Green 2001: 102). As one woman put it:

> Not that I immediately entered into a uniform, but there was an extra degree of reflexivity about that . . . I wanted to be an individual, I wanted in a sense to have something appropriate to the position but that was a style that I was comfortable with, or that reflected certain sorts of things about me. There was no sense of just going to the shop and buying things off the peg and thinking . . . here is my work uniform . . . it had to be much more consciously selected and tailored [but] I don't fool myself that my real self shines through. (Sheila, quoted by Green 2001: 102)

Women used clothes to "stage manage" their professorial role and announce "to themselves and others that they are serious academics and powerful women" (Green 2001: 113). But while they saw "clothes or the way that I appear as part of my sort of professional image . . . as a positive contributor to my profession" (Barbara, quoted by Green 2001: 110), the women went to some lengths not to dress like men in male-style power suits but to vary the codes of formality and status to introduce a note of femininity and individuality. Said one woman:

> I decided that I was definitely going to dress as a female . . . I was not going to look like a clone of a pinstriped suit . . . I

Figure 33
A medical technician.

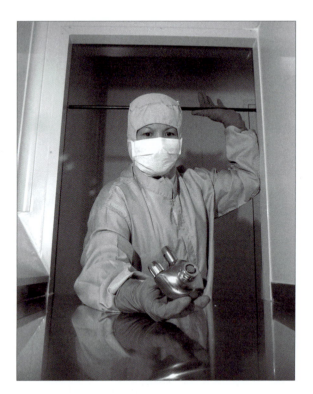

have a soft crushed velvet jacket and a long skirt . . . I have
to project a huge amount and therefore dress is a part of that
for me. In other words, I don't "mouse dress!" (Jenny, quoted
by Green 2001: 113)

In order to make sense of these experiences of wearing formal and
informal uniforms as part of establishing and maintaining a
professional occupational persona, a more systematic way of
categorizing uniforms, the attributes and their rate of change was
needed. To this end, I developed a typology that could cross-
reference different kinds of uniforms – official, unofficial or quasi,
and informal dress – with the likelihood of change. To do so, a
typology of stability–instability and tradition–innovation was
developed (see Table 5.1).

The typology shows that there is a trade-off between classicism
and fashion – the greater the departure from classic design, the
sooner the imperative to restyle a uniform. Those uniforms that
embody classic elements and resist change, such as full academic

Table 5.1 Typology of Occupational Uniforms relating to Stability–Instability and Tradition–Innovation

	Resist change	Slow change	Periodic change	Rapid change	Quasi-uniforms	Informal uniforms
Characteristics of uniforms	Traditional, historic, classical elements resist change	Retain distinctive elements, stable	Updated periodically, classic elements plus conservative fashion motifs, generally stable	Change regularly, derived from high fashion mixed with normative elements, date quickly, unstable	May change arbitrarily (e.g. women's corporate wear) or be reasonably stable (e.g. men's suits), normative, influenced by fashion	Apparently personal choice, no rules, prestigious imitation, unstable
Occupations	Ecclesiastic, legal, formal academic dress, blue-collar trades, funeral directors, laboratory workers, orchestral conductors (male)	Medical (doctors, nurses), dental, etc. butchers, chefs, military	Corporate – banks, service providers/ customer interface, healthcare and allied police, park rangers	Airline, cosmetologists, restaurants and food outlets, sports teams	Quasi-corporate, e.g. administrative, education, social work politicians, gardeners, professional choirs	Artists and cultural workers, hairstylists popular musicians, boutique staff, university students, demonstrators, street market vendors

dress, formal judicial dress, blue-collar workers, funeral directors and laboratory workers, maintain their occupational specificity and status ranking partly by use of their easily recognized vestimentary codes. These codes both reassure bystanders and establish the kind of body techniques performed by that occupation – whether it be furthering knowledge, dispensing justice, fixing or servicing things, burying the dead or practising scientific techniques. The uniform of each occupation conveys an immediately perceived sense of skills and knowledge as well as expectations of the relationship between the worker and others.

Other occupations retain some distinctive elements while slowly changing their occupational dress. Examples include doctors and nurses, dentists and dental nurses, butchers, chefs and – perhaps surprisingly – the military. The slow rate of change seems to be a guarantor of reliability and constancy, though slow change also indicates that the occupation updates itself over time. Many doctors have abandoned the tweed jacket and leather patches on the elbow – or switch, from white lab coats to coloured ones, or perhaps just an apron – but some markers of the occupation remain, and media representations of these occupations often opt for the traditional dress code. For example, doctors doing hospital rounds usually carry a stethoscope in their jacket pocket as an easily recognized sign of being a doctor. In their surgeries and clinics, some doctors wear a lab coat while others wear street clothes. Surgeons dress in surgical uniforms for the operating theatre and after surgery when reporting to a patient or patient's relatives, but on regular rounds, they dress like doctors – in a suit, or jacket and trousers – thus downplaying their specialist medical status. Dentists have evolved a distinctive uniform of a narrow striped lab coat (dress for nurses) usually in white and a calming colour like blue or pink.

Like dentists and doctors, uniforms have evolved for those handling food. We have already mentioned butchers whose distinctive navy and white striped aprons are still worn, although elaborations of the number and thickness of the stripes to denote high-ranking butchers have largely disappeared. Often, the butcher wears the apron over a white lab coat, creating a uniform link with workers who are involved in food processing. Whether they work in factories, delicatessens or retail, specialist food processors typically wear a lab coat – and perhaps an apron – with the hair covered by a disposable "shower" cap (replacing the maid's cap or scarf).

Cooks and chefs are generally accorded a higher occupational status, indicated in vestimentary terms by a more elaborate uniform. Fussell (2002: 154) suggests that the typical chef's outfit has changed little since its aristocratic origins two centuries ago. The uniform is "precisely described and proudly worn". The most distinctive element is the toque, the tall white hat consisting of a cylindrical crown and pleated "balloon-like" top, traditionally composed of between 48 and 100 pleats, depending on the height of the toque. The tallest toque was, of course, worn by the most senior chef.[6]

The origin of the toque is purportedly that it emerged during the sixteenth century (others say the Byzantine empire) when artists and chefs were persecuted and took refuge in monasteries, adopting the same garb as the priests for disguise (Kane 1998; George 2003). Later they retained the tall hat – in white instead of black as a mark of distinction. Toques were high maintenance and chefs were expected to keep them looking pristine. Inevitably, perhaps, this part of the uniform has undergone significant change. In this throw-away society, toques are now made of disposable paper except in the most exclusive restaurants. Chefs have experimented with variations on the headwear, ranging from modified toques with no pleating, caps that are a cross between a forage cap and a fez, berets, captain's caps and scarves tied at the back (usually black). Increasingly, and despite public health regulations, top chefs wear no headcovering at all, suggesting that they are relying more on personal recognition than standard uniform.

Chefs' jackets have remained more stable, typically consisting of a white cotton stand-collar double-breasted tunic jacket with either white or black buttons and optional trimming and embroidery designating the restaurant or chef. Ostensibly, these jackets were worn for insulation against the heat, protection against spills and because they were reversible (George 2003). These jackets seem to have derived from the cavalry tunic adopted and modified by Napoleon and popularized in the 1960s along with the Nehru or Sun Yat-sen jacket (with a stand-collar and centre-front opening). The Sun Yat-sen suit was itself "a complex synthesis of the Japanese Meiji-period student uniform, German military dress and the western suit" (Roberts 1997b: 18). Other chefs choose more of a Qipao style jacket (*ao*) of a mandarin collar and side fastening (cf. Hume 1997: 49; Roberts 1997c: 18–21, 50–1; Szeto 1997: 57; Finnane 1999: 129). Designer jackets for elite restaurants and kitchens are also proving popular, with special touches and variations to indicate distinctiveness.

Despite the impracticality of white uniforms around food preparation, the white jacket or coat persist as the norm; some restaurants have introduced black jackets, although these also show marks and spills. While some chefs have kept the traditional white trousers, many have opted for black and white houndstooth check trousers that have become something of a global norm, though Fussell (2002: 154) laments the fashion for chefs' trousers "patterned with little pictures of vegetables (onions, artichokes, peppers), revealing that the age of cute leaves its mark everywhere." Other chefs have opted for pinstriped or baggy trousers and trousers with CIA (Central Intelligence Agency) logos (George 2003). This example

indicates that the chef's uniform may be moving from the slow
change category to periodic or rapid change as stylistic and fashionable elements enter the traditional design. Moreover, the theatrical
element of the restaurant trade seems to be reflected in the increasing importance of distinctive uniforms that designate a chef,
restaurant or specialist task. Nonetheless, we can recognize a chef
anywhere due to the classic elements of the uniform.

Other occupations have uniforms that undergo periodic change,
such that classic elements are combined with some nod to conservative fashion trends. Examples include corporate uniforms of service
providers (for example, in banks, travel agents, chain stores, auxiliary healthcare providers) and regulatory occupations (police, park
rangers, security guards, prison officers). Bouncers (in nightclubs
and pubs) are another example. Black trousers with a white shirt
were the norm but as threats and violence from patrons has
increased, bouncers have adopted black shirts and trousers, ostensibly so that the blood from altercations does not show but perhaps,
too, in order to look more menacing to patrons, perhaps alluding
to the all-black uniform of the Nazi SS and Fascist Italian Black-
shirts as a sign of intimidation, power and menace (Fussell 2002:
23). At best, black is associated with evil and/or authority and
seriousness.

Some uniforms are highly susceptible to fashion updates and
these are generally unstable. The case of airline uniforms has been
discussed above. In some occupations, uniforms may or may not
be worn, and sometimes quasi-uniforms (similar types of fashionable dress, for example, each worker in black everyday dress). So
while some chains of cosmetic treatments may have a distinctive
uniform, others and solo workers may simply wear a modified lab
coat or coverall over their everyday dress. For students at beauty
colleges, however, a uniform is mandatory – perhaps indicating
their low status yet contributing to their initiation into the occupation rather than for a functional reason associated with their
exposure to chemicals and equipment. While barbers usually still
wear a white jacket, hairdressers tend not to wear a uniform as
such but fashionable everyday dress that conforms to the "style"
of the salon. Hair colourists, however, do don protective coveralls
and gloves owing to the harsh chemicals they work with – but
perhaps too, as a mark of specialist occupational status.

In addition, I have added two other categories – quasi-uniforms
and informal uniforms. Quasi-uniforms are dress codes that are

held normatively but not officially enforced. This follows on from Stone's (1970) discussion of using dress to fit in with one's peer group, as a kind of game, or sign of acceptance and incorporation into a group. The case of women professors wearing modified suits is an example of the assumptions of the occupational role and status being internalized by incumbents as part of the performance of those professorial duties. These informal dress codes can also be found in administrative workplaces, in schools, among politicians, professional photographers, non-uniformed gardeners (ever seen one in pink shorts and thongs?) and semi-professional choirs.

Informal uniforms refer to occupations where there are no acknowledged rules or pressures and where practitioners believe they dress according to personal choice. However, there is a systematic set of conventions that they display suggesting internalized attributes of the occupational role are translated into modes of apparel and accessories. For example, artists and some types of cultural workers (such as curators, art gallery and museum staff, hairdressers and fashion designers) can be easily identified by their penchant for black, severe spectacles and haircuts, outrageous jewellery, sharp, colourful and avant-garde clothes and unusual boots or other footwear. Other distinctive modes are worn by popular musicians, fashion boutique staff, hair stylists, university students and demonstrators. Other examples of the variability of uniformed and quasi-uniformed occupations include restaurant waitresses and waiters and professional sports people (especially when competing in special competitions such as national teams, Olympic Games and international events) – tennis players and golfers are cases in point.

Interpreting Occupational Uniforms

The typology shows that there are four key components of the adoption of a certain kind of uniform and its cycle of redesign.

Occupational Role and/or Skill

Most overtly, the design of an occupational uniform relates to the status, qualifications and membership of an occupation. At a practical level, some uniforms reflect the kind of skills and specialist activities that a worker undertakes. As Steele (1989: 66) observed, some jobs require protective clothing (coveralls, face masks or

Figure 34
Miners.

goggles, hard hats, gloves, boots) while other jobs require specialist clothing and equipment (astronauts, divers, rescue teams) that equip them for the job but many uniforms combine "the practical and the symbolic" (Steele 1989: 66) such as the lab coat or hostess uniforms discussed above.

While uniforms may indicate either professional status or a service function, they also convey a combination of authority, hierarchy, specialist knowledge or techniques, and a sign that the wearer possesses occupational authority rather than simply displaying individual personality. The body – through the uniform – constructs the attributes of the occupational role. This is especially important when specialised training and qualifications have been obtained to enter the occupation. Some of the most extreme markers of uniforms can be found in occupations where there is a closed shop and membership is restricted and regulated – e.g. judges, specialist medicos, senior clerics. The status and hierarchy are made super visible.

Transactional Forms of Occupational Interaction with Others

The idea of transactional body techniques refers to the use of uniforms as statements for others. Here the uniform provides clear signs about the nature of the worker – special skills (of the plumber or bodyguard), the demeanour or attitude and values of the worker (the caring nature of the nurse or funeral director), the authority and perhaps ability to intervene (of the police, welfare officer or lawyer) and the nature of the service that can be provided (by the cleaner, phone company, mechanic, tax agent). As the Bickman (1974) study cited above showed, those wearing uniforms of authority have a taken-for-granted ability to get respect and persuade people to obey orders.

One unexamined aspect of these transactional techniques is the importance of tailoring and colour in the design of uniforms. High authority uniforms – particularly involving the use of force (e.g. police, military, security guards) – adopt uniforms with severe tailoring, sharp lines and dark colours (navy, black) while high-status jobs involving knowledge or power (e.g. academics, judges, specialist medicos) adopt an almost fancy dress kind of uniform which may designate strength (e.g. the bold colours of judges' and clerics' garb) or compassion (e.g. the pastel shades of the specialist).

Habitus of the Worker and Pressures on Performativity

Equally important is how the uniform transforms the wearer into an occupational persona of a suite of trained body techniques and mental attributes. It is well known that people report feeling different in a uniform as if the clothes themselves bolster the persona of the wearer and equip them to perform. The uniform constitutes the occupational habitus of the worker in the transformation from civilian self to worker persona.

Gendered Attributes of Occupational Uniforms

Gentle in manner, resolute in deed. (Women's Royal Army Corps [WRAC] motto, cited by Ewing 1975: 136)

As we have already seen, gendered attributes are an important
element of occupational uniforms. The quotation above, although
used in the Second World War as the rallying cry of the women's
armed forces in Britain, encapsulates the enduring ambivalence
between the attributes of femininity and the body techniques and
demeanour of occupational roles. Where uniforms are concerned
as much attention is paid to how the uniform is worn by women
as to the apparel itself. The constant refrain is that women must
retain their femininity ("maintain your modesty" as a trainer of
female recruits in the Australian army put it) yet not be coquettish
(alluring to male recruits) while acquiring the ostensibly non-
gendered attributes of being a soldier. The police force has also
grappled with the issue of appropriate wear for women (see Chapter
1) oscillating from designing quasi-male uniforms to outfits more
appropriate to social work and public relations (Steele 1989: 69-
73). Skirts were retained until the 1970s although they became
shorter and replaced the helmet with "a cute, little stewardess-type
hat" in the mid-1960s in order to "feminize the policewoman's
uniform" (Steele 1989: 70). The campaign to introduce trousers
for women police was protracted and controversial despite the
obvious practical benefits. Young (1997) has argued that

> the endless re-designing of the uniform and the resultant air-
> hostess-type gear . . . symbolizes the male view that uniform
> fashion must match the obsessive changes in fashion for
> women in the outside world, which rarely affects men in a
> similar manner. (Young 1997: 273)

Even in the 1980s, it was still common to find male police denouncing
female colleagues as butch and unfeminine (see Chapter 4). The
retention of military motifs in policewomen's uniforms and regulations about the wearing of hair, jewellery and make-up indicate that
the female gender is still problematic in occupational roles of
authority, security and forcefulness.

Corporate, Quasi and Informal Occupational Uniforms

One uniform retail company, Focus Uniforms, includes a section
on "Why have uniforms in your company?" It suggests that "first

impressions are extremely important and often the most lasting" and when staff are making contact with clients, they "need to look and feel smart and stylish". This in turn "gives the company a co-ordinated image" allowing "customers to easily identify your employees". Finally it argues that uniforms increase employee satisfaction:

> Statistics show that employees who wear a smart uniform more readily identify themselves with the company they work for and feel like they are truly part of the team. They are also more interested in the company's profile and how the company is regarded by the public at large. This leads to higher job satisfaction and lower employee turnover. (Focus Uniforms 2004)

Employees in courier companies that deliver goods to businesses and private residences support these arguments. Not only do couriers share the feeling that they are more part of the team in uniform than in casual dress but also they report that, when making household deliveries, many people simply will not answer the door unless the courier is in a readily identifiable uniform (Personal Communication with a courier team). So the uniform acts as a security device to allay anxiety and articulate a professional transaction.

Despite the quest for individuality and criticisms that uniforms suppress the ability of the wearer to be themselves, in fact uniforms are increasingly being adopted in new occupational contexts. The growth of corporate uniforms is one example, including uniforms in banks, some administrative bodies, face-to-face service occupations, healthcare, childcare, hospitality, tourism and travel, animal carers and park rangers. These uniforms are designed to convey a sense of solidarity and uniformity among the staff as a whole. Uniforms which tend to opt for the "soft" approach – shirts, slacks and jackets for men, blouses and skirt/trousers or (quasi-auxiliary medical) dresses for women – are designed to embody attributes of professionalism, identity and identification. While the mix-and-match range of garments enables individual workers to decide whether "this goes with that", all together, uniformed corporate staff display a sense of us versus them – the client or customer. On the other hand, many uniform designs are shaped by the dictates of management and public relations who favour stylishness over comfort. Employees often complain that uniforms suit only some bodies (slim and young) and those with irregular shapes find difficulty selecting comfortable corporate wear.

Even where a uniform is not formally adopted, workers often mould their clothing and appearance to unwritten norms of the job. By a combination of prestigious imitation and taken-for-granted codes of appropriate dress, informal dress at work – such as that of businessmen and women, female lawyers and museum/gallery curators quickly adopt a particular style appropriate for the workplace. While there may be more variation among clerks and administrators, university students, educators in the classroom, people attending boardroom meetings and conferences, social activists, demonstrators and protesters, commonalities usually outweigh differences. We absorb the minutiae of rules and stigmata of transgressions and adapt our vestimentary behaviour often imperceptibly and sometimes (as in the case of female professors) deliberately.

Ambiguity and Occupational Identity

Throughout this chapter, we have seen that while some uniforms are normative and unremarkable to their wearers and bystanders, other uniforms have posed a series of issues and tensions. These include uniforms for policewomen (colloquially denigrated as "old trouts or sexpots"), women in the military, judicial workers (from the archaic gowns and wigs of judges to the balancing act of female legal counsel), the relevance of academic gowns in an increasingly informal vestimentary workplace, the national team uniforms worn at the Olympic Games opening Ceremony, women undertakers and civil celebrants. These examples illustrate not only the importance of clothing as a part of occupational attributes and demeanour – as the habitus of the individual worker – but also the ambiguities and tensions enmeshed in particular sartorial choices.

Three ambiguities are noted in particular. First, gender is often involved especially when a normatively male occupation is opened up to women. Uniforms match ideal attributes of western masculinity but challenge ideal attributes of femininity. This is even more pronounced in the case of Islamic women where a particular code of femininity (modesty in dress and avoidance of public display) contrasts so markedly with occupational roles and outlooks.

Figure 35
Australian universityvice chancellors.

Second, where uniforms disrupt authority and status, they are especially problematic. The adoption of police-like uniforms by private security firms may have had its rationale in signalling widely understood signs of order and authority. Yet the adoption of a police-like uniform – for example, by nightclub bouncers – has been a topic of debate in Australia as enabling security officers to assume an inappropriate mantle of authority and unwarranted exercise of force (including bashing and even murdering patrons deemed undesirable). Other examples include taxi drivers, chauffeurs, lift or bell boys, concierges, traffic wardens, car park attendants, guards at cultural institutions.

Third, occupational dress is used frequently in contexts of sexual excess. The preference for clothing and props including nurses' uniforms, maids' uniforms, school uniforms, military dress including boots, whips and guns, ecclesiastical garb, icons and paraphernalia in sado-masochistic performances, above all confirms that alongside normative codes of gender and sexuality are transgressive codes of rebellion, rejection and misidentification. This trend has been exploited by so-called school discos where patrons meet a "strictly enforced dress code of real or imitation school uniforms

– braces and pigtails optional" (Zamiatin 2003b: 47). Fans like the chance to misinterpret the rules for wearing school uniforms as a pretext for abandoning their inhibitions and having a good time. The idea of the naughty schoolgirl or delinquent schoolboy is at the heart of the appeal. As a Melbourne designer, Nevada Duffy, who customizes school uniforms for clubbing, commented:

> I like the way school girls modify generic uniforms, projecting their own identities on to them, making them really short and tight and turning a demure look into something tarty. (quoted by Zamiatin 2003b: 47)

Indeed, the outfits "work" only to denote ambiguous sexual allures because of the cultural anxieties about women that are woven into the very fabric of the uniforms. This is the basis of the longevity of uniforms for work and their proliferation in the workplace and leisure venues.

Working Uniforms for Postmodern Sensibilities

In sum, occupational uniforms wear the body and construct occupational techniques and persona. Central to this is negotiating the tension and "fit" between the civil self and occupational persona. Of prime importance is the fact that there is a mismatch between occupational attributes involving authority and normative feminine attributes.

Given this, we might conclude that occupational uniforms and the rules about how they are worn may constitute a partially codified form of sumptuary laws where internalized regulation of behaviour and dress conduct has replaced externally imposed sanctions.

6

Sports Uniforms to Sportswear

Sporting Bodies and Disciplined Selves

This chapter explores how customized clothing or uniforms developed for sport and subsequently became a correlate of wider developments in the history of everyday dress. Above all, sports uniforms have at their core a tussle between tradition and innovation and, as such, have become the hallmark of fashion and the pulse of style more generally.

Why do people wear specialist clothes for engaging in sport? What has influenced the development of those specialist clothes? Why have sports uniforms provoked not just attention but also controversy, especially in relation to women? To what degree have sports clothes influenced trends in fashion generally? Apart from histories of individual sports, little has been written directly about why sports uniforms and sportswear emerged or why they exerted such a profound influence on contemporary streetwear and leisurewear. Indeed, the fact that casual everyday clothing is called "sportswear" in the apparel industry is a testament to how comprehensively the development of specialist sports clothing has shaped our ideas about clothing. To avoid confusion, I distinguish between *sports clothing* (sporting wear worn by people engaging in sport, exercise or active leisure activities) and its subset *sports uniforms* (for official sporting events by teams or individuals) from *sportswear* (casual clothing and leisure fashion that has borrowed from sports clothing).

Four features of sportswear stand out. First, sports uniforms developed from other apparel, usually more as a statement of contemporary fashion than as a functional solution to the demands of different types of physical exertion. Second, changes in sports uniforms have mirrored changing ideas about the body and third, about gender. Fourth, the history of sports uniforms is intertwined with the history of consumer culture. In short, the emergence of sports uniforms reveals tensions and plays between a number of polarities: regulation versus experimentation; morality versus immorality; discipline versus transgression; modernity versus postmodernity; and masculinity versus femininity. In this framework, sports uniforms have become such an integral part of our fashion language and clothing habits that sports clothing has been adopted as the epitome of everyday dress, constantly playing out appeals to tradition against innovation and experimentation.

The only integrated commentary on either the forces shaping the emergence and development of sports clothing or on its gradual impact on fashion, leisurewear and casual wear within popular culture has been written by Schreier (1989). This is perhaps surprising given the ubiquitous genre of sports clothes and their visibility in cultural history. Possibly, the fact that sports clothing is so common has made it unremarkable – something so pervasive and taken-for-granted that analysts have not found a need to comment on it. In the themes of Marcel Mauss, this would translate into the status of sports clothing as a body technique and habitus that marks out a distinctive characteristic of western culture. Yet, Braddock and O'Mahony (2002) have argued that:

> the origin of contemporary sportswear can . . . be found in the protective and performance clothing designed by the first hunter-gatherers. This clothing was designed to be functional, protecting the wearer from the elements and allowing them to move with greatest ease and comfort. (Braddock and O'Mahony 2002)

Such clothing included garments with symbolic motifs designed to frighten or attact (a feature still prominent in sportswear) and fabrics or furs with special properties (such as sealskin, feathers, furs and wool) designed to be waterproof and weatherproof.

In addition, the development of sports clothing is inextricably linked to the emergence of modern forms of social organization and patterns of human movement, particularly to and within the New World. So we find that the history of sportswear and the history of clothing in North America are closely connected. Despite attempts to emulate the formal clothing practices of Europe, the thread through American clothing history is the emergence of more informal clothing codes, mass production, marketing and new practices of consumerism. Sportswear is, then, an intrinsically American phenomenon albeit one that has travelled globally, including back to Europe.

There are histories of specific sports that include descriptions of sporting wear and uniforms and changes over time (e.g. cricket, baseball, football, swimming and tennis).[1] There are intermittent references in histories of fashion.[2] The development of women's sports and appropriate sportswear has also received attention.[3] There are some (mostly journalistic) accounts of contemporary sportswear brands,[4] and some on sportswear as leisurewear.[5]

So, how can the history of sports uniforms and sports clothing be pieced together? Rather than being a new phenomenon, as we often think, sporting apparel has quite a number of progenitors. Indeed, the fashion historian, James Laver, argued that sports clothes were an intrinsic part of the development of modern men's clothing. In the seventeenth century, he suggested, "forms of male dress originated as sportswear" (cited by Wilson 1985: 27; cf. Laver 1995: 149, 168–74, 202–6). Laver nominated riding clothes as the first type of specialist sporting clothes. These were derived from the clothing of the rural aristocracy. Later, riding clothes were adopted as everyday wear for men anywhere.

By contrast, specialist sporting apparel for women occurred later and although influencing everyday women's dress, tensions between the "sportif" woman and contemporary ideals of womanhood have characterized subsequent developments. In other words, while ideas of male sporting and everyday dress have been compatible and the sportsman has epitomized masculine ideals, this has not been the case for women's sports clothing and ideas of femininity. As Schreier (1989) put it:

Figure 36
Italian tennis star Lea
Pericoli.

To an extraordinary degree, definitions of the virile male and the athlete have been synonymous. Only war has rivalled sports as the proving ground for masculine behaviour. The female athlete, however, has long been considered a contradiction in terms ... we seek reassurance that womanly instincts supersede athletic aspirations as we scrutinize sportswomen's appearances for tangible signs of femininity. (Schreier 1989: 92)

Therefore, women's sports clothing has had a more controversial history and set of associate motifs, relating to the revelation of the body, implications of sexuality and sexual transgression and unfeminine conduct and appearance. Above all, the most contentious theme that runs through the development of women's sports clothing concerns the wearing of "bifurcated" garments – trousers, shorts, leotards, and bare limbs and exposed flesh. Wilson (1985) has argued that:

Figure 37
Tatiana Panova.

It is possible that the advance of the trouser for women is the most significant fashion change of the twentieth century. For centuries, western women's legs had been concealed, trousers and pantaloons worn only by actresses, acrobats and others of dubious morality. Paradoxically, in Islamic cultures women wear trousers and men robes, but in the western world until the 1900s only working women, and then usually only those engaged in the coarsest labour, and entertainers, wore trousers or showed their legs, and when they did so their morality was impugned. (Wilson 1985: 162)

If we accept Wilson's contention, it seems that the issue of female sexuality has been at the heart of developments in women's fashion generally but highlighted in the specificities of sporting wear for women. The bifurcated garment seems to be controversial because it highlights the upper thighs and groin/pubic area, drawing attention to the area of the female sex organs. So, any design of sports clothing that reveals the lower torso – for men but especially for women – has attracted controversy. Pants, leotards, tights, swimwear and exercise wear epitomize this tension. Whereas such garments take a while to be accepted for women, revealing wear for men is more quickly incorporated and naturalized. Examples can be seen in the history of men's sports such as swimwear, gymnastics, track and field, fencing, ice skating, cycling, weightlifting and surfing.

Given the attention to female sexuality in the emergence of women's sports clothing, the adoption of trousers, pants and bodysuits has also characterized this history and debates. In sport after sport, including cycling, swimming, tennis, netball, hockey, lawn bowling, the development of specific outfits for women repeats controversies about maintaining modesty in the pubic area via modesty panels, skirts or loose shorts more than any other issue.

The arguments of Laver (1995) and Wilson (1985) highlight a key gender difference about sportswear. For men, there has been *continuity* between the development of sport uniforms and modern forms of masculinity (as expressed in identity and dress codes). That is, male sports clothing is normative of modern masculinity. For women, sport uniforms have highlighted *discontinuities* between ideal concepts of femininity and the actualities of women's lives, reflecting debates about women's role, femininity and role in public culture. In this sense, female sports clothing is transgressive or sexually charged just as female sports stars and women in sports clothing convey ambiguous messages. While this might seem like a fairly recent preoccupation, the history of sports clothing tells a different story: one of anxiety and controversy about new twists and turns in the design, manufacture and uptake of sports clothes.

Defining Sports Uniforms and Sports Clothing

There are a number of distinctions and categories that need to be noted. First, while we probably think of professional sports people seen in the media every day as epitomizing sports clothing, there are a number of different *groups who wear sports clothing. Players and participants* are the most common, although these may be amateur, informal, institutional or professional, each group adopting a different convention of sports clothing. While professional sports people are endorsed often by major sports clothing companies – some having special outfits and lines designed for them –

other groups may adopt the sports clothing of a club, school or region. Others may wear individual selections of sports clothing or everyday wear. We must distinguish *team* and *group* sports from *individual* sports although the latter may be formed into group teams to represent a region, state or nation. Another group of sports clothing devotees are the *fans* and *spectators* of sports who may wear replica outfits (e.g. football strips) or leisure sportswear suitable for the art of spectating (e.g. tracksuits, T-shirts, shorts, sports shoes, baseball caps) and indicating allegiance. Another growing group of sports clothing fans is to be found away from the sporting arena in the high street, in clubs, shopping centres, non-uniformed schools and the like. The impact of sports clothing on sportswear has become generic to *everyday dress* especially associated with leisure and youth.

In addition, we must distinguish different *types of sports clothing* in terms of function and/or style. Some sports clothing, especially some of the earliest forms, developed out of *traditional* modes of dress or contemporary fashions that subsequently were designated as conventional sportswear. Cricket was, for example, influenced by succeeding fashions for breeches, shirts and jackets only to be supplanted by the fashion for white trousers, coloured shirts and, for a period, top hats (Cunnington and Mansfield 1969). These were rather genteel uniforms. The preference for white flannels and blazer persisted with the choice of colour – or use of stripes – denoting the team identity. Alternatively, the blazers borrowed the military use of coloured braid edging. Over time, white leather shoes became the desired footwear. Some teams added further contrast by adopting coloured ties and sometimes sashes around the waist. The top hat was eventually replaced by a straw hat, again reflecting fashion rather than function. The changing elements of the cricketing uniform seems to relate to the more aristocratic origins of the sport and its gradual popularization among the middle class.

By the 1860s, the kind of wear we associate traditionally with cricket – white flannels, white shirt, team blazer, Arran-style knitted pullovers and cricket cap – was standardized and remained the convention for over a century. This outfit was not always practical – white trousers were hard to clean, especially when grass stained, caps gave little shade from the sun, blazers were impractical, and long trousers were hot, particularly when cricket became an obsession in British colonies (West Indies, Australia, South Africa, New Zealand). Yet, changes were resisted.

When change did happen, it was motivated by the development of Australian media mogul Kerry Packer's One Day cricket that sought to repackage the game in a shorter, more audience-friendly format that exploited televisual possibilities. The traditional cricketing outfit now contrasts with One Day cricket's brightly coloured "pyjamas" – loose polo-necked shirts, loose track pants gathered at the waist, with a choice of cap or hat, long or short sleeves, and mouth, groin and shin guards. Instead of white, the new cricket outfits are often garish and emblazoned with stripes and sponsorship insignia (Anon. 2003). While function has, to some degree, replaced tradition, whites have been retained for test matches and the pyjamas commonly ridiculed as infantile. Yet, youth cricket teams still play in the traditional all-white, long-sleeved shirts, trousers and hat. Other sports with traditional elements of outfits include tennis (historically), croquet, lawn bowling, hockey, fishing, golf and martial arts.

Some sports are primarily motivated by the need for *protective* clothing requiring some specialist outfit – such as outfits for fencing, boxing, American football and wetsuits for scuba diving and surfing. Still other sports are shaped by the desire for *performance-enhancing* designs that give an edge to the performer. These include swimwear, athletics shoes and bodysuits, gym and cycling wear. Other sports have seemingly more *functional or practical* outfits such as football (soccer, rugby, union, Australian Football), hockey, traditional track and field, basketball, fishing, walking, and gymnastics/physical education. And some seem to have been influenced above all by dictates of contemporary *fashion* that has then become convention or timeless – e.g. yachting, shooting, early cycling wear, motoring wear, surfwear, contemporary tennis wear and beach volleyball. We must also distinguish *customised or preferred sports clothing* (e.g. for casual tennis or soccer training) from sanctioned *uniforms* (for competition). The latter have a close parallel history to that of school and military uniforms.

Shaping Sports Uniforms: Some Historical Currents

Most accounts of sports uniforms are English-centred and focus on the impacts of industrialization, the emergence of leisure time and the development of private schools. Those histories are elite

Figure 38
Women's hockey team.

oriented and concerned with the rise of modernity (Cunnington and Mansfield 1969; Davidson 1990). Recounting a similar set of concerns are histories of sportswear in former British colonies and dominions such as Australia, New Zealand, South Africa, India and Canada where many of the elements of English sports wear were adopted – irrespective of climatic differences and social structure (Joel 1984; Routh 1993; Joel 1998; Wolfe 2001; Maynard 2002). By contrast, histories of sports uniforms in America focus on citizenship, democratization, women's issues and the rise of ready-to-wear manufacture and modern sales techniques (e.g. Kidwell and Christmas 1975; Warner 1988; Schreier 1989). As noted earlier, "sportswear" is virtually synonymous with American fashion since leisurewear and informal clothing in general form the backbone of its clothing industry.

Yet, sports clothing is not as modern as one might think. Within European court society, informal clothes were worn for times of "surcease" or leisure. Henry VIII had lounged around in an early form of the dressing gown adapted from the caftan. Henry was also a keen player of real tennis and wore specially made outfits: linen shirt, velvet jacket, breeches and stockings, as well as specially made felt shoes (Cunnington and Mansfield 1969: 83–5). French courtiers at Versailles during the reign of Louis XV wore pastoral costumes for elaborate charades at the palace retreat, the Petit Trianon (Joseph 1986: 168–9). Affluence permitting, different clothes were worn for different occasions and activities, a habit that inevitably extended to particular leisure and sporting activities. The origins of consumer culture and trickle-down fashion trends was in its infancy (cf. Roche 1996).

Mansfield (1969: 353) suggests that the earliest sports of modernity were hunting and riding in Britain and hunting (shooting, fishing and hawking) in North America. Specialist outfits for riding were created in the sixteenth century followed by outfits for hunting and shooting in the eighteenth century. While the rider's outfit was tailored and tight-fitting, hunting outfits emphasised comfort by adapting the "frock" coat as the basis. By the end of the century the frock was worn on dress occasions: "an example of how sports or leisure clothes of one generation become the formal attire of the next generation but one" (Mansfield 1969: 353). So we can see a play between a number of forces that from early on characterize the genre of sports clothing: formality versus informality; restricting versus loose; leisure versus official occasions; and functional versus fashionable.

The eighteenth century witnessed a number of developments. Many of these were products of wider social transformations that accompanied industrialization. The formation of cities and organized workplaces and routines as well as the emergence of non-work periods for leisure and holidays made sport an attractive option. Clubs became popular and attracted members to partake in organized activities such as hunting and cricket with the gradual emergence of distinctive club colours initially designed to distinguish teams from each other. Factories and mills would form teams to compete. Schools also formed sporting teams as part of enhancing the school's ethos and for competition. Cricket became one of the most popular team sports and seems to have been the first to adopt and codify a distinctive outfit – namely white clothing – "long before the players of other games had got around to considering what they should wear" (Mansfield 1969: 354). There was a class difference between the elite and the masses, the latter playing in their everyday clothing. For a time, club uniforms and specialist clothes were the province of the elite.

During the nineteenth century other sports – football, handball, hockey, wrestling, golf and athletics – gained in popularity and new games like lawn tennis and croquet developed. Why this proliferation? Mansfield (1969) others puts it down to the consequences of industrialization that took the rural population into the cities, and the urban dwellers to seek leisure in the country; the rise of leisure time; the reformed school movement; and the popularity of spa towns, seaside jaunts and bathing activities. In clothing terms, the rural aristocracy adopted everyday riding clothes (sports clothes) as everyday dress; for men, this meant tweed jackets and trousers. This trend spread to the city and became the everyday norm – so appeared the first identifiable sportswear (in modern times) and the connection between sport and a more casual approach to dress and dress codes. Women remained more formally dressed.

By the mid-nineteenth century, some sporting teams wore similar kinds of clothes (e.g. sleeveless jersey, white flannels, peaked cap and jacket) though not identical uniforms. But this was about to change. Perhaps inevitably, the growing popularity of sport spawned a demand for "appropriate clothing for sports and games" met by the fervent development of "new cloths, processes, and inventions at the disposal of the growing ready-made clothing industry" (Mansfield 1969: 356; cf. Kidwell and Christmas 1975: 117–23). And so, spikes for cricket shoes were patented in 1860, canvas shoes with rubber soles in 1868 and knickerbockers in the 1880s. Many of the early garments became staple fixtures in sportswear, such as the blazer that – as we have already noted – had made its appearance as "sporting" apparel in the 1860s and was popularized because it was both stylish and readily identified team membership and prestige. Likewise, knickerbockers were first adopted by the American baseball team, the Cincinnati Red Stockings, in 1868, upstaging the convention of white flannel shirt, wool trousers and straw hat, an adaptation of cricket garb. The knee-high knickerbockers proved to be "convenient and comfortable" and "showed off . . . their red stockings". Although arguably a rather unlikely outfit for virile males, knickerbockers have nonetheless remained the basis of contemporary baseball uniforms (National Baseball Hall of Fame and Museum 2002; cf. Schreier 1989: 103, 99). Later on, other elements were added – collarless jerseys, player numbers, script lettering, patriotic motifs and logos, caps, double-knit jersey fabric, and the like.

As baseball has gained an international following, other countries' teams have adopted American-style uniforms (e.g. Safe 2004). In Japan, enormous effort goes into simulating American-style baseball. One team, the Nippon-Ham Fighters (NHF), from the northern island of Hokkaido, changed its name to the Fighters as part of a bid to gain credibility (by losing the "lunch-meat gladiators" tag) and reverse their form (Stevenson 2003). In their search for a new uniform and a new logo, the team mocked up four

Figure 39
Australian Rules Football
uniforms.

graphic directions: traditional heraldic (knight badge and "F"), contemporary heraldic (a modernized badge depicting a shield, a baseball and mountains plus lettering "Fighters"), contemporary baseball (a "fast and forward-leaning" baseball diamond with letters "NHF") and baseball forward (an abstract geometry of baseball diamond and the high tech Sapporo Dome stadium – "where sports-mark design is right now". All these designs were rejected and the final choice was a contemporary heraldic of a baseball centred on a seven pointed star (a symbol of Hokkaido and also the logo for Sapporo beer).

The new uniform repeated the gold hue of the beer, potatoes and hills of Hokkaido, livened by a single black shoulder. The old team mascot (a pink bird) was replaced by "an attitudinal bear". Whether the new kit will guarantee success on the field, this example of uniform design reveals the historic legacy in contemporary uniforms and the global reach of arbitrary uniform design in a sport.

Between the 1860s and 1880s, uniforms were adopted in school and club sports. A photo from 1867 shows the sporting stripes at the Forest School (later known as Snaresbrook) in England as horizontally striped jerseys and long white flannels (like long johns) – the garish stripes designed to frighten the opposition (Davidson 1990). Even more frightening would have been the skull and crossbones embroidered onto the shirts of the Kings' School rugby team. It seems that during the late nineteenth century, outlandish gameswear became the norm – e.g. striped shirts, coloured gaiters, neck scarves, etc; and from the 1880s, knickerbockers and knee-length shorts were also introduced. Some of these uniforms resemble those now popular in American baseball – striped or patterned jerseys and long socks with white knickerbockers and "baseball" caps.

During the late nineteenth and early twentieth centuries, white gained dominance in many sporting outfits. Not only did cricketers and rugby teams wear white, so too did participants in tennis, baseball, lawn bowls, fencing, gymnastics, wrestling, rowing, yachting, croquet, soccer – and almost invariably for the blouse and tops in women's sport. Umpires, too, were frequently dressed in white. How do we account for the preference for white? It may have been because it was an easy colour to launder – early dyes were limited in hue and colourfastness. But, on the other hand, laundering was not an everyday occurrence except for the very rich, so white was also a marker of status (in the sense of access to washing facilities or staff to do the washing) (cf. Kidwell and Christmas 1975: 141). Others have accounted for white as reflecting contemporary fashion (Cunnington and Mansfield 1969: 19; Wigley 2001). Thus, white again became the preferred colour for active sports in shirts, trousers, shoes and sometimes headwear during the 1920s and 1930s. It was probably a combination of symbols of purity, cleanliness, healthiness, status and style that made white synonymous with sport. Sparkling white also made the participants easily visible so perhaps too the rise of the spectacle as a dominant motif in popular culture played a part.

The development of modern schooling also played a big role in aligning exercise and physical discipline with attributes of the ideal student. As early as the fifteenth century, children dressed in less cumbersome clothes for playing sport from early times, but these were ordinary clothes and often did not stand up to the wear and tear of rough play. There are records of pupils of St Omers (later known as Stonyhurst) in the seventeenth century playing football in their cumbersome soutanes (cassocks) tucked in at the waist (Davidson 1990). By the nineteenth century, the school had settled on wearing old clothes (often old cricket suits) for play and sport. Etonians wore tweed jackets and breeches for hunting until farmers complained that they could not tell them apart from themselves. Surprisingly, though, swimming was often done naked (at Eton until 1936).

Not only did the design of school uniforms reflect trends in military uniforms, but also, in turn, sports clothing reflected the design of school sports uniforms. On the reasons for this was the popularity of gymnastics, callisthenics and other physical education regimes that were integrated into the school curriculum and beyond.

The Gendering of Sports Uniforms

The history of men's sports clothing neatly matches the emergence of modern sensibilities and preoccupations especially those concerning modern ideas about masculinity as something virile – strong yet disciplined and restrained. By contrast, the history of women's sports clothing is a counterpoint, revealing the anxieties and contradictions within modernity. As Warner (1988: 49) noted, although many commentators of women's sports clothing argue that "women expressed a newfound freedom through involvement in sports", their outfits reflected fashion not function and came complete with "hat, pompadore, tight sleeves and bodices, corsets, petticoats, and sweeping skirts". Indeed, corsets were worn to play tennis into the 1920s and women were still covered up on the beach at this time. Why, when men had been wearing specialist outfits that embodied fashion *and* function for over half a century, did it take so long for women to wear loose or unrestricting clothing for sports without attracting controversy?

Warner (1988, 1993, 1995; cf. McCrone 1987; Horwood 2002) suggests that there are two histories of women's sports clothing: a private and a public one. The private history emanated out of girls'

Figure 40
World Cup cricketers.

schools and academies that had enthusiastically taken up the cause
of promoting exercise and healthy living for women in the 1830s
and 1840s. From the 1860s, a growing number of these establish-
ments advocated physical exercise (gymnastics, callisthenics) as
part of the curriculum and introduced special gym clothing consisting of versions of the "Turkish" look, loose trousers gathered at
the ankle worn under a loose frock gathered at the waist. Over time,
the loose trousers were transformed into bloomers and the frock
turned into either a gymslip (pleated skirt on a yoke) or became a
two-piece outfit of blouse and skirt. This became "standard gym
wear from the end of the 1880s through the end of the 1920s"
(Warner 1988: 50; cf. Routh 1993: 16, 25). In 1893, Butterick
published a pattern for the gym bloomer for home sewing, thus
reflecting the growing demand for cheap and functional clothing
(Warner 1993: 154).

In turn, the gym suit became the basis of the controversial
bloomer debate and dress reform movement. But wearing gym suits
did not mean that women were free to reveal their oddly clad bodies
in public. These outfits were strictly private, confined to the
gymnasiums and playing fields of the schools and academies, away
from the eyes of the public, especially men. This ostensibly liberat-
ing clothing was strictly out of bounds. In public, women wore the
constraining and restraining fashions of the day – even when

women's sports became public events, such as tennis tournaments from the 1900s.

By the 20th century, girls were wearing special sports uniforms – white blouses with (pink) bloomers or knickerbockers (modestly tied at the ankle) for cricket; ankle-length serge skirts for hockey; and aprons with pockets for tennis. In the gym, girls often removed their skirts and bloomers, though only when prying eyes were not there. As the importance of physical education in the curriculum took root, gym uniforms became adopted for other games, sports and physical activities – jerseys and shorts for boys and white blouses and gymslips or skirts for girls. Plimsolls (or tennis shoes – that is, rubber-soled canvas shoes) were worn for many sports activities and distinctive headwear became a handy marker of excellence and distinction. Increasingly, specific colours would be repeated on the blazer, tie, hatband, jersey, skirt, and socks or stockings.

The invention of the bicycle led to the popular pastime of bicycling and suitable garb to ride in: tweed jackets and flannels for men. It seemed like the perfect occasion to introduce functional clothes for women but despite the best efforts of reformers to persuade women to wear bloomers or divided skirts, women cyclists stuck to long flowing skirts and tight short jacket (Schreier 1989; Winkworth 1989–90; Sims 1991; Russell 1994). The arrival of the car, in the late nineteenth century, spawned the habit of motoring for leisure complete with specialist fashions and more casual clothes (dust wrappers and golfing jackets). Yet women's fashions continued to reflect high street fashion not sporting function.

Tennis was already the most popular sport for women by the 1880s and became "one of the first – and one of the few – sports in the twentieth century in which women were able to display their abilities to public acclaim" (Horwood 2002: 36). It was a sport that cried out for functional clothing but even here, it was slow to arrive. Women wore floor-length full skirts – the more daring raising them to ankle-length, with tight bodices or blouses – and jackets. When May Sutton appeared in 1905 in a short-sleeved blouse and a skirt 4–6 inches off the ground, her opponent complained and Sutton was not permitted on court until she dropped the hem to regulation length (Warner 1988: 53). Corsets were mandatory. Even at Wimbledon, the women's dressing room sported an iron bar above the stove over which players could dry their – frequently blood-stained – corsets, "never a pretty sight," recalled former English tennis star, Betty Ryan (Wilson 1985: 99; Warner 1988: 52). In fact, she removed the boning from her corset before a match on a hot day in 1921 (Horwood 2002: 48). Rules dictated that women players wore long dresses and long sleeved shirts: "modesty and decorum" ruled (Horwood 2002: 47).

The first world war was a particularly significant time for women's sportswear, although as we have seen, conservatism and controversy remained a keynote. Women were co-opted into factories, occupied war support roles and many wore uniforms (Ewing 1975). Generally, women began to play more active roles in public life – as well as earning their own money and having more independence. Developments in black and white photography were also involved; new aesthetic codes suited sporting movements, motifs and sports clothing, which were enhanced still further by film-making (especially Hollywood) and the development of moving images.

Suzanne Lenglen shocked Wimbledon in 1919 with her Patou-designed skirt and blouse but no stockings or petticoat. Through the 1920s, avant-garde cultural forces including the popularity of the "boyish look" and the popularity of dance music all combined to make clothing more suitable for active lives – sport and leisure frequently overlapped and sports clothing and leisurewear began to converge. For example, it became popular for men to wear white trousers and casual shoes (often white) at the weekends – an adaptation of cricket and tennis wear. During the 1930s, shorts became acceptable for men; they were first worn at Forest Hills (New York) by Bunny Austin in 1932 and at Wimbledon in 1933 (Schreier 1989: 115–16). Not to be outdone, two enterprising American players known as the two Helens – Helen Wills-Moody and Helen Hull Jacobs – also wore shorts at Wimbledon (Wilson 1985: 162; Warner 1988: 53–4; Schreier 1989: 115).

Despite the uproar, Horwood (2002: 49–53) argues that the popularity of players such as Lenglen – akin to the film stars, pop stars and celebrities of later decades – meant that their outfits were popularized as fashion and this gave them the legitimacy to be grudgingly accepted on court. Quickly, the long skirts and restrict-ive blouses were replaced generally by loose white outfits and fashionable bandeaux – though hardly risqué by present day standards. Subsequently by the 1930s shorts were accepted as casual wear for women for the beach and similar venues. However,

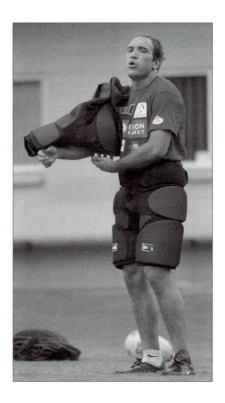

Figure 41
Rugby League player
removing his protective
tackle suit.

shorts have remained controversial in major women's tennis tournaments, showing that sensitivity about trousers has persisted.

The importance of Coco Chanel cannot be underestimated in revolutionizing our ideas about casual clothing and the relationship between fabric and body. She virtually single-handedly popularized men's fashions for women during the 1920s and 1930s (Charles-Roux 1995: 252; see also Wilson 1985: 40–1). Chanel borrowed English aristocratic country (i.e. sporting) dress codes and incorporated elements of these into women's fashion. She also adapted the sailor suit and men's pullovers for women. Perhaps her most daring innovation was the use of knitted jersey, then used only for men's underwear. Karl Lagerfeld (who designed for Chanel after her death) commented that Chanel's use of jersey for outerwear was more shocking than any fashion statement he could make. Chanel liked jersey's clean, flowing lines for dresses, cardigans and skirts and established her own factory to produce a variety of types suitable for a range of women's clothing. The properties of jersey for active wear were quickly recognized and it became a staple for the manufacture of many types of sports clothing, including T-shirts, tracksuits, leggings, lyotards and swimwear.

The Transformation of Sports Clothing Under Consumer Culture

While many of the modern trends in sports clothing were already in place, these received a fillip during the Second World War. By now, lifestyles on both sides of the Atlantic were more casual and ordinary people aspired to better themselves. The war once again provided opportunities for women to work, play active roles in public life and enlist in military and support jobs. The donning of special uniforms became a fashion statement, with fashion magazines promoting women in uniform and uniforms influencing everyday fashion. Shortages in raw materials and rationing were circumvented by the popularity of home sewing and the ingenious adaptation of old clothes and substitutes.

Perhaps the most significant long-term factor in the explosion of the sportswear industry was the development of new fabrics like nylon and parachute silk, for these unwittingly created entirely new possibilities in clothing. Nylon was a particular winner. While the military had taken to it with alacrity, it quickly proved versatile off the battlefield. It was first used as sports clothing in the knickerbockers worn by the Notre Dame football team in 1941. An assessment pre-empting recent debates about the practicality of sports uniforms concluded that the nylon knickerbockers were an excellent choice in the rainy, muddy conditions (Handley 1999: 48–52):

> The nylon pants, which weighed [a quarter the weight of] ordinary moleskins, proved a boon in the quagmire because they retained little moisture and picked up little mud . . . The same ones were worn by the South Bend varsity for six seasons. (Handley 1999: 183)

With the US entry into the war, nylon and rayon were prioritized for military purposes. If anything, this increased its fashion value and production could not keep up with demand. Although synonymous with stockings, nylon found more and more uses: in underwear, outerwear, household textiles and soft furnishings. The escalation of post-war consumer society, with demand-driven manufacture and consumption, enhanced further the popularity of synthetic fibres, assembly-line goods and pre-fabricated materials. Another development was also critical. Fashion photography increasingly reflected the more informal and consumer-oriented trends in society, depicting sportswear and leisurewear in fashion spreads as normative, since sporting imagery suited the technology and new ideas about the body, guaranteeing a positive reception by keen consumers.

Despite these changes, women's tennis outfits have provoked ongoing controversies since then. In 1949, the designer, Ted Tinling dressed Gussie Moran in lacy panties and short skirts (Routh 1993: 93). The glamorous Italian tennis star, Lea Pericoli, shocked spectators in the 1950s with her body-hugging shorts and frilly underpants. Tinling continued dressing star players into the 1970s, introducing lace and frills, visible knickers, miniskirts, sleeveless tops and lots of colour. His sense of style outraged the conservative elements of the tennis fraternity but delighted players and the public. Such outfits became the norm. Then, in 1985, Anne White wore a figure-revealing bodysuit at Wimbledon and created another furore (Warner 1988: 53). In the twenty-first century, Serena and Venus Williams' often ill-fitting, body-revealing lycra and micro-fibre outfits in garish colours created further controversy. In 2004, Serena adopted skimpy navy denim-like outfits with denim boot-like leggings (rather like military puttees), sparking more censure. If history tells us anything, it is that the controversy that marked early women's sports clothing persists with issues of decency and modesty simmering under the veneer of postmodernity.

The basic elements of sports uniforms have largely remained in the twenty-first century, although new synthetic fabrics, body spectacle and the retreat of the shame frontier have triggered some revolutions in the design of sports clothing. Generally, it can be said that major developments in sport – particularly involving new approaches to sports clothing – have, after initial controversy, spearheaded the uptake of that dress code into everyday clothing habits. Examples include Annette Kellerman's neck-to-knee, one-piece bathing suit made in jersey; Suzanne Lenglen's white shirt, skirt and gym shoes for tennis (without stockings, petticoat or sleeves); Jan Stephenson's miniskirts for golf; Martina Navratilova's shorts (and muscularity) for tennis; the World Series cricket "pyjamas"; the bodysuit controversy in swimming and athletics;

Figure 42
Speedo fastskin swimsuits.

and microfibre tennis outfits. Taken together, these sports clothing moments trace a history of increasingly informality, orientation to performance enhancement, and closer body fit.

As we have seen, sportswear has merged genres of everyday dress due to a number of factors associated with key social developments – industrialization; urbanization; various phases of the women's movement; world wars; cycles of economic prosperity; technological and technical developments (e.g. photography; moving images and new media; new fabrics and materials; mechanized manufacture; mass production). From the outset, sports clothing has had a tangled relationship with fashion and everyday wear. That relationship was about to become more intertwined than ever.

7

Fashioning Sports Clothing as Lifestyle Couture

Sports Clothing as Fashion

> Sportswear exists because American women were the first to live the modern, fast-paced life. (designer Michael Kors, quoted by Seeling 2000: 578)

This chapter explores how sports clothing has shifted from specialist apparel to enhance sporting performance to become a mainstay of stylistic trends in fashion and the basis of contemporary everyday dress. Sports clothing is not only the dominant form of clothing and footwear manufacture and marketing but also an increasingly important segment of designer fashion. So-called sports couture has taken the functionality out of sports clothing and transformed it into hyper chic.

In the post-war period, sports clothing developed both more refined and specialist genres and influenced increasingly the commercialization and democratization of fashion into everyday streetwear and high street fashion. Sportswear has become a huge international business with brands becoming synonymous with sporting apparel both in and out of sporting arenas. Brands such as Reebok, Nike, Adidas, Puma, Ripcurl, Billabong, Hot Tuna, Quiksilver, Speedo, Jantzen and Canterbury have become the currency of youth-oriented "hip" style (O'Mahony and Braddock 2002; Quinn 2002: 185–200; Chalmers 2003; Weinstein 2003). In addition to sports clothes, sportswear has proliferated into an unimaginable array of associated paraphernalia, such as heart monitors, sports watches, computerized devices, sports radios and CD-players, sports bags, sports drinks, sports cosmetics and body products, sports cars, sports bikes, sports underwear and socks, sports shoes, sports parkas, sports exercise equipment, training devices and facilities.

The marketing and selling of this paraphernalia and sporting merchandise in general has become extremely sophisticated: e-selling, club merchandise, high street chain merchandising, special-ist stores (e.g. Niketown in Chicago) and sports superstores and malls. Sports clothing has become an integral part of subcultures and youth identification with sporting heroes vying with movie and pop stars as role models and whose dress sense has influenced youth clothing since the 1950s. Increasingly, everyday fashion and prosaic dress has its origins in sportswear since sporting apparel offers clothes that are cheap, practical, casual, multipurpose and stylish (Kidwell and Christmas 1975; cf. Joseph 1986: 177–80; de Teliga 1995; Danielsen 1999). This trend has been explained in terms of the apparent blurring of class and status, the rise of leisure time and decline of formality in everyday life.

Functional imperatives have dominated over form and design or aesthetic sensibilities increasingly shaped by the elements and details of sports clothing. In Chapter 6, we discussed the important contribution made by Coco Chanel to transforming sports fabrics and clothing into high fashion and thereby reshaping ideas about comfort and style. In the United States, Claire McCardell played a similar role in the post-war period. She experimented with jerseys, knitted fabrics and nylon that she manufactured into clothes with a practical cut and more relaxed styling, thereby influencing the consumer culture of clothing and influencing the designers who followed (O'Mahony and Braddock 2002: 14). By the 1960s, sports clothing had become an integral component of designer fashion. This occurred first in North America, but quickly spread to Europe, then globally.

From the 1950s, sports clothing dominated the cinema, popular music and consumer culture. American popular culture became a major influence elsewhere reflecting an obsession with leisure, informality and less conservative social mores. Wetsuits, for example, were developed in California as part of the culture of surfing with the development of neoprene fabrics to cope with cold water and long immersion (Hall, Carne and Sheppard 2002). Innovations in swimwear soon followed.

To meet demand, many clothing companies specialised in "sportswear" and leisurewear. Some also became heavily involved in the development of new artificial fibres that were cheaper than wool and cotton as well as having other advantages; they were lightweight, resisted water and dirt, and streamlined the body. Companies like Du Pont, Courtaulds and ICI developed new synthetic fibres, based on nylon, rayon or polyester, such as dacron, orlon, tricel, bri-nylon, terylene, courtelle and a lycra forerunner – fibre K – that were quickly popularized. Synthetic fibres and fabrics were marketed as "miracle" materials with "easycare", "wash and wear" properties.

Because of their "resistance to outdoor exposure", light weight, durability, and wash and wear character, they were perfect also for sports clothing, and made appearances in swimwear, skiwear, anoraks and many sports uniforms (gymnastics, baseball, basketball and so on), though other sports resisted their allure, e.g. athletics, boxing, hockey, football. Skiwear, however, adopted these new fabrics with alacrity and, as skiwear was emulated in fashion, streetwear followed suit. Quilted nylon anoraks and polyester ski pants were popularized both for practical reasons (e.g. warmth) and for fashion (as après-ski wear) (Handley 1999: 63). The image of Emma Peel in the British television series, *The Avengers*, dressed in a body-hugging futuristic flying suit had a major impact on redefining the ideal female form and popularizing body-hugging fashions and fabrics (O'Mahony and Braddock 2002: 16). These fabrics also influenced developments in camping and outdoor equipment (such as sleeping bags) again popularizing outdoor, sporting lifestyles.

Increasingly, acrylics (e.g. terylene, orlon, dacron and crimplene) were adopted in sport and on the street with their benefits of being drip-dry, permanently pleated, non-fading and durable. These wonder fabrics were weatherproof, breathable and durable as well as being adaptable for hot or cold environments in which sport occurred (O'Mahony and Braddock 2002: 41–4). Their uptake in sport quickly led to fashion knock-offs such as 1960s one-piece stretch jumpsuits, pantyhose, sleepwear, underwear revolutions, skivvies and stretch slacks. Indeed, Handley (1999: 75) regards the 1960s and early 1970s as "the heyday for synthetic fashions". A big breakthrough in securing public acceptance of synthetics was the growing use of synthetics by Parisian – and later American – designers. And, as American fashion was dominated by casual wear, synthetics quickly became the staple of everyday clothing.

Perhaps it was the impact of 1960s pop culture and "Swinging London" fashion that catapulted experimentation with these new fabrics and new approaches to design and wearability into global prominence. According to Handley (1999: 89–112), the period saw the growth of a specific teenage culture with distinctive consumer habits, new designs that were skimpy, bold and body revealing and new looks that were ultra-fashionable, lurid, synthetic and neon. Above all, they were sporty. A revolution in streetwear and sports-wear was occurring. By the 1970s, sportswear-influenced fashion had been elevated to the status of haute couture and renamed sports couture, a label attributed to the American designer, Roy Halston, who reworked sportswear as fashion for the mainstream market. He favoured understated elegance using jersey and body-hugging fabrics for tube dresses, jumpsuits, pantsuits and cashmere twinsets (Danielsen 1999; Seeling 2000: 417). Halston "gave sportswear a sophistication which had seemed impossible beforehand" (Seeling 2000: 588).

As marketing companies mastered the art of making sports clothes "cool" for the youth-oriented market, sports labels have increasingly produced "diffusion lines" alongside sports perform-ance gear aimed specifically at the mainstream market. According to O'Mahony and Braddock (2002):

> The latest designer sports labels are aimed at the 18–34 age group, with the result that anyone wearing them can seem young, healthy and active by association. Sports-inspired fashion advertisements suggest links with a clean-living active life: sport is fashionable, and sporty references give collections a contemporary edge. (O'Mahony and Braddock 2002: 132)

At the moment when it seemed that synthetics had swept away all before them, a convergence of factors in the 1970s burst the bubble.

Figure 43
Olympic athletes' Nike
uniforms.

Synthetics became synonymous with bad taste, tackiness and superficiality: "disco dacron" became a term of abuse, despite the popularity of commercial bands like ABBA and John Travolta's groundbreaking performance in John Badham's *Saturday Night Fever* (1977). Manufacturers were desperate to revive the fortunes of synthetics with all kinds of marketing and promotional campaigns. Although the public turned away from synthetics, companies continued to experiment with new fabrics, especially by developing blends that disguised the essential ingredients of the fabrics and could incorporate some natural fibres. In particular, new approaches were developed to produce better fabrics for sports clothing, especially action sports clothing for elite athletes. Low cost, high quality leisurewear was now available in turn producing a "more practical mix-and-match aesthetic" (Danielsen 1999). Thus ironically, at the time when the masses turned away from synthetics, major advances were occurring in the sporting arenas that were to revolutionize approaches to fabrics in the future.

Handley (1999: 129–42; cf. Quinn 2002: 141–61) attributes the breakthrough to the impact of Japanese designers such as Rei Kawakubo, Issey Miyake, Yoshiki Hishinuma and Junya Watanabe on western fashion in the 1980s. They used radically different ideas of line, cut and combination with technological savvy and technical sophistication in producing sculptural body outfits using the latest developments in fibre manufacture. Instead of sewing machines, clothes were made by industrial techniques:

Polyester, shrunken nylon, microfibre taffetas and monofila-
ment gauzes undergo unspecified chemical and heat treatments to emerge as textured cocoons for the body. Waves or
wrinkles are technologically fixed into the fabrics or, con-
versely, creaseless, glassy acetates produce wrinkle-free
clothing. (Handley 1999: 134)

So there was a convergence of factors: clothing designed for
enhancing sporting performance was taken up by high-street
fashion; revolutions in fabrics to improve comfort, durability and
environmental conditions were challenging traditional natural
fibres and fabrics; and subcultures associated with certain sports
(e.g. surfing, skiing, ski-boarding, bushwalking, riding, cycling)
had become the defining parameters of youth culture.

The Lycra Revolution

By these techniques, fabrics were more responsive to the body –
acting like the pores of skin, almost a second skin – and therefore
perfectly suited to designing performance-enhancing sports clothing, such as the skiwear of the winners of the 1988 Winter Olympics. Epitomizing this fabric revolution – as far as public opinion
was concerned – was lycra, which is perhaps the wonder fabric of
postmodernity (O'Mahony and Braddock 2002: 143; Quinn 2002:
192–4). Developed in 1958, it was not popularized in fashion until
the 1980s. However, as a synthetic elastic, it had an immediate
uptake in foundation garments (corsets and bras) because of its
profound "stretch and recovery" qualities and because it could be
blended with anything.

In 1964 the lycra body stocking was invented; swimwear manufacturers immediately adapted this for swimwear because it was
body hugging, lightweight, colourful and moisture repellent. Other
sports and leisure manufacturers soon followed, e.g. skiwear. This
trend really took off in the mid-1970s coinciding with the new
body-conscious culture of self-improvement, body sculpting and
healthy living. Lycra could be found in exercise wear, sportswear,
lingerie and fashion. Films like teen-oriented *Grease* (1978) and
Fame (1980) reflected the convergence and triggered the manufacture of sportswear as leisurewear on an unprecedented scale.
By the 1980s, lycra leggings, bodysuits, tops and tights were
everywhere from the catwalk, the starting blocks and the gyms to

shopping centres, offices and backyards (Joseph 1986; Schreier 1989). It was not too long before specialist clothes for sport could be worn in a multiplicity of venues: gym wear, dance wear, aerobics wear, swimwear and even evening wear all drew on the same synthetic body-hugging elements (see Schulze 1990; Li 1999; Skoggard 1998; O'Mahony and Braddock 2002: 143; Sawyer 2002; Taffel 2003; Zamiatin 2003a).

The popularity of underwear as outerwear, a trend from the 1980s and still fashionable, further enhanced this convergence. Lycra became a key attribute of postmodern popular culture because of its flexibility, suitability for a relaxed, pleasure-seeking lifestyle and connotations of sexuality and eroticism. Inevitably it infiltrated popular music and celebrity culture – a mainstay of stage clothes for example (e.g. Madonna, Kylie Minogue, Cher). If a celebrity wore a designer label garment, increased sales were sure to follow. The success of Tommy Hilfiger, Stussy and Massimo in the 1990s has been largely attributed to celebrity promotion (Danielsen 1999). The fusion between sportswear and streetwear was deepened with the fad for the styles of American basketballers and rappers. Streetwear became black, baggy and bold – and accompanied by the ubiquitous baseball cap and "athletic" shoes or sports shoes (Chalmers 2002; Weinstein 2003; Zamiatin 2003c). The widespread acceptance of the highly charged allure of urban black culture produced globalized fashions for teens, especially young males based on the sportswear and streetwear of sporting heroes (cf. Maynard 2004: 34–6). In turn, selected sports stars were used as the face of sport labels' promotions, such as Michael Jordan for Nike. Nike was the first company to exploit the sportswear as fashion promotional tactic, leading the industry for more than a decade "in both technological innovation and style" (Quinn 2002: 186). Simultaneously, Nike produced advanced sports gear for professional sports people and parallel lines aimed at amateur sport and leisure, "urban streets and city parks":

Nike's signature Lycra and fleece silhouettes leapt into main-stream casual wear, creating a look that went beyond sporty associations to identify the wearer as an active, trendy, health-conscious individual. Nike's body-hugging designs were produced in vibrant colours or basic black – creating shapes and tones that mirrored those worn on the nightclub scene. (Quinn 2002: 187)

Before long, Nike gear was the cool gear for clubbers and ravers. As other companies began to compete for the youth market for sportswear, Nike invested in designing a "Swift Suit" that could give the body aerodynamic properties and thereby enhance performance (O'Mahony and Braddock 2002: 127; Quinn 2002: 187–8). Other companies soon followed. Clothes that emanated from sport-music contexts were turned into fashion for everyday everywhere (Li 1998; Skoggard 1998). This has spawned a proliferation of brand names and companies specializing in sports goods and popularized on the street by brand-name trainers visibly promoting sports brand names.

These trends persisted through the 1990s with the ubiquitous lycra and sportswear never far from headline fads and celebrities. The designer label Prada, for example, was credited with turning nylon into the cashmere of the 1990s (Handley 1999: 163). Miuccia Prada has experimented with new lightweight fabrics that breathe and float to produce a "synthesis of design and function" leading to "new styles and types of clothing" (Danielsen 1999). While Prada is associated with couture, her Prada Sport line is aimed at the well-heeled mass consumer who can also display her comfortable yet sexy outfits for leisure or for active pursuits (Quinn 2002: 192–4). Inspiration from sports clothing has become the defining theme of fashion:

> Hybrid clothing – between sports clothes and pure fashion – is where action clothing, prêt-a-porter and the rarefied world of haute couture meet. Fashion also influences sports clothes in its turn, and sports collections are becoming more glamorous. Track runners can now wear aerodynamic one-piece garments in low-resistance synthetics; beaded stretch tulle may be used for sports tops, and sequinned hotpants for running. Practical and decorative, they are suited to action and fashion alike. (O'Mahony and Braddock 2002: 140–1)

Body Technologies

The development of full bodysuits for competitive swimming raised the stakes still higher. Released to coincide with the 2000 Olympics, the new bodysuits created controversy because of their acute figure-hugging qualities and rumours that they were performance-enhancing apparatuses rather than simply swimming costumes. The suits – based on the swimming capacities of a shark and the unusual characteristics of sharkskin – were designed to streamline the body's silhouette, cut down drag and resistance through the water, compress the muscles into performance and control bodily deviations from maximum performance (O'Mahony and Braddock 2002: 119–24). Despite the initial controversy, the suits quickly transformed the sport of swimming.

The revised Fastskin FSII, designed for the 2004 Athens Olympic Games, "mimics sharkskin and employs the same 'computational fluid dynamics' used in the design of Formula One racing cars and America's Cup yachts" (Jeffrey 2004b: 3). Not only does the new Speedo suit follow the flowlines around the body", but also the suits are now "gender and stroke specific" (Jeffrey 2004b: 3). So confident of the suits, Speedo launched an international advertising campaign featuring leading swimmers (including Grant Hackett, Michael Klim, Jenny Thompson, Lenny Krayzelburg and Inge de Bruin) as "human fish" with "shark gills" simulated on their necks (Cowley 2004: 69).

Once again, the bodysuit technology has been adapted for other sports (e.g. athletics, netball) and other garments (e.g. lingerie, gym wear). So-called gym wear combines the latest in action sports clothing design with high street fashion and recognizable brand names and motifs. Leggings and legwarmers are one example of an undergarment that has become high fashion and everyday wear (O'Mahony and Braddock 2002: 143; Thompson 2003). Epitomized by beach volleyball uniforms, almost all this sports clothing contains synthetic fibres (Schulze 1990; Sawyer 2002; Taffel 2003). Microfibre technology has transformed the properties of many sporting items, from bodysuits to shoes to footballs.

The latest chapter of the sports clothing saga is the promise of wearable technologies, that is, through smart-fibre technology for the manufacture of smart clothes (Handley 1999: 140–2; Marzano 2000; Harkin 2002; O'Mahony and Braddock 2002: 48–52; Quinn 2002: 191–2; Fynes-Clinton 2003). Products such as Fabrican, an aerosol spray-on fabric, are already being used in fashion, for example, by the New York-based label DDCLAB to produce super-tough hip urban wear. Other fabrics have been Teflon-coated, Kevlar-treated or Tyvek-infused to produce practical, lightweight and extremely durable clothes that have been endorsed by American film and music celebrities.

Figure 44
Australian Olympics team
members in parade.

These new age fabrics can offer thermal control, built-in air
conditioners, performance-enhancing attributes and control mech-
anisms, and body adjustment or maintenance – hydrating, vitamin,
perfume or steroid release, for example. In the lead-up to the 2004
Athens Olympic Games, the Australian Olympic team had an
exclusive deal with Nike to provide uniforms that included a "pre-
cool vest" constructed to incorporate eighteen ice packs that allow
"athletes to perform for 19 percent longer before their body
temperature reaches the critical point where it compromises their
efficiency" (Jeffrey 2004a: 3). While Nike believed its vest was
state-of-the-art, the Australian Institute of Sport advocated the
adoption of its "new high tech cooling jacket that uses a phase-
changing polymer rather than ice to reduce the athlete's core body
temperature", a jacket it claimed was "vastly superior to our old
ice vest . . . We believe that technology is outdated". Although the
ice vest was favoured at the 2004 Athens Olympics, one could
confidently predict that high-tech vests will make their appearance
in international competition very quickly. Other components of the
Olympic team uniform include other heat-countering features such
as "ventilation panels, lightweight materials and breathable fabrics".
Applications of new technologies into competitive sports uniforms
illustrate the rapid uptake of innovation and refinement of traditional approaches to sportswear.

Still at the experimental stage are sports uniforms and sports
clothing that incorporate inbuilt communication systems in clothing. Although the circuitry currently creates a problem for launder-

ing, ultimately such garments will be manufactured with machine-washable circuitry. Already Phillips has manufactured underpants and bodysuits for athletes and clubbers with body-monitoring sensors, flashing lights and pagers (Marzano 2000: 55, 91; O'Mahony and Braddock 2002: 80–4). The possibilities for applications in sports clothing as well as streetwear are clearly mind boggling.

Even the staid tracksuit has undergone a revolution. It was one of the earliest applications of new synthetic fibres to sportswear, producing fleecy jersey that kept sports people warm, comfortable and dry, first manufactured in the 1960s. From the late 1970s, tracksuits incorporated then switched to synthetic fabrics that were lighter, water resistant, warmer and more stylish. During the 1980s, the tracksuit was popularized for leisurewear (indeed, it has been regarded as Australia's national costume) and in the 1990s, the tracksuit gained popularity for travellers and among elderly people, e.g. preferred clothing in nursing homes. Although this could well have been the death knell for the tracksuit – unstylish (baggy, faded and misshapen) beyond belief – it has been revived in celebrity circles as the fashion look of hip hop artists, rappers, pop stars, sports celebrities and film stars. The tracksuit in the new millennium is ultra cool streetwear. The tracksuit worn by the soccer star, David Beckham, at the Manchester Commonwealth Games opening ceremony in 2002 confirmed its high fashion status: here was a specially designed shiny white tracksuit with cubic zirconium detail highlighting, among other things, the brand name, adidas – surely synonymous with cutting-edge sports clothing and sporting excellence (Sawyer 2002).

From Stylish Sports Clothing to Sporty Style

Over time, but especially during the twentieth century, clothes have become looser, are more informal and more suited to leisure and recreational activities "all-purpose clothing [has] transcended role demarcation" (Joseph 1986: 178). Sports clothing has been the obvious beneficiary of this trend. As well as using sports uniforms for other activities, designers are increasingly designing and producing sports-influenced casual clothing (e.g. T-shirts, leggings, sports shoes, lycra swimwear and exercise wear, sports jackets, facsimile sports jerseys, football strips and baseball caps). These garments and their details focus on the utilitarian and the egalitarian with the "emphasis as much on the structural quality and everyday practicality as on the visual surface of the garment" (Danielsen 1999).

Designer cargo pants, military-style trousers, jumpsuits, hooded jackets, fleecy vests and zippered tops proliferate in recent collections. These borrow heavily from winter wear and mountaineering apparel, with brand names like Himalayan and Patagonian. Sports clothing has become the mainstay of many designers and the last resort in hard times. There is an increasing incidence of specialised wear for leisure activities for those who may not actually be sports people – for fishing, horse riding, golf, tennis, martial arts, yoga, and so on. The quasi-uniform has been derived from the appropriate sports uniform and outfits then commercialized into specialist activity wear and popularized as leisure and recreation fashion.

The theme of this chapter has been the play between the maintenance of tradition and the impact of innovation – factors that have simultaneously characterized the development of the modern fashion industry and the manufacture of outfits specifically for sport. From the earliest appearance of sporting outfits, fashion has either been never far behind in incorporating elements of the sporting look into mainstream fashion or influencing the design and/or acceptability of new sporting looks. As the cult of the body has asserted itself cyclically, the credibility of sports clothing has been enhanced. This has created opportunities for manufacturers to increase sales to non-sporting consumers and develop everyday sports-look lines. Competitive teams often change their strips each season and have different home and away colours. This increases sales among supporters who want the latest team look – and sometimes a star player's number. Clubs and sporting stores satisfy this demand while creating new ways to enhance it further. Sports stores have proliferated in airports offering accessible stock to new markets. Chain and department stores are quick to manufacture facsimile versions for the cheaper end of the market.

Of course, this becomes a double-edged sword, for while a sports-core of consumers may prove reliable, the fashion-conscious consumer is not. One of the notable success stories of sports clothing being mainstreamed is that of sports shoes (O'Mahony and Braddock 2002: 105, 169–74; Quinn 2002: 197–9). While soft shoes or slippers for sport were systematized in the invention of plimsolls (or tennis shoes), it was relatively recently that manufacturers reworked the design of sports shoes to maximize flexibility, support and sport-specific requirements by rethinking support and cushioning. What they did not count on was the translation of the sports shoe into youth culture to become the generic shoe of young people. They have become the tip of new trends, necessitating constantly updated models and features – with fashion and style as much in mind as practicality for sport.

Manufacturers of sports shoes produce and retailers stock only limited numbers of high-end street designs to make purchases more exclusive: "We only get a limited number usually in the low hundreds, of each style, which can sell out in a couple of weeks. Then we move onto the next one. It keeps up the excitement over the shoes" (Zamiatin 2003c: 37). At Niketown, a sportswear mega-complex, some buyers acquire special edition shoes as an investment – never to be worn. Indeed, collecting sports shoes and sneakers has become a popular hobby with enthusiasts owning up to 500 pairs and specialist websites and magazines serving the collectors (Lunn 2003: 9).

According to Alderson (2002: 29), an estimated 430 million pairs of sports shoes are sold annually accounting for a quarter of the footwear market. Yet only a fifth of these are worn for sport; the rest are "lifestyle" purchases. In the United States, the "athletic footwear" industry has been valued in excess of $16 billion a year (Lunn 2003). Perhaps not surprisingly, couture designers have joined the fray producing "status sneakers" for the "fashionista" and bowling shoes (a cross between a "nanna" shoe and a trainer) for the chic urban worker. Sportswear manufacturers must not only produce garments that enhance performance and are durable but also be equally concerned with producing goods that are received as looking stylish: cool vies with function in the sports clothing war and, all too often, cool has won out.

Not always though. Some sports have resisted new approaches to uniform and sports clothes' design – for example, tennis, baseball and football. So while some sports embrace new developments, others lag behind. Thus we find that cycling, skiing, scuba diving, swimming, luge and so on have adopted one-piece outfits as standard wear while other sports resist. One case in 2004 concerned the decision of the Cameroon soccer team to wear a one-piece microfibre bodysuit in the African Cup of Nations in Tunisia. As a result, they were docked vital championship points on the grounds that football's governing body, FIFA, had rules insisting on a two-piece outfit (BBC Sport) 2004. The Cameroon team's defence was that they had merely joined the two pieces together. Despite this setback, it can be predicted that the sport of soccer will, in time, permit one-piece bodysuits in new climatically suitable and ergonomically appropriate fabrics.

According to Quinn (2002), we are seeing a new dialogue between sports technicians and fashion designers:

> forever disrupting the historical narrative of fashion, making it less apparent where the boundaries between fashion and sport now lie. From sportswear, fashion has learnt to protect and equip the body, while from fashion, sportswear has learned to decorate the body and tailor clothing to follow its shape . . . The combined sense of utility, functionality, performance and transformability inherent in sportswear is moving fashion forward. (Quinn 2002: 199)

But is this as radical as some commentators suggest? Quinn (2002: 200) concludes that the sports-techno revolution in fashion is overdue – a belated recognition of the centrality of characteristics of "functionality, performance and transformability" in clothing. In a sense, this is a revival of fundamental principles of clothing design developed among early societies such as the waterproof, weatherproof clothes of the Inuit (parkas and sealskin boots) and Scandinavians (two-thumbed mittens knitted from human hair to repel water and provide a wet and dry thumb for fishermen) (O'Mahony and Braddock 2002: 92, 4, 111–12). The wheel of fashion may have turned full circle with the sports obsession redrafting our ideas about clothing, dress and bodily performance in general.

Part IV
Uniform Culture

Figure 45
Demonstrators.

8

Uniforms in Fashion and Popular Culture

Uniforms and Popular Culture

The use of uniforms in popular culture has become endemic. We have already examined the uptake of uniforms from sporting arenas to everyday leisure sites, from formal uniforms to consensual quasi-uniforms at work, and the concluding chapter explores transgressive contexts and subcultures. So, why this proliferation of uniforms and the associated obsession with uniforms in contemporary popular culture? Alan Hunt (1996) has related the legislation of sumptuary laws to the moral regulation of popular pastimes and emergence of popular culture. For Hunt, sumptuary laws were not just about the arbitrary imposition of idiosyncratic laws from above, but a contested response to wider social changes and political challenges from below. The discourse of this moral regulation was centred on ideas of idleness and luxury, both of which were perceived as problems to be managed. These twin targets were a manifestation of the growing "insubordination of the labouring classes" (Hunt 1996: 274) attendant on the extension of wage labour, industrialization and urbanization which brought

in its wake, the origins of leisure time (time to be idle and degene-
rate) and consumerism (the ability to desire luxuries previously
restricted to the elite).

Pastimes, too, were regulated. The medieval regulation of games
was replaced by the specific regulation of dangerous activities like
idleness, drinking and gambling in the late Middle Ages. Games
that provided possibilities for gambling were especially despised
as were popular festivals, sports and recreations of the working
class, especially those that occurred in and around the alehouse.
As people became more mobile the problem of the vagrant became
a major concern, resulting in strategies like issuing licences, pass-
books, wearing badges and restrictions on movement being used
to attempt to monitor behaviour and distinguish "the deserving
from the undeserving poor" (Hunt 1996: 287). Hunt identifies a
moral panic surrounding repeated plagues as a factor in the
succession of sumptuary laws as a means to control outbreaks and
contagion from afflicted persons:

> The interpenetration of poverty and plague was productive
> of major social tensions and anxieties; in many cases rulers
> expressed a contempt for the masses who were perceived as
> presenting a threat to the health and well-being of the respect-
> able classes. The result was a sharper social dichotomy
> between civic rules expanding state authority and the poor
> who resisted these regulatory measures. (Hunt 1996: 294)

Increasingly important, too, were sartorial devices to allude to
distinction, role and place. Some of these were sanctioned, others
a deliberate form of fraud. In the late fifteenth century, beggars
evaded vagrancy legislation by dressing as pilgrims or discharged
soldiers or sailors, leading to legislation "requiring evidence of
status – authorisation from parish priest or discharge papers from
naval or military authorities" to be carried (Hunt 1996: 137). The
adoption of a specifically recognized dress code was a (reasonably
successful) strategy to project certain attributes of persona that
fooled enough people to necessitate remedial legislation. Yet, there
is little evidence that such legislation worked. As Hunt emphasises,
the adoption of prohibitive strategies – only certain persons can
wear certain items and others must not wear these items – if
anything fuelled a desire for the prohibited item ("the elicit").
Economic changes meant that increasing numbers of people had
the possibility of acquiring prohibited items:

Figure 46
Schoolgirl performing troupe.

The right of an aspirant group to wear some symbolic item of apparel or to participate in some rituals are important forms of social conflict. The history of sumptuary law reveals a general pattern of a widening of the privileged circles as successive waves of pressure come from below and concessions are granted. The result is that far from clarifying social differences, sumptuary law actually provokes increasing competition and imitation since it is "cheaper" (economically and politically) for all parties to compete over the symbols than over what those symbols represent. The result is the generation of fierce tensions and rivalries over symbolic distinction. (Hunt 1996: 105)

By making social distinction visible, the regulations "became a source of significant resentment and thus became a site of struggle". Hunt likens this to the role of brand names in contemporary society. "Known" brands create a specialist clientele and knowledge of their deemed attributes and associated status. Those in the know are prepared to pay more for the cache of association. While this conspicuous display of "accumulated cultural capital" works for a niche market, should a brand become "'too popular', the *cognoscenti* 'move on'" (Hunt 1996: 106).

Hunt relates the proliferation and longevity of sumptuary laws to broad transformations of the economy, gender relations, urbanization and politics. Clothing the body became a key element of the project of modernity. Of all forms of clothing, those with instantly recognizable codes and signifiers became a convenient form of shorthand – hence the uptake of uniforms in modern civic life. What we have now is the legacy of that recognizability. Uniforms have percolated every aspect of contemporary existence and sartorial codes.

This is especially the case in popular culture today. There are a number of versions of the adoption of uniforms and creation of uniformity through quasi and informal uniforms. These include the

- transformation of military uniforms into high fashion (e.g. Haymes and Lafitte 2001; Colls and Smith 2003)[1]
- adoption of youth dress codes by revolutionary and resistance groups (e.g. the hip denim jeans and jacket look of the women soldiers of the Liberians United for Reconciliation and Democracy engaged in the 2003 civil struggle in Monrovia)[2]
- borrowing of the (fetishized) leather wear of the military (especially Nazi uniforms) into fashion and sexual allure dress (e.g. Jane Fonda's black leather bustier, stockings and boots in the film *Barbarella* (1967), Garner (2003: 117); Paris designer, Chantal Thomas's 2004 "love, whips and lingerie" collection)[3]
- construction of distinctive codes of dress and body decoration within subcultures (Molitorisz 1998) (e.g. Goths (Morris 2001), bikies, mods, rastas, rappers, hippies, Sloane rangers, punks, skinheads, etc.)[4]
- imitation of filmic codes of dress by certain groups (e.g. of iconic mafia dress by crime families and associates (black suits, collarless shirts and sunglasses for men and bottle-aided brassy blonde hair teamed with black designer clothes and accessories – such as designer handbags and sunglasses by women)[5]
- establishment of consensual appropriate modes of dress for film premieres and award nights (penguin suit for men,[6] remarkably similar so-called Goddess evening dresses for women)[7]
- fashion conscious uniformity of "free" leisure wear among young people
- overwhelming presence of sportswear and leisurewear influences in fashion and everyday dress.

Trends such as these can be commonly seen in fashion magazines and spreads. For example, the April 2001 issue of *Nova* (UK) magazine features a fashion spread sporting the title, "Off Duty. Because Every Girl Loves a Uniform" (Haymes and Lafitte 2001). It contained a series of intriguing fashion photographs of female models in outfits that borrowed items of military dress. One photograph featured a model in an airman's peaked cap (Camden Market) worn with a Gucci bodysuit. Another showed a model wearing a plain military-style brown button-up shirt (Miu Miu) decorated by a row of medals (Greenwich Market) and webbed canvas and metal belt (Jean Colonna). The military touch was provided by a leather officer's belt (Lawrence Corner) worn over a Celine black vest and camouflage green flounced skirt (Bernhard Willhelm) in another shot.

One of the most spectacular images was of a model wearing a military-style jacket with extensive gold braiding (Ter et Bantine) and (fake) bearskin hat with metal chin strap (Lawrence Corner). A less obvious military theme was evident in an image of a girl in a black 1940s-style tailored wool dress (Comme des Garcons), while in another, a model wore a plain white cotton shirt (Paul Smith) with khaki tailored shorts (MaxMara) and khaki socks. A more dramatic image showed a model in a white gaberdine cropped jacket with narrow lapels (Balenciaga le Dix) decorated with three star (military style) brooches (Cornucopia). This was worn over a black and white striped shirt with a Racing Green hat (the latter modelled on that of the French gendarmes, designed by Lawrence Corner) and leather and metal belt (Hermes).

Finally, the theme was completed by a girl in an army green cotton flight suit (Lawrence Corner) worn with a leather and brass belt (Celine). Clearly, uniforms were a key reference point for major designers and brands – complemented by second-hand and army disposal items. There was also another outfit in the spread that had a more remote link to uniforms but alluded to a central preoccupation of military life. This image showed a model (seemingly as a dominatrix) wearing an Oriental Blue body-hugging satin waistcoat with a concealed front opening and high collar (Louis Vuitton), brown leather suspender belt (A. F. Vandevorst), satin lingerie (Passion Bait) and stockings.

In all of the images, filters produced a sepia-tinted mise en scene to set off the demure yet seductive poses. These female bodies may have been wearing male uniforms but their demeanour conveyed

Figure 47
First communion.

bodies on display – open and available – at least to the gaze. The uniforms connoted an aura of sado-masochism and sexual licence or transgression and a tension between the officialdom and authority they conventionally stand for against their appropriation in other contexts. Uniforms were not just clothes or props but encoded in the language of the photography. This chapter contends that the aesthetics of uniforms structure contemporary fashion systems and in turn form the aesthetic codes that underpin fashion photography and forms of representation and seeing in popular culture more generally.

In particular, the superficial "look" of uniforms as markers of group belonging, authority, discipline and order masks equally important inscriptions that – though often unacknowledged – shape the unconscious resonances of and responses to uniforms. And while one uniformed body is striking, uniforms are most effective when they appear en masse as a display of identically kitted-out persons. So the impressions and connotations of the sight of uniforms – singly and multiply – is a key element as to how uniforms "work" as a body technique and cultural technology. Consequently conventions of how uniforms are displayed, depicted, denoted and represented become inextricably tied up with the twin forces of their history as the visible sign of the disciplined persona.

Equally techniques that are used to represent uniforms as spectacle have come to encode aspects of the uniforms in their essential aesthetics. As discussed earlier, two factors have shaped over-whelmingly the meaning and significance of uniforms in a succession of cultures by embodying an acknowledged and unacknowledged set of connotations about uniforms derived from ecclesiastical dress and military uniforms as discussed earlier. An example of how uniforms have influenced our postmodern ways of seeing is evident from the frequent use of uniforms in popular film.

Uniforms in Hollywood Musicals

Motion pictures were a new technique of aesthetic representation as well as becoming a new cultural form. This arguably bridged portraiture and fashion illustration and the emerging technique of fashion photography. Inevitably, the aesthetics of motion pictures – especially those concerning the representation of clothing and gender heavily shaped the aesthetics of early fashion photography. In turn, fashion photography influenced aesthetic codes in other visual forms of twentieth-century popular culture.

In particular, musicals played a big role in this process. For the musical aesthetic developed around display and spectacle, e.g. in chorus line-ups, synchronized swimming, boy-meets-girl plots and coupling (Fordin 1984). For a number of reasons, military themes were prominent,[8] including recent and contemporary wars and political threats, the suitability of military uniforms to this aes-thetics of spectacle, the added frisson of putting women in uni-forms, the transformative effects (from "civvies" to "mufti") and the popularity of cross-dressing spoofs. Some of the best known choreographers – such as Busby Berkeley – had been drill instruct-ors in the US Army before working in Hollywood. This experience in synchronization, repetition, discipline and authority undoubt-edly influenced the style of choreography that became a keynote of musicals.

Wills (2000) argues that the use of women in uniforms and military-influenced female fashions enabled musicals to address issues about emerging identities for American women, realign ideas about femininity with new ideas about national identity and to deal with a series of turbulent incidents in national and international life (e.g. wars, depression). The use of women in uniforms served simultaneous functions – it was humorous (due to its origin in burlesque and carnival) and it was erotic (evoked all the tensions about women in uniforms and displaying attributes of power and authority). This combination "made this potentially provocative image . . . innocuous" (Wills 2000: 318).

In the 1920s and 1930s uniforms took on additional connotations of changing gender roles and gender confusion. Military uniforms were incorporated in fashions, but as Wills (2000: 319) notes they were not those worn by women but "bastardised versions of male uniforms," especially the sailor suit "which connoted a strangely sexual innocence derived from children's fashion and girls' school uniforms." She concludes that: "In the 1920s military-influenced fashions and women-in-uniform costumes were no longer funny, they were sexy" (Wills 2000: 319).

By the 1930s, women in uniforms had acquired new meanings. When used as costume, uniforms retained their dramatic and spectacular functions but as fashion, military uniforms conveyed the threats posed by the increasing role of women in public life. Within musicals, women in uniform came to signal transgressive femininity and sexuality signalling ambiguity and misplaced eroticism. The emphasis on spectacle was thus combined with "an unruly feminine overabundance of unstable female bodies" epitomized by the Busby Berkeley chorus lines (Wills 2000: 323). Indeed, the use of women in uniform provided a cinematic space for the partial rehabilitation of troubled tropes of masculinity (cf. Mrozek 1987). Uniforms as costumes served to give credence to strong notions of masculinity but problematic notions of femininity. Female characters were portrayed as problems (threats, unstable, ambivalent and weak). Generally, their cinematic predicaments were resolved once the female characters abandoned their uniforms for civvies and exchanged the public sphere for the fantasy of domestic bliss.

In this process we can see that uniforms were a highly effective language that bridged the screen and real-life tensions and contradictions whether they were employed as costumes or as fashion. As screen actors became stars and stars became role models in a rapidly expanding consumer culture, uniforms were omnipresent in projecting identities and negotiating difference. This was reflected in the frequent derivation of uniform motifs, garments and cut in mainstream fashion and its translation in the aesthetics of representing fashion in photography.

Figure 48
Mrs Winter on holiday.

The Uniform in Fashion Photography

So, why are uniforms such a pervasive factor in how we develop and express our sense of ourselves through the aesthetics of popular culture?

Clothes are about dressing the body but the way they are perceived is as important as the garments themselves. Indeed, Hollander (1978: 311) argues that dressing "is always picture making, with reference to actual pictures that indicate how the clothes are to be perceived." In other words:

> People dress and observe other dressed people with a set of pictures in mind – pictures in a particular style. The style is what combines the clothes and the body into the accepted contemporary look not of chic, not of ideal perfection, but of natural reality. (Hollander 1978: 311)

Thus the clothes and the look are united in knowing and recognizing a shared aesthetic code of desirable ways to perform the self. These are culturally specific and historically contingent: there are no universal or unchanging ways of seeing and looking. Hollander continues:

> And the difference between the way clothes now look (at any given time) and the way they used to look is made most clear

to the eye through changes in the style of their pictorial
representation – including styles of photography and cinema-
tography. (Hollander 1978: 311)

She argues that it is visual desire that structures the look, rather
than practical needs or necessities. As wearers of clothes and
observers of others in clothes, we are dictated to by our desire to
present a certain image and to be seen as that image as well as being
able to interpret the images of others. Even when practicality
dictates certain clothing or modes of dress, stylistic factors may
subvert that reason. Hollander (1978) gives the example of military
lapels:

> The lapels on early military uniforms . . . which were intended
> to cross over and keep the chest warm, were speedily atro-
> phied into decorative flaps, worn buttoned open to show the
> colour of the facing. They could still button across, too, but
> they were never worn so. (Hollander 1978: 312)

Consequently, clothing should be interpreted not only in terms of
iconographic or symbolic meanings but also in terms of its formal
properties and their fluctuation. It is changing looks that determine
how garments will change to embody a new symbol or statement.
It is only when a new look (visual desire) coincides with a new
sensibility (habit or moral outlook) that a particular mode or style
captures the public imagination. When the two do not coincide,
there are called fashion failures. Hollander (1978) argues that:

> It has always been fashionable to copy certain elements of
> dress that have public timeliness, such as military motifs in
> wartime or foreign motifs while public attention is focused
> on the foreigners in question. But fashionable mimicry does
> not occur unless the look pleases for itself and blends with
> what already pleases. If Garibaldi's blouse and hat in 1865
> and General Eisenhower's jacket in 1945 had not harmonised
> with the most satisfying shapes in the female dress of their
> day, they would never have been imitated as elements in
> modish clothing, no matter how complimentary to those
> heroes the ladies wished to appear. Nobody copied General
> Pershing's jacket; it was out of line with the current feminine
> shape in 1918. (Hollander 1978: 313)

As we have already seen, military motifs and allusions have spiked our cultural history and, as such, have been incorporated in our aesthetic and stylistic regimes of looking. They have, accordingly, become part of the very fabric of the succession of looks (clothing systems) and ways of looking (representational codes and conventions). Thus Hollander (1978: 312) argues, visual desire feeds into a range of factors that account for our love of the uniform and its fetishization.

Military uniforms encode ambivalent iconographic messages though ostensibly they are technical devices that submerge personality, create distinctive group identity, and convey authority and status. But they also "enhance machismo and glamour" (Wilson 1985: 36). Hollander (1978) cites the popularity of the country sportsman's look among city businessmen in the nineteenth century. The look was

> overlaid on a vestigial military look – but clothes embodying such meaning carried their significance in suspension, while their formal properties (dull wool fabric, cutaway coattails, crisp lapels, extra buttons) produced an independent satisfaction. The connotation of soldiering or riding to hounds was not central but peripheral and irrelevant to the pleasure taken in the look. (Holland 1978: 313–14)

Over time, individual elements of uniforms have acquired highly specific meanings and erotic allusions to the point where they have virtually developed a life of their own: body-hugging jackets buttoned to the neck convey one thing; epaulettes another; jodhpurs and knee-high boots another; frogging another. It is the desire to achieve a certain look that prompts people to cannibalize motifs in the clothes they wear and influences how they wear them. To that end, military uniforms have had a profound influence on fashion and its aesthetics of representation. This can be seen in conventions of painting (especially in portraiture), illustration (for example, in magazine covers and fashion plates: Packer 1983; Robinson 1986); photography (Lloyd 1986; Scott 1999); and film making (Gaines and Herzog 1990).

Ways of representing clothes have been one component of these representational systems. The first recorded use of photography to record fashion was in 1856 but it was not popularized until the 1920s when it appeared alongside fashion illustrations (Craik

Figure 49
Major Steel and
tiger.

1994: 97). It was initially favoured because of its technical ability
to record details faithfully – unlike the flights of fancy employed
by illustrators – but the photographers quickly tired of the mechanical portraiture convention. The move to mechanical reproduction
of images became a contest of experimentation and innovation. The
photographers rejected the conventional notions of docile femininity and embraced new roles for women, new technical developments in photography, new art movements (cubism, fauvism,
surrealism) and new contexts (mise en scène).

Movie making – and particularly the impact of Hollywood in
popularizing ideas about femininity and masculinity, social change,
fashion and cosmetics, and American versus "Other" cultures –
also had a significant role in shaping the aesthetics of fashion
photography. The impact of documentary and social realism was
tangible in the location shots and emergence of a distinct aesthetic
that turned on narrative, fleeting impressions and blurred actions.
Black and white photography was replaced by colour but the
starkness and ability to manipulate light and dark in monochrome
photography ensured that it was the iconography of modernity and
a staple in the language of fashion photography.

The culture of fashion was saturated with debates (explicit and
implicit) about femininity although the dominant visual aesthetic
was, as Mulvey (1989) identified, a voyeuristic, normative "male"
point-of-view. This was evident across representational forms and
perhaps reached its apotheosis in advertising as consumer culture

grew and took hold of image-conscious citizens. Although popular culture was based on mass availability, reproducibility, distribution and consumption, individuality was its keynote and people strived to differentiate themselves through their looks and ways of living. In the world of fashion individuality was embodied in the cult of couture, the notoriety of designers, the stables of known photographers and an elite core of models and actresses as role models.

Uniform Influences on Design

Alongside the froth and bubble of the cultural moments shaping fashion and photography were historical forces that produced turbulent and threatening times. Military undercurrents persisted. As the memory of the First World War became the threat of even worse conflagration, the role of photography and film reflected the new realities. Sparke (1986) argues in her suitably titled chapter, "Democracies and Dictatorships", that design aesthetics during this period were heavily influenced by the orientations of governments, their ideologies and forms of government support. She contrasts the design legacies of Sweden, the United Kingdom, Germany and Italy in these terms, suggesting that the distinctive aesthetics of each can be directly related to the political contexts that shaped them, especially different versions of – and responses to – nationalism, fascism and totalitarianism.

In addition to the aesthetic systems of design, Moneera Laennec (1997: 81) argues that bodies themselves were produced in politically charged ways. She examines the increasing use of the machine aesthetic in the representation of women, influencing fashion photography and "how the (fashionable or desirable) body was being defined." The "connection between photography and the machine was not coincidental" but stemmed from technical developments in mechanical reproduction and their recognition as an art form.

The machine aesthetic later worked its way into popular culture: consumer-oriented industrial design, "streamlining" and a preoccupation with function continued throughout the 1930s, 1940s and 1950s. The iconography of the machine itself entered aesthetics as the canonical image and crowning convention. It also informed fashion photography: "woman as a mechanical (and thus reproducible) realisation of man's desires remained merely implicit in fashion photography, which functioned much more intuitively in conveying an image of what was up-to-date, glamorous and modern" (Moneera Laennec 1997: 83).[9] Photographs typically depicted movement, fragmented body parts, repetition, duplication, uniformity, angular shapes, and plays with light and shade.[10] Images of machines as the setting for the models was also common.[11]

Often images borrowed from conventions of chorus lines, which, as we have already noted, incorporated the techniques of the military drill. Military implications were ever present. When used to frame women the constant theme was "implicit violence and the threat" they posed (Moneera Laennec 1997: 96). By the late 1930s, machines had a sinister edge to their aesthetics signifying:

> A somewhat frightening, inhuman force which no doubt became more and more identified with impending war (as exemplified by such terms as *war-machine* and *military-industrial complex*). When in 1940 photographs of women interacting with machines appear in fashion magazines, the women in them are not representatives of an elegant, stream-lined modernity, but are soldiers and nurses fighting in the war, or women once again in munitions factories. After 1939, the presence of machines in fashion photography is less a sign of the machine aesthetic than it is a simple documentation of the world in which women lived. (Moneera Laennec 1997: 96)

One reason for this was that fashion photographers were also acting as war photographers, for example, Lee Miller and Cecil Parkinson. The gritty realism and horror of war contrasted greatly with the rationale of fashion spreads. Although magazines initially tried to keep the war out of their pages and concentrate on the more pleasant things in life, circumstances dictated that they address issues of rationing, lonely women missing their men on the front, supporting the war effort, and so on. Bombing of *Vogue*'s London offices in 1940 (Hall 1985: 10) and the dangers faced by staff on assignment reinforced the reality of the war.

In the event, fashion magazines produced an unexpectedly rich and textured coverage of the war years probably because of the tensions and contradictions they tried to negotiate. It was neither pure documentary nor pure amnesia but an almost dreamlike allusion to desperate days. In particular, the war provided new

Figure 50
US naval cadet officers
on leave.

avenues to explore ideas of femininity and push the boundaries of
convention. For many women, they had no choice: joining the war
effort in some capacity was essential. For others, displacement and
the lack of basic essentials were traumatic but also a challenge.
Many women found new identities and possibilities throughout the
war. In these various manifestations of femininity, images of
machines and military themes were prevalent in the forms of
military equipment, uniforms, military and homefront mise en
scène, and negotiations of heroism – masculine and feminine.[12] And
although the woman machine aesthetic became uncommon after
the war, it lurked in the background as "an early precursor to the
fashionable techno-body of the late twentieth century" (Moneera
Laennec 1997: 82). Indeed, in discussing modernist aesthetics and
and ideas of the body, frequent references have been made to the
influence of Leni Riefenstahl's images of the 1936 Berlin Olympiad
on fashion photography (e.g. Jobling 1999: 25).

Postmodern Sensibilities

In the post-war years, covers and fashion shoots returned to more
familiar refrains. Women were actively retuned to hearth and home
and lavished with consumer goods and mother's little helpers as if
this would blot out the experiences they had endured and enjoyed.
Fashion photography evolved and stabilized around images of

glamour, elegance and consumerism. But in chasing constructions of images redolent with "what is exotic, dramatic, glamorous and different", fashion photography has heavily drawn on anthropological references to emphasise the difference of consumer culture (Ramamurthy 1997: 177).

Other influences and aesthetic forms have also contributed to the emergence of a distinctive genre that ironically destabilized conventions of femininity and constructed contrary images. The cult of Hollywood continued apace with new stars and new role models, many of whom were young: youth culture was born. These were rivalled by up and coming popular music artists. But it was also the age of the Cold War and military themes continued to proliferate and unsettle the cosy conventions. One manifestation of the uniform was in the safari suit, a jacket and trousers or shorts made of lightweight cotton material, typically in khaki or beige, with buttoned pockets, narrow lapels and pleated lines. The suit was popularized in tropical countries as a modernist approach to administration. The suit was practical, climatically suitable, western and supposedly stylish but despite extensive promotion and slavish devotees, a rather unsympathetic portrayal of the safari suit as a fashion garment has become its memory. Nonetheless, Norman Parkinson featured a model in a safari suit in a *Vogue* (UK) issue set in the Bahamas (July 1959: see Lloyd 1986: 105).

The 1960s manifested major upheavals. Fashion photographers such as Richard Avedon, Irving Penn, Lord Lichfield, David Bailey, Terence Donovan and Brian Duffy threw out established conventions and shocked the magazines, models and themselves. Fashion photography (only recently acknowledged as a distinctive aesthetic) was rewritten in radical ways that have continued to shape its contours. The photographers became stars and celebrities – as bad boys – and fashion photography became a symbol of anti-establishment sentiments and resistance. Couture was swapped for street fashion, racy lifestyles, radical politics and a new coalition between aesthetic regimes were established: fashion photography, popular music and radical film became bedfellows. Their shared practices rested on subversions and cannibalization. Uniforms and military motifs were perfect sources of appropriate imagery for the burgeoning youth culture and counter culture.

Uniforms featured strongly in the heady world of street fashion, exemplified in 1960s pop culture (as discussed in Chapter 7). The uniform became a symbol of anti-establishment feeling, rebellion and revolution. The uniforms of resistance groups were especially popular – such as Che Guevara's beret and bandana, and the Palestinian head scarf. Other examples include the Black Panthers in the United States and the IRA (Irish Republican Army) in Northern Ireland, both of whom favoured black berets and dark glasses. What began as a radical statement was quickly normalized in mainstream youth fashion. Even *Vogue* showcased army surplus clothing on its covers.[15]

Subcultures and Uniforms

Out of the youth culture and popular music culture of the 1960s emerged the proliferation of subcultures as a dominant component of young people's lifestyles. Subcultures are, above all, out of the mainstream – a social group that defines itself in opposition to dominant values, beliefs and codes. They reject mainstream power relations, authority and status hierarchies by establishing a counter-set of meanings, hierarchies, values and modes of appearance as a visible sign of symbolic resistance.

As children transform into teens, they – to varying degrees – reject what their parents stand for and "adopt a look, a pastime, a lifestyle. You adopt a tribe" (Molitorisz 1998: 6). But to do so involves trading one look for another. Visibility is one of the distinctive features of subcultures, hence members aim to create an instantly recognizable appearance so that both fellow travellers and non-members can identify who they are and are not. In short, in creating a distinctive look, subcultures create quasi uniforms, sometimes with secret codes for other members.

This symbolic resistance and visible difference may become entrenched over time as a subculture develops a mainstream following (e.g. punks, mods), its members' age (e.g. bikies), it is appropriated in popular music or fashion (e.g. grunge, hip hop, surfers, rappers, Goths). So subcultures have an accommodative relationship with mainstream culture that necessitates constant reinvention and the imposition of new forms of distinctiveness. In the twenty-first century, subcultures have changed in three ways: they are changing faster than ever; they have proliferated in type and subtypes; and they are increasingly hybrid (Molitorisz 1998: 6).

In this sense, maintaining dress codes that are distinctive, recognizable yet different means continually updating the quasi-uniform.

Figure 51
Cheerleaders.

Ironically, then, subcultures have become as dependent on the codification of the quasi-uniform as business people have on wearing a formal suit and female actors to showing off their assets in the latest designer evening gowns. In many ways, subcultures epitomize the relationship between the contemporary body and postmodern senses of identity as arbitrary yet contingent, unstable yet legible, changing yet distinctive.

Even in subcultures where difference is paramount – for example, the piercing and tattooing subculture adherents, each dressed in their "unique" outfits – fit together like a patchwork quilt to produce a coherent and recognizable "look" and community. And of course there are fashions in piercing and tattooing, in terms of which body parts are decorated (face, navel, genitals, limbs), the number and types of piercing or tattoos, and so on. Equally important is the accompanying jewellery and clothes to match in order to look consistent with the body modification.

So, we can see that subcultures institute quasi-uniforms as strict codes of adherence as the hallmark of their resistance or opposition to the mainstream culture. In fact, the more radical the subculture, the more cohesive the subcultural codes of dress, behaviour and beliefs. Not only can these tendencies be seen in western societies but especially in cultures that have recently modernized or westernized – such as Japan, China and Asia more generally, Eastern Europe and African states. The global visibility of sub-cultures acts as a passport to the international stage through the instant recognizability of the quasi-uniform of particular "tribes".

Indicatively, subcultures have not been immune to the creeping scope of consumerism instead becoming a creative impulse in product design and marketing. Subcultural markers, such as baggy pants, sports shoes, bleached hair, baseball caps, leather jackets, bomber jackets, surfwear, Gothic black and so on, have shifted from niche boutique or custom-made items to high-status high street fashion in high mainstream demand. The more refined version of this is brand-name appropriation where items become synonymous with their marketing label – for example adidas, Nike, Billabong, Quiksilver, Mambo, Dr. Martens, Vans and Airwalks. While brand-name appropriation secures elite mainstream uptake of subcultural motifs as fashion paraphernalia, translation into department and chain store labels and marketing creates main-stream adoption of such motifs, obliging the reference subculture to reinvent itself and create new looks and distinctive motifs. And so the proliferation of youth-oriented markers of resistance con-tinues producing in its wake the genesis of new fashion trends and new quasi-uniforms.

From West to East – and Back Again

The influence of uniforms on dress and fashion was not confined to western cultures. Like other cultures subjected to colonial incursions, China was ambivalent about balancing traditional cultural habits with so-called modernizing influences from Europe. This directly stemmed from political upheavals and ideologies especially with respect to modernism, nationalism and global connections (Roberts 1997C; Finnane 1999; Steele and Major 1999).

The gradual infiltration of European-style uniforms into the ranks of the leadership (political, military and administrative) quickly influenced styles of civilian Chinese dress (Finnane 1999). The popularity of high collars, close-fitting jackets, gold buttons, gold braid, frogging and epaulettes were a legacy of military uniforms. Sun Yat-sen's influence was especially significant "chang-ing from western suit to Chinese robe and back again, and even coming up with a style of his own – the Sun Yat-sen suit" (Finnane 1999: 130). This outfit was modelled on military dress and was just one of a succession of influences of military culture on Chinese dress. Another was the *qipao* that was popularized in the 1930s and 1940s serving as a de facto national dress for women until it was "displaced by the dress of the women's revolutionary army" (Finnane 1999: 131). Finnane concludes that:

> The green and blue army and naval suits sported by Mao Zedong's teenage fans during the years of the Cultural Revolution were thus not a quixotic or aberrant fashion, but rather a logical product of a process of dress reform which had its origins in new uniforms for the soldiers in the service of the Manchu dynasty. (Finnane 1999: 131)

Chen's (2001) study of women's dress from the 1940s through to the Cultural Revolution in China argues that there were two interlinking forces. First, clothing habits were much more complex and varied than officially sanctioned modes of dress seem to suggest. Far from looking "shapeless" and "sexless", Chinese women experimented with all kinds of modifications and uses of colour to personalize their clothing. Second, the Communist Party quickly realized the importance of dress as a technique to produce particular kinds of citizens and preferred codes of femininity. In this process, women mixed traditional elements of dress (such as patterned blouses) with newly sanctioned ones, such as the *quipao*, belted Mao jacket and soft cloth cap. The Mao suit was an interestingly ambiguous outfit. On the one hand, it promoted uniformity and an image of the new nationalism of the Cultural Revolution. But it also functioned to make distinctions within the party, between the party and ordinary citizens, and between some ordinary citizens and others. According to Chen (2001):

> During the Maoist period, sartorial discourse increasingly placed value on the uniformity of militaristic fashion and promoted this form of clothing and its concomitant behaviour as that towards which all citizens should work. This increased presence of militaristic uniformity did not destroy other clothing conventions; but it did necessitate that alternatives to the uniforms be measured against the uniform. (Chen 2001: 156)

This resulted in fine distinctions being made between "the various manifestations of the Mao suit as well as between the Mao suit and clothing made from coloured fabrics" (Chen 2001: 157). Despite the importance of dress reform to the implementation of the Maoist doctrine, the elaboration of dress habits and subtle resistance to officially sanctioned modes of dress illustrated the complexity and multiple responses to the regime (Scott 1965).

A little later, the opening up of China and ambivalent fascination with an exotic yet austere culture led to an on-again, off-again love affair with the Mao suit – and derivations in fashion design. The Mao suit had been designed as a uniform of nationality – to provide a garment worn by all classes – but its appropriation was as a marker of difference (Steele and Major 1999). In western fashion, it represented a deliberate though insincere allusion to the drab reality of the Cultural Revolution.

The Mao suit even made it to the cover of *Vogue*. In October 1979, *Vogue* (UK) went to China and featured a model in a Mao suit in front of a silk tapestry.[14] An even more startling cover on *Vogue* (Australia) (in March 1981 showed a model in a Mao suit, a cap with a red star badge, sunglasses and a red scarf.[15] These images guaranteed that the Mao suit gained a new life as high fashion (Lloyd 1986: 198, 204). The red star became a ubiquitous fashion accessory while jackets adapted from the severe lines of the Mao jacket, high collars, caps and military insignia created something of a controversy. While some derivations intended to make a sympathetic political statement, fashion aficionados preferred an irreverent appropriation purely as style. It was a very different fashion statement from the longstanding derivations of the elegant *cheungsam* or *qipao* (long fitted dress fastening on the right with stand-up collar), *qianlian mei* ("pretty face" jacket typically worn by peasants) and *xiao'ao* (wedding jacket: Clark and Wong 1997; Szeto 1997; Ye 1997).

The military theme has continued to recur in fashion and fashion photography both in haute couture and street fashion. It has a remarkable ability to both give a sense of authority, discipline and stylish cut as well as being used subversively. Fashion photography ostensibly is about picturing clothes but its history shows a genre that constantly seeks to escape the outfits and construct other possibilities and mise en scène (Scott 1999: 154–5; see also Jobling 1999). That multiplicity of references and play between visual language, historical references and narrative allusions constitute fertile ground for encapsulating the ambivalent registers of uniforms as fashion.

The themes of sex and militarism have provided the punch for more familiar themes of gendered roles and body decoration. Jobling suggests that "body fascism" has come to characterize male fashion photography in an especially strong form. He notes the similar impulses of narcissism and fascism that has spawned a distinctive iconography within fashion photography, such as that of Bruce Weber and Herb Ritts:

> Nazism fascinates in a way other iconography . . . does not
> . . . For those born after the early 1940s, bludgeoned by a
> lifetime's palaver, pro and con, about communism, it is
> Fascism – the great conversation piece of their parents'
> generation – which represents the exotic, the unknown.
> (Susan Sontag, quoted by Jobling 1999: 147)

The legacy, according to Jobling, is that contemporary conventions of representing masculinity and male fashions draw heavily on the military dress of Nazism and ideal images of male bodies as captured by Leni Riefenstahl.

Contemporary fashion design has been heavily influenced by military themes. Designers who have incorporated military references include Emanuel Ungaro, Thierry Mugler, Claude Montana, Giorgio Armani, Vivienne Westwood, Jean Paul Gaultier, Karl Lagerfeld, Kenzo (Takada), Rudi Gernreich, Walter Albini, Hardy Amies, Kansai Yamamoto, Geoffrey Beene, Ralph Lauren, Antony Price, Luciano Soprani, Gianni Versace and Perry Ellis (McDowell 1997; Baudot 1999; Seeling 2000). Indeed, designers who have not drawn on motifs from uniforms at some point in their careers are the exception.

The Popularity of Uniforms and Sexual Frisson

In sum, uniforms have lent themselves to particular ways of looking and seeing as a hallmark of fashion and fashion photography in contemporary culture. In turn, fashion photography laps up any "uniform theme" in fashion. Uniforms serve to fix identities surrounding femininity and masculinity especially when these are diverse, crossing the boundaries between public and private, and where sexual ambiguity is involved. The uniform is, then, a primary aesthetic of the language of fashion photography. It is both its mise en scène and rationale – referencing our outer skin and our underworld. In turn, the aesthetics of other ways of looking and seeing have equally been shaped by the iconic design elements and best remembered examples of uniforms – in particular the Napoleonic legacy and uniforms of Nazi Germany. More recently, historic groups have taken to recreating uniforms of the past – even recreating famous battles re-enacted by costumed participants. For example, "thousands of men and youths in Confederate grey and Union blue, and women in black hoop skirts and veils escorted the crew of the Confederate submarine HL Hunley, the first submarine in history to sink an enemy warship, to their final resting place". (Associated Press 2004). A similar re-enactment takes place annually in Australia commemorating the 1804 Battle of Vinegar Hill in which government troops in facsimiles of their distinctive red coats confront escaped convicts (Sandrejko 2004).

If clothing and dress are given their appropriate significance in ordering social relations and specifying cultural messages, then the uniform is a key subtext of the formation of the self, persona and collective identities. Without this encoding of the aesthetics of uniforms, the *Nova* fashion spread discussed at the start of this chapter could not so decisively convey the multiple and ambiguous connotations of the uniform as a defining body technique of the postmodern self. For modes of clothing the body in instantly recognizable ways has become the marker of the shift from the external governance of bodies and selves to the self-governance of the body via how the body is wrapped and place ballets produced. The adoption of uniforms in popular culture epitomizes this process.

9

Transgressive Uniforms in Contemporary Culture

The Power of Uniforms

Why is it that countless instances of transgressive behaviour involve the adoption of some form of uniform as part of the costume or play? Why is it that the markers of discipline, authority and order are spontaneously subverted and inverted by transgressive uptakes? Garber has speculated on this phenomenon in cases of cross-dressing, for example, where women become a "spectacle" when dressed in men's clothing, especially in men's military and lay uniforms. She suggests that this leads "back to the question of male cross-dressing and its relationship to structures of hierarchy and power" (Garber 1992: 55). As mentioned earlier, Max Beerbohm derided one of the witnesses at the 1895 trial of Oscar Wilde as "wearing Her Majesty's uniform, another form of female attire" was not just sarcastic but

> Focuse[d] attention on the "fancy dress" aspect of soldiering
> – an aspect that came under serious and sustained scrutiny

by the man who coined the term "transvestite", the German homosexual rights advocate, Magnus Hirschfeld. (Garber 1992: 55)

In relating the fetishization of uniform to the nexus between sexual identification and desire, and rank and authority, Hirschfeld identified the implicit sexual references exuded by uniforms. He supported this theory with evidence from research into transvestites in the military. He argued that there was a huge over-representation of cross-dressers in the military, a fact he linked to "the intense love of the uniform" among likely recruits. According to Hirschfeld:

> Women joined the army . . . because they liked to dress up in uniforms. Men who wore uniforms did so in part because they unconsciously understood them to be "fancy dress". (Garber 1992: 55–6)

As Garber noted, the attraction – or obsession – stemmed from the nexus of attributes signalled by uniforms: normative masculinity (and its counterpoints – homosexuality and effeminacy); carnival-esque and parodic release from everyday conventions; and unequal power relations and their actualization in sartorial and gestural codes. This nexus is both visible in military displays of transgression witnessed by the popularity of drag shows that often included female impersonators as well as the popular use of military uniforms as costumes or props in musicals, films, plays and novels. Indeed the word, "camouflage", now synonymous with modern military uniforms (Newark, et al. 1998),

> became a term covering costume, set design, camouflage design for combat – and gay identity. Many of the camou-fleurs had held civilian jobs as set designers, fashion designers, or window dressers. (Garber 1992: 56)

In her study of cross-dressers, Bloom (2003) found that:

> Heterosexual cross-dressers are disproportionately repre-sented among the retired military; they are often first-born sons, and often quite masculine looking, which is why the rest of us struggle so with their appearance. (Bloom 2003: 37)

Bloom cited Ray Blanchard, head of a sexology services centre in Canada, who claimed that cross-dressers seek out occupations with archetypal "masculine" uniforms in order to hide their "feminine" side:

> "All of these men will tell you, 'I had to hide my femininity. I became a cop, a firefighter, a black belt in karate, a construction worker, in order to compensate, in order to put these fears to rest and to hide my true nature'." Blanchard thinks that what they fear is actually ridicule and exposure – not of their own femininity but of their drive to cross-dress. They want to believe that their wearing of women's clothes expresses this femininity rather than an erotic compulsion. (Bloom 2003: 35)

Bloom's study highlights the diversity of men who become cross-dressers – and the varying difficulty of their partners to accommodate this compulsion. She concluded that the "world of cross-dressers is for the most part a world of traditional men, traditional marriages and truths turned inside out" (Bloom 2003: 37).

The majority of cross-dressers revel in the performance of cross-dressing rather than the erotic or sexual possibilities apparently encoded in cross-dressing. Cross-dressing is explained away as a sartorial desire where the uniform (women's clothes) enables the subject to perform authentically. Yet it is clear to the partners and the public that the cross-dressing "uniform" itself is imbued with erotics and sexual references. In other words, there is an ever-present tension and sexual perversion in the most archetypal ostensibly non-sexed uniforms.

Even in politics, transgressive use of uniforms has made its mark. The Nazi hierarchy surreptitiously tolerated cross-dressing and gender-bending outfits. The US Senator Edward Kennedy once dressed as a blonde miniskirted woman at an office Christmas party, while legendary violinist, Isaac Stern, was entertained at his 70th birthday by cellist Mstislav Rostropovich masquerading as the ballerina "Natasha Milanova Rostropovich" (Garber 1992: 52).

But whereas these episodes were treated as humorous, other politicians' forays into transgressive dressing have not. British conservative politicians became notorious for sexual peccadilloes and cross-dressing dalliances. The insinuation that the US presidential candidate, Michael Dukakis, might cross-dress (or be gay) initiated a scathing attack on his moral stances by night-wing groups (Garber 1992: 53–4). The Australian Foreign Minister, Alexander Downer, never lived down the occasion he wore fishnet knee stockings for a dare on a politically satirical television show. He has invariably been depicted in sexy fishnet stockings with suspenders in cartoons ever since, even though the episode was accepted as a one-off humorous joke at the time. So the transgressive wearing of uniforms and transgressing codes of dress remain culturally fraught practices.

The wearing of a uniform provides points of identification for audiences – sometimes of painful memories, clashes with authority, or fancy dress – as well as allowing a performer to adopt a special persona relating to the uniform. An example discussed later in this chapter is the use by the group, The Village People, of distinctive characters (Sims 1999: 213). These in turn, may be usurped by the fans, as in the fetishization of The Village People in New York gay culture or the adaptation of school uniforms in punk regalia (Sims 1999: 87). But how did these double entendres about uniforms become entrenched in cultural practice? The origin of the popularity of using uniforms in transgressive contexts stems from vestimentary practices and sartorial codes in the military (as discussed earlier) and religions.

Ecclesiastical Dress: From Carnival to Carnal

The use of particular dress and decorations to signify those with religious, spiritual and magical powers is deeply ingrained in human culture. Yet, in the Early Christian Church, before the fourth century, the religious dressed like the laity. Only after the invasions of the Roman Empire did the clergy adopt distinctive dress, based initially on Roman civilian dress and later on liturgical dress (Ribeiro 1999: 120). These garments shaped subsequent ecclesiastical garb and consisted of layered garments starting with a cassock embellished by robes, capes, mantles and decorative bands, girdles, scarves and fastenings. Monastic dress was introduced in the sixth century, consisting of a habit, hood or cowl, and a scapular (protective apron).

Over time, ecclesiastical dress became more and more distinctive with the high church opting for opulence and splendour and the low church (and Protestants) opting for austerity and simplicity. The emergence of specific garments was the vestimentary encapsulation of moral and spiritual principles associated with Christianity: for the high church, status, authority and power; for the low church, poverty, chastity and obedience. In a ground-breaking article examining the eroticization of ecclesiastical dress, Keenan (1999: 391–2) characterized this garb as a "dress of innocence" that signalled "the body's renunciation of the desires of the flesh": "the habit stood for a chaste life". The habit served both a religious function and as a force of moral order among believers. Hence it had to be instantly recognizable and sufficiently distinguished from the dress of ordinary people as well as instantly conveying religious messages about "good" and "bad" behaviour. So, from the outset, religious garb simultaneously embodied sexual and spiritual purity and stood for surveillance and punishment for impure behaviour. Figures in religious habit unwittingly posed ambiguous and highly charged messages.

This was irrespective of whether the preferred religious garb was highly decorative or puritanical. The Roman Catholic Church, in particular, adopted more and more extravagant outfits featuring luxurious materials in bright colours with lashings of gold trimmings and precious stones. The Protestant reformers rejected this ostentatious display and opted for simple gowns in dark colours devoid of decoration and embellishment. Elements of both of these types became synonymous with religious garb: surplices, cassocks, habits, dog collars, crucifixes, rosary beads, headwear (mitre, skull cap, hood, wimple), shawls and crosier. Colours too acquired religious significance after papal regulations were introduced in 1570: white or silver symbolized joy, purity and innocence; red symbolized martyrdom and sacrifice; purple stood for preparation and penitence; green was a neutral colour; gold could be added to any of these colours; and black was associated with death and solemnity (Ribeiro 1999: 21). These associations carried over into civil life, but they could be used mischievously to subvert their religious connotations.

Significance was placed on the perceived tradition carried by religious dress as something static and stolid. This perception gave rise to the phrase "changing fashion means moral decay" (cited by Keenan 1999: 393). And yet, irrespective of whether the religious adopted the peacock or austere look, elements of both looks became the symbol not just of the intended attributes of religious values but of their opposite: immorality, licence, depravity, excess and disorder. Religious motifs became ingrained in carnivalization and fetishism with discarded religious garments being especially prized. Such garments have become central props in erotic games and fantasies. The desire for actual or copies of ecclesiastical garments and props has produced a minor industry in buying and selling religious accoutrements for non-religious purposes, a theme picked up by many fashion designers who use religious garb or motifs to shock and titillate the fashion industry.

Even within religious orders, there was a carnivalization of the religious body and its dress in many non-sanctioned pursuits of the pleasures of the flesh, a tradition that still besets the church. As noted at the outset there is a long history of the resonance of ambiguous meanings of religious garb in carnival and as kitsch in popular culture. Keenan (1999: 395; cf. Bakhtin 1968) emphasises the "carnivalesque aspect of popular culture generally when it comes to religious dress modes". He continues:

> Carnival does not belong exclusively to the streets or to those with an ideological "vested interest" in cross-dressing. More fundamentally, it is an attitude of mind, one that pricks the bubble of strait-laced, "serious" and "respectable" culture by infiltrating the comedic, the ludic and the erotic into otherwise controlled and "responsible" modes of social and cultural expression. Relevant instances here occur with some frequency within mainstream Hollywood mass culture in the inversion of the serious religious import of the religious habit to secure comedic effect. (Keenan 1999: 395)

At stake is the signification of "not statements" by religious garb. The more religious authorities attempted to convey purity of the body and spirit through clothes that signified the renunciation of fleshy pleasures, the more the suppressed and forbidden was signalled and made desirable. The concealment of the body only provoked curiosity and sexual interest. Clothes became coda of what was repressed, namely, sexual desire as a denied and forbidden pleasure (cf. Murdoch 2000). As Keenan put it:

> Part of the lure of the religious dress fetish lies in the frisson obtained when carnal and spiritual bodies juxtapose and commingle, when "the lusts of the flesh" commune with "the

Figure 52
Masks at the
Carnivale di
Venezia.

garments of God", when the conventional morality of dress is overturned. (Keenan 1999: 397)

While the appropriate modes of religious dress and behaviour of clergy wearing such outfits is highly regulated around restraint, ritual, authority and the regulation of action, emotion and attitude, this set of "not" statements and prescriptions simultaneously evokes their opposites by highlighting unrestrained behaviour and erotic connotations. In this process, ecclesiastical dress joins a parade of other kinds of uniforms as common props in sexual desire, transgression and perversion. "Religionwear" appears alongside other fetish wear, including school uniforms, maids' uniforms, traffic wardens' uniforms, nurses' uniforms, police uniforms, military uniforms and "rubberwear" as the basis of sado-masochistic practices, cross-dressing and mardi gras costuming.

Religious garb embodies "integrity and innocence" as well as conveying "a sense of *jouissance* about the 'fallen' or 'depraved' body". This double face exemplifies "the dynamics of purity-in-passion/passion-in-purity" (Keenan 1999: 396). The formation of the Sisters of Perpetual Indulgence in San Francisco in 1979 marked another transgressive use of ecclesiastical garb. The Sisters were a group of gay men trying to draw attention to gay activism dressed in habits based on Flemish fourteenth-century nuns. Their "vows are to promulgate universal joy and expiate stigmatic guilt" (The Sisters of Perpetual Indulgence 2002; see also Kellerman 2002). Over time, orders have been set up in many cities in the United States and elsewhere, including South America, Russia, Australia and Europe. The excessive adoption of the garb of female religieuse and the Sisters' outrageous form of activism has guaranteed media attention, church condemnation and a conservative backlash. In short, their appropriation and de-sacralization of ecclesiastical wear has become more noteworthy than the causes they espouse.[1] Tellingly, one of their favourite chants is: "The Pope wears a dress and so will I" (Sisters of Perpetual Indulgence 2004).

In short, it signifies excitement and difference and is incorporated in aesthetic conventions and fashion design. Motifs, themes and exemplars of religious wear - not only in transgressive cultures of carnival - are intrinsically part of the ways we look and see, and shape our clothing conduct.

Transgression and Culture

The use of transgressive dress is culturally coded as part of carnival (as discussed above) and in part produces the abject and grotesque.[2] Carnival refers to licensed transgression, usually a kind of temporary liberation in which people are given permission to transgress from everyday norms and mores in their behaviour, dress and emotions and engage in excessive or extreme behaviour (Russo 1986). According to Bakhtin (1968):

> As opposed to the official feast, one might say that carnival celebrated temporary liberation from the prevailing truth and from the established order; it marked the suspension of all hierarchical rank, privileges, norms, and prohibitions. Carnival was the true feast of time, the feast of becoming, change, and renewal. It was hostile to all that was immortalised and completed. (Bakhtin 1968: 10)

Examples include festivals (such as marking the seasons), festive or ceremonial occasions (Christmas, New Year, mardi gras) and rites of passage (birthdays, naming ceremonies, weddings, funerals). Folk culture especially embraced the idea of carnival and became "a parody of extracarnival life, a 'world inside out'" (Bakhtin 1968: 11). This is a "world of topsy-turvy, of heteroglot exuberance, of ceaseless overrunning and excess where all is mixed, hybrid, ritually degraded and defiled" (Stallybrass and White 1986: 8). Over time, the impulse of the spirit of carnival has been restricted and commoditized: "The carnival spirit with its freedom, its utopian character oriented toward the future, was gradually transformed into a mere holiday mood" (Bakhtin 1968: 35). And yet, the principle of carnival "still continues to fertilize various areas of life and culture" (Bakhtin 1968: 34).

While there are boundaries placed on the acceptable performance of carnival, such events are liable to spill into the arena of the grotesque, that is, to displays and performances that go beyond the limits of carnival. As Bakhtin argued:

> The essential principle of grotesque realism is degradation, that is, the lowering of all that is high, spiritual, ideal, abstract; it is a transfer to the material level, to the sphere of earth and body in their indissoluble unity. (Bakhtin 1968: 19–20)

The grotesque refers to something that is bizarre or distorted, ludicrous from incongruity, or absurd. Accordingly, grotesque phenomena are open to exchange, multiple readings and are mobile (Russo 1986; Johnston 1996; Greer 1999). For example, while it may be permissible for a woman to wear a nun's habit at a fancy dress party, it may not be should she carry a whip or wear bondage underwear underneath. Equally, a man in a nun's habit may be regarded as an even more extreme example of the grotesque, especially since the institutionalized adoption of habits by the Sisters. Bakhtin (1968) observes that:

> This is why the main events in the life of the grotesque body, the acts of the bodily drama, take place in this sphere. Eating, drinking, defecation and other elimination (sweating, blowing of the nose, sneezing), as well as copulation, pregnancy, dismemberment, swallowing up by another body – all these acts are performed on the confines of the body and the outer world, or on the confines of the old and the new body. In all these events the beginning and end of life are closely linked and interwoven. (Bakhtin 1968: 317)

Yet even the grotesque body has its normative framework of

> Impurity (both in the sense of dirt and mixed categories),
> heterogeneity, masking, protuberant distension, dispropor-
> tion, exorbitancy, clamour, decentred or eccentric arrange-
> ments, a focus upon gaps, orifices and symbolic filth . . .
> physical needs and pleasures of the "lower bodily stratum",
> materiality and parody. (Stallybrass and White 1986: 23)

Where transgression well exceeds the boundaries of licence, performance is regarded as abject, that is, embodying something that
is repulsive, degrading or debased. But as well as a repulsion factor
abject phenomena also contain an attraction factor. Abject performances encode desire, fascination, revulsion and repulsion in
the same moment. Examples include the Sisters of Perpetual
Indulgence, drag queens, excessive cosmetic surgery (e.g. Performance artist Orlan, singer Michael Jackson, singer/actress Dannii
Minogue,[3] actress Lolo Ferrari,[4] singer Dolly Parton), overly
"masculine" female sports stars (especially those who are openly
gay – e.g. Amelie Mauresmo, Martina Navratilova, female body
builders), fetishistic sexual practices or displays of excess bodily
fluids (blood, faeces, semen). Whereas the film *G.I. Jane* (1997),
or the famous *Vanity Fair* cover of singer k.d. lang and model Cindy
Crawford (to be discussed later in this chapter) were regarded as
grotesque by the heterosexual mainstream, sumo wrestlers are
regarded as abject by the western mainstream. So whereas carnival
can be used to harness populations by the licensed performance of
excess – or letting off steam in a world turned upside down –
grotesque and abject performances can threaten to destabilize
social order and performative identities.

There are a number of motives associated with cultural transgression: the compulsion to subvert and invert the established
order; the exaggerated performance of display and spectacle; the
demonstration of cultural excess often as a one-off or occasional
"letting off steam" and ignoring social rules; and the creation of
polarities and oppositions. Above all, cultural transgression is a
means of simultaneously undermining *and* reinforcing rules of
uniforms since an effective transgressive performance relies on
shared understandings of normative meanings, designated codes
of conduct and connotations. Once a cultural phenomenon is
transformed into a transgressive culture, the original impulse is

never the same – e.g. since air hostesses became the butt of parody, it has been hard for the profession to regain credibility. In a similar way, recent exposes (and court cases and financial settlements) concerning sexual improprieties among the priesthood in many countries have significantly dented those religious institutions.

The Transgressive Uptake of Uniforms in Contemporary Culture

Discipline and Transgression

> [Cross-dressing is] central in our culture, it calls attention to the artificiality and constructedness of gender roles, it is a rebellion and a critique. The more rules and borders in the society, the more someone will want to cross them. The "trans" in transvestite is the "trans" in transgression, right? (Marjorie Garber, quoted by Purves 1992: 5)

Much of the transgressive use of uniforms in culture occurs as the "not" statement of social rules and everyday conventions. Examples include the popularity of "camp" parody in the military; the common use of school uniforms in pornographic costumes and sexual games; the penchant for leather (belts, boots, whips) in sado-masochistic and dominatrix performances; the retention of traditional uniforms of servility (such as "French" maids, nurses) in pornography and prostitution; and the long history of the appropriation of almost every kind of ecclesiastical wear in scenarios of immorality and excess. Examples can be found in more "respectable" arenas of life, too. Transgressive uniform conduct is common in schools, military forces, celebrations (such as festivals and carnivals) and theatre. Moreover, over time, transgression becomes inscribed in the accepted routines and regimes – even if distanced from ostensible ethic

Radicalism and Transgression

The other side to transgression as a counter to discipline is the use of transgression as a force for radicalism – that is, to explicitly challenge conventions or norms. This can be observed across a range of cultural sites – in popular music, in avant-garde art and cultural movements, in subcultures and in everyday codes of dress and adornment. There are connections between these spheres and to illustrate this, the example of rock music culture sets the scene of the deployment of uniforms in radical transgressive situations.

The culture of popular music has been long linked to the adoption of uniforms and uniform style. In the 1940s, zoot suits – synonymous with gangsters – were popularized as the look of black music and radical nightclub sounds (Cosgrove 1989; Sims 1999: 19–20). This look remained popular:

> Its louche style – long jackets and high-cut baggy trousers – worn with braces – was a natural for rebel rockers and imitated by the likes of 1980s bands Kid Creole and the Coconuts and Blue Rondo a la Turk. (Sims 1999: 18)

The zoot suit influence established a code of stage dress for performers of popular music, many opting for coordinated suits or other outfits.[5] What started as a black musician's habit quickly became a norm in the mainstream. Through to the 1950s and early 1960s bands could be readily identified by their formal or informal "uniforms", for example, The Righteous Brothers, The Temptations, Little Richard, Jerry Lee Lewis, Sam Cooke, Bill Haley and the Comets, Chuck Berry, and Billy J. Kramer and the Dakotas. Even the bouffant hairdos and extravagant evening gowns of The Supremes became a kind of uniform for female singers.

One outrageous entertainer was Liberace, who adopted elaborate sequinned and/or gold lamé jackets and jumpsuits as his moniker, creating a quasi-uniform for performance, one copied by subsequent performers such as Elvis Presley (in his later years) and Peter Allen. When pop and rock culture developed in the 1960s, the strategic use of official and quasi-uniforms in the language of radicalism was reinforced. Here the adoption of quasi-uniforms was an effective means to establishing distinctive identities, and recognition and identification with audiences, as well as making social comment and attracting growing media and public interests in this burgeoning phenomenon. Accordingly, arguably the centrepiece of 1960s music culture, The Beatles, adopted a common look, initially black leather but later – styled by their manager, Brian Epstein – collarless jackets, stovepipe trousers and "mop" haircuts (Sims 1999: 24–5, 171).

Those who did adopt stage "uniforms" bred a counter-reaction. Other bands promoted difference in each and every band member

– each striving to be distinctive and cultivate a "unique" look. These sartorial games were a key feature of pop music. Often there was fierce rivalry between bands – such as The Beatles and The Rolling Stones – and their actions were driven as much by turf wars as they were by musical motives. Frank Zappa, for example, competed both with The Beatles and Jimi Hendrix. Zappa was preparing to release a new album when a "Sergeant Pepper" appeared and made " a vast cultural impression" so Zappa retaliated by substituting "female transvestite clothes for The Beatles' military uniforms, and replaced the flowers with carrots and sliced watermelon" (de Lange 2001). Hendrix (a former soldier) seemed to adopt military stage gear after he witnessed the effect of Zappa's manipulation of a party of uniformed marines "to mime the act of killing" on stage: "The show was often grotesque or sexual. But a fascinated audience always lapped it up" (de Lange 2001). Coinciding with youth disillusionment with politics, foreign policy and suburban consumer culture, Hendrix sensed the benefits of disrespectfully appropriating the United States' iconic military dress. Lehnert (2000: 60) has argued that Hendrix "was the embodiment of the 1960s generation's revolt against the establishment" in his improvised guitar-playing, his non-conformist lifestyle and his stage outfits: "the colourful, richly embroidered jacket that he often wore is an ironic reference to traditional military uniforms and a subtle expression of the anti-Vietnam protest among the young."

As the 1960s moved into a rampant era of radicalism in dress, gender codes, lifestyle that accompanied the explosion of a popular-music-fuelled youth culture, an increasing number of artists adopted formal uniforms or elements thereof – e.g. The Beatles wore candy-coloured replicas of eighteeth-century military uniforms for the LP record cover of "Sergeant Pepper's Lonely Hearts Club Band"; Jimi Hendrix adopted a confederate jacket and other military paraphernalia in the latter stages of his career (McDowell 1997: 69);[6] Pete Townshend (The Who) wore a suit made from a Union Flag with much controversy and the band subsequently was photographed draped under a Union Flag (Sims 1999: 4; see also Chenoune 1993: 254–5);[7] Public Enemy wore NATO Arctic camouflage kit (Sims 1999: 223), The Kinks made hand-crocheted vests with fur edging a quasi-uniform; Duran Duran favoured versions of military uniforms (Sims 1999: 67)); New Order wore Third Reich uniforms (Kohn 1989); and Adam and the Ants popularized romanticized versions of the costumes of "18th century highwaymen, pirates,

Figure 53
Cartoon by Jon
Kudelka.

rogues and dandies" (Sims 1999: 60). Others chose to parody
school uniforms such as the dishevelled stage wear of Angus Young
of ACDC, Chrissie Hynd (The Pretenders), Chrissie Amplett (The
Divinyls) and later Kelly Osbourne. School uniforms were also
commonly adopted by Japanese pop groups such as YMO (Yellow
Magic Orchestra) (Kinsella 2002: 220).

Retail outlets in the 1960s reflected the obsession with the
irreverent use of uniforms which became a central element of
Swinging London's mod look (Fogg 2003: 55–75). This was perhaps best epitomized by the iconic *I Was Lord Kitchener's Valet*
shop in Carnaby Street, the source of avant-garde psychedelia, its
shopfront covered in multiple images of Lord Kitchener in military
dress (Sims 1999: 63; cf. Fogg 2003: 64–5). This sold Nazi paraphernalia, Union Flag-adorned clobber, iron cross pendants,
military surplus wear such as great coats, boots, belts, hats, jackets,
etc. The largest selling item was a recruiting poster of Lord Kitchener exhorting "Your country needs you" that adorned the bed-
rooms of countless young people.

Other popular boutiques included *Lord John, Mr Fish, John
Stephen, His Clothes, Male W1, Mod Male, Domino Male* and *Just
Men* – while *Bazaar* (Mary Quant), *Biba* (Barbara Hulanicki), *His
& Hers, Gear, Bird Cage, Kleptomania* and *Pop* catered for a
female and "unisex" clientele (Chenoune 1993: 256–9; Fogg 2003:
64–89). Although not all these boutiques were on Carnaby Street,
this was the street that became synonymous with Swinging London
and its reputation as the epicentre of new trends and styles in pop

culture. Celebrities and musicians – and their girlfriends and families – became a significant feature of the high profile of ever-changing London emporia. Above all, these boutiques aimed to subvert conventional ideas about clothes, colours, combinations and gender roles. They aimed for shock value and nonchalant subversions and parody of treasured cultural icons.

One of the recurring themes of this period was the challenge to traditional gender roles and sexual conventions. Not only was much of the mod and pop look castigated as effeminate or (worse) pandering to homosexual desires, but also pop celebrities took to parodying conservative values by "unisex" and cross-dressing. A now infamous example was the decision by Mick Jagger to wear a white semi-sheer "tunic" over trousers when he played the 5 July 1969 Hyde Park concert, which had become a memorial to Brian Jones, who had drowned in mysterious circumstances two days before. Instead of a sombre "respectful" outfit, Jagger's choice was denounced as a "dress" and seen as a mark of disrespect for Jones (Wilson 1985: 165). In fact, Mr Fish had designed two customized outfits that were based on Greek National Guard uniforms. How-ever, both customers had decided against wearing them.[8] Not so Jagger, and his costume made international headlines. According to rock historian, Joshua Sims (1999):

> By wearing what was essentially a white moire mini-dress over white trousers . . . , Jagger, his lips smeared with blood-red lipstick, his hair newly washed and hanging over his shoulders, gave a performance of unprecedented sexual ambiguity. It was a theme he would explore famously on film in *Performance* (again in an Indian inspired "dress" designed by Michael Fish) and on stage for the next twenty years. (Sims 1999: 116)

In a "fashion note", the popular newspaper, *News of the World*, announced that "Mick Taylor's lilac mini-length jerkin adds a pleasant splash of colour. Mick Jagger's button through dress is cool and summery."[9] Jagger himself retrospectively seemed puzzled by the reaction, describing the outfit as "a funny, flouncy thing . . . sort of peasant blouse, gathered here [upper thigh]" (quoted by Parker 2003). His choice to wear the "dress" and the controversy it created became a turning point. It redefined the importance and impact of stage costume as an adjunct to rock music culture. Jagger was quick to capitalize on the pay-off of creating shock value. As Sims (1999) observed:

> While Jagger's cross-dressing had a minimal direct effect on street fashion, it undoubtedly helped promote the unisex trend. Other male rock stars, however, quickly latched onto the "dangerous" notion of wearing dresses. (Sims 1999: 116)

David Bowie was one such artist who favoured men's dresses and subsequently invented other personae – such as Ziggy Stardust – taking the artful construction of stage identities to new heights (Frith 1989; Costantino 1997: 114–15; Sims 1999: 116–17; Bolton 2003: 122–5).

Jagger quickly learned the importance of having the right "stage clothes" to become "a stage person" (Parker 2003):

> Clothes were an integral part of this performing, Jagger said. "Part of the process of going onstage is to become a stage person. And even if I wore these trousers" – he had arrived at rehearsal in a T-shirt and Dick Schonberger trousers – "on the day that I put them on for the stage they're stage trousers."
>
> ". . . if you're wearing the wrong thing you're in trouble. The clothes are important. Guitar players always think it's about what they play, you know, Lead singers have another attitude". (Parker 2003)

He devoted considerable time to commissioning clothes made to "rigid specifications",[10] and trying out different outfits and combinations "but made in stretchier fabrics or brighter colours or with extra crystals to catch the light" (Parker 2003). But, as his fashion stylist said:

> "In the end, it's all about the trousers." According to Jagger, the problem with stage trousers is that they need to have some give – allowing him to run around on stage like a teenager – but he wants them to be properly cut, not mere leggings.
>
> "You're in them a lot, more than anything else," he said. "They've got to keep their shape. And the trouble is, stretch fabrics start to bag. Round your bum or wherever, it all starts bagging, and you're forever pinning." (Parker 2003)

Jagger's obsession with stage clothes stems from the influence of the first manager, Andrew Oldham – a "clothes fanatic" – who devised their early stage personae and outfits:

> In the '60s, Jagger wore suits and thin ties (briefly), then mod shirts and corduroy jackets, then scarves and devilish frills, and the Uncle Sam hat and the black "omega" T-shirt at Altamont, California.[11] Later, the eyes of the fans were directed more towards the Jagger crotch, which was clothed in embroidered, unzipped Ossie Clark jumpsuits and tight-laced knee breeches during sporty, gay-quarterback phase.[12]
>
> Throughout Jagger's career, one look has remained constant: the hard male core (tightly covered Nureyev abs and crotch) that is teasingly revealed beneath a layer or two of something more feminine. (Parker 2003)

One of the trademarks of the rock culture legacy was costume changes during a performance:

> On the Licks tour, as before, Jagger is likely to take to the stage in a three-quarter-length coat, then do a striptease during the first songs; later, he will leave and reappear in amore ornate coat, creating a moment of fashion drama. [His stylist] and Jagger call this all-important piece a "fantasy coat."[13] (Parker 2003)

Madonna – undoubtedly picking up from The Stones, David Bowie and others – has adopted a succession of looks (including a serious military phase, a pinstriped suit phase, and a fetish and dominatrix lingerie phase) in her diverse career. She especially conflated "religious and erotic themes" (Garber 1992: 211), expressing ambivalence about her Catholic upbringing and deliberately setting out to shock and subvert public expectations. During her Blond Ambition tour, she

> Evoked Hasidic as well as Catholic images when she and her back-up singers, dressed in long black caftans, waved their hands above their heads as they danced in a "church" lit with votive candles. (Garber 1992: 211)

Her other stage outfit for the tour – Jean-Paul Gaultier's conical bras and corset – "saved her career" (Sims 1999: 130–1) and later she turned to Dolce and Gabbana to create costumes for her "Love Kylie" tribute, design "Rocco" T-shirts celebrating the birth of her son, and "in 2001 sen[t] her on stage in a re-interpretation of a 'rhinestone cowboy'" (Cole 2002a).

The adoption of a particular look – or increasingly changing looks – has become part and parcel of the pop-rock scene. Some artists, for example, have adopted distinctive "class" gear, such as Cindy Lauper in her role as "trailer park trash" or Jimmy Barnes (Cold Chisel) in the Australian "working man's" uniform of singlet and jeans. Michael Jackson also invested heavily in inventing stage personae and "deftly manipulated the stage vocabulary of gender" (Garber 1992: 295), creating a highly marketable commodity and public mask: "his signature white socks, single glove, and sequinned clothing are readily identifiable – and often imitated – marks of his personal style" (Garber 1992: 296). Annie Leibovitz's photograph of him for *Vanity Fair* depicted him in "a familiar Jackson uniform of epaulets, gold braid, and black tailcoat with red cuffs that is somehow reminiscent both of a mythical middle European dynasty and of a matador's costume" (Garber 1992: 296). But in framing him in front of several mirrors, his multiple reflections suggested multiple personae – or perhaps only mythic ones. His fall from musical popularity and subsequent legal and ethical dilemmas perhaps indicate that Jackson was ultimately swallowed by that constructedness.

While some artists were refining marketable images and associations as pop-rock became mainstreamed and its radical challenges muted, newer artists began to rebel against the quasi-uniform of the 1960s music culture. Glam rock took stage costume to the limit with more and more extreme outfits and identity shifts – for example, Freddie Mercury. Musicals like *The Rocky Horror Show* turned uniforms and costumes into performing arts – theatre as well as music. Phenomena like punk, grunge, anti-fashion, heavy metal and gritty realist rock generated a new approach to stage wear that aimed to challenge. Typical artists of this breed included Johnny Rotten, the Sex Pistols, Kurt Cobain, Boy George and Culture Club, Siouxsie Sioux, Alice Cooper, Kiss, Lou Reed, the Smiths, and Marilyn Manson. Punks typified the new irreverent approach to stage dress: "Punk uniform in the 70s . . . became an anarchic anti-fashion statement of rubber, latex, vinyl and leather plus a safety pin or two." Gear like this was sold in boutiques like *Sex*, the punk shop of Malcolm McLaren and Vivienne Westwood in the Kings Road, Chelsea.[14] In this company, uniforms were distinctly uncool.

Yet another kind of uniform began to emerge among the rap and hip hop artists that began as black subcultural rallying points of radicalism and resistance but were quickly mainstreamed. Their sartorial influences were black street culture and black streetwear – typically shiny baggy trousers or trackpants, bomber jackets, sunglasses, headwear (cap, scarf, beret, hat), sneakers and heaps of chunky gold jewellery. Occasionally, official uniforms appeared as a point of controversy or repudiation, but essentially pop-rock had moved from the appropriation and reworking of uniform culture to inventing a new quasi-uniform of global urban street-wear. At least this was the case for male artists. Female artists have increasingly appeared in versions of fetish lingerie – or "slut" wear – potentially undermining the growing presence of women in popular music by presenting them as objects of desire to be despised rather than admired. If there is a common theme of contemporary music video clips it is shock value and debasement of moral codes.

During this period, one group above all epitomized the love affair with uniforms. In 1977, the Village People were formed as a "group of [Greenwich] Village icons from various American social groups".[15] The group was composed of "gay male stereo-types or objects of desire" (Williams 2002) or "clones" (Cole 2000: 133–5) – a cowboy, GI (soldier), biker/leatherman (in vest, trousers, boots and bike cap), construction worker (with hard hat), American Indian (complete with feather headdress), and a policeman on a bike.[16] In an effort to capture the New York club crowd, the "gay-themed" band adopted the uniforms strategically.[17] Their catchy songs that were "odes to male bonding" (Williams 2002) – includ-ing "Macho Man", "YMCA", "Hot Cop", "In the Navy", "Go West" and "Sleazy" – and colourful costumes attracted mainstream attention, initially primarily female. In 1980, their music was the basis of a "song and dance" feature film, *Can't Stop the Music*. This was a major success and "remains a popular cult film around the world",[18] appealing both to mainstream and gay/queer audiences.

In the early days, the band was generally regarded as innocent – "light and fluffy" recalled a friend whose mother took her to see the film when she was 12 as her first grown-up evening out (pers-onal communication). However, while this image persisted in the mainstream, and they sold an astonishing 65 million records

(Williams 2002), The Village People soon became a major icon in gay, transexual and transvestite subcultures. In fact, as Healey (1994) has observed:

> The Village People are probably the most famous macho drag queens in recent history, and obviously so to us now. Yet their sexuality was by and large invisible to the popular mainstream in their heyday; arch homophobe Anita Bryant was quite happy to appear alongside them on the *Johnny Carson Show*. In such cases, when the mainstream remains blissfully ignorant, butch queens simply pass, and the field of masculine identities is not disrupted. (Healey 1994: 89–90)

In short, popular music – especially rock – has accommodated uniforms as costumes as normative stage dress. And, as Garber (1992) noted:

> Cropped hair, menswear suits, thin flanks – these are not only the signature characteristics of "cross-dressed" entertainment figures like Annie Lennox or k.d. lang or Madonna, but also then high-style looks of the mainstream fashion magazines since the sixties. (Garber 1992: 136)

Sexuality and Transgression

Of all the forms of transgressive uses of uniforms, sexuality is the most contentious. Some transgression is intended – sometimes it is not. Garber (1992: 24) related the dilemma of West Point, the US Military Academy, in 1976 when women were admitted for the first time. The concern was about dress codes – but in reality it was about implied sexuality and destabilizing sexual mores. When a dance was held for the new intake, there was

> Consternation at the sight of "mirror-image couples dancing in short hair and dress grey trousers." The rule book was swiftly amended; women were still permitted to attend future hops in trousers, but if they wanted to dance they were required to wear uniform skirts. (Garber 1992: 24)

The uniforms themselves were differently cut from men's – trousers had no back pockets and coats were cut off at the waist – changes probably intended to "de-emphasise the curve of a woman's buttocks, but the changes in fact called attention to gender differences they were designed to conceal" (Garber 1992: 24). These garments were also altered. Later, the academy became concerned that women in trousers with short hair "didn't look like women" and instituted a mandatory lecture on how to apply cosmetics (Garber 1992: 24–5). These sartorial dilemmas stem from the lack of fit between normative ideas about femininity and the normative masculine attributes of performing "military" activities – and indeed displaying appropriate "military" characteristics. The constant tinkering with women's uniforms suggests that instabilities remain.

While this example is comic, it reflects ongoing debates about women in military forces, many of which circulate around appropriate dress codes, including (elements of uniforms as well as around codes about make-up, jewellery, gesture (don't sit with your knees apart) and conduct (don't chat up male colleagues).[19] In short, women in military forces create "problems" because they look like normative males yet are expected to perform as military machines while retaining feminine attributes. This is a problem that afflicts other women who appear to be "masculine" or chose to wear normative male clothing. One example is Grace Jones' androgynous image which she accounted for because of being mistaken for a man:

> I always like to wear my hair very short, and my voice was deep. So even before creating that [androgynous image] for the public, I used to go in to buy bread and they would say "Bon jour, monsieur," and I would try and say "No, I am a mademoiselle," and forget it, they'd say "Bon jour, monsieur" again. I think I have the features of an African man ... When I put on a wig with long hair, I look like a hooker or a drag queen. So I look actually more feminine when I'm dressed as a man. (quoted by Williams 2002)

While Jones has strategically "worked around" her normative "masculine" identity, singer k.d. lang flaunted her "butch" lesbian identity in the 1993 cover shoot for *Vanity Fair* where she posed "lounging in male drag in a barber's chair with Cindy Crawford hovering teasingly over her" (Gianoulis 2002). But whereas women in men's clothes – especially uniforms – is still a controversial thing to do, men in women's dress has a long and at least partially tolerated

history. A history of drag in Britain cited a former "sea queen"
recalling the prevalence of queens and drag shows on voyages:

> The Sea Queens were all drag Queens and we all had a frock
> tucked away, just in case. We did shows on a little stage on
> the ship: the crews got the dirty version, while the passengers
> got the cleaned-up one. (quoted by Garber 1992: 57)

Over time, a public perception of "sailors and cross-dressing"
emerged – as reflected in musicals and Hollywood films – embodying "anxiety about gender, or about policing, or breaching, the
borderline between gay and straight" (Garber 1992: 57, 58). In
short, concerns about the instability of sexuality and gendered
codes of dress and conduct underpin the prevalence of uniforms in
sexually transgressive episodes.

We have already noted the preponderance of gay people in
creative occupations, such as "fashion, design and show business"
(Cole 2002b: 3) that inevitably shaped the contours of style and
aesthetics. Yet this "web" of homosexuality was something of a
secret society and gays strove to appear mainstream to the public
at large while simultaneously sending signals to other gays about
their sexual preferences:

> The adoption of a series of secret codes allowed gay men and
> lesbians to spot each other, while remaining invisible to the
> outside world. The gendered nature of clothing led some gay
> men to adopt overtly feminine dress and some lesbians to
> adopt overtly masculine garb as markers of sexual identity.
> (Cole 2002b: 1)

Often certain colours or accessories have acted as codes. During
the 1980s – when Oscar Wilde was tried (as referred to earlier) –
a green carnation was the marker. Later the colour green retained
gay connotations, only to be replaced by a red necktie in the
interwar years, and by suede shoes in the 1950s and 1960s (Cole
2002b: 1).

By contrast, gays who openly flaunted their sexuality often chose
extreme motifs of feminine "mannerisms and dress: plucked
eyebrows, rouge, eye make-up, peroxide blond hair, high heeled
shoes, women's blouses" (Cole 2002b: 1). This overt masquerade
became another kind of uniform that signalled "flaming queens"

and became a quasi entry pass to "the subculture of gay society" (Cole 2002b: 1).

Gay women, too, adopted vestimentary markers including a masculine collar, tie or trousers – that subsequently became the vocabulary of androgyny (Wilson 1985: 128, 164). Throughout the twentieth century, the markers shifted including "butch" or "femme" personae, the "dungaree wearing, crew-cut lesbian feminist" of the 1970s, S&M dykes, lipstick lesbians and so on (Cole 2002b: 2; see also Wilson 1985: 240–1).

The popular music culture revolution of the 1960s, however, was perhaps the most significant force in loosening up the codes of gay dress with the Carnaby Street push diversifying the range of possible looks for straights and gays alike. Similar shifts occurred in Greenwich Village, West Hollywood and Haight Ashbury in the United States, copied elsewhere in other fashion centres. The "clone" movement was a particularly key moment of transition from the closet to the public arena for gay men (Wilson 1985: 202; Cole 2000). Clones adopted the dress of archetypal examples of American masculinity. Clones included the lumberjack (jeans, plaid shirt, hooded sweatshirt, lace-up work boots) and the athletic look (Lacoste tight-fitting shirt, 501 Levi jeans, adidas runners). Other popular clone styles included:

> Cowboy – Cowboy hat, cowboy boots, denim jacket, leather chaps; Military – flight jacket, army fatigues, leather bomber jacket, combat boots, khaki army shirt, army cap; Construction Worker – construction boots, hard hat, cut down Levi's; Uniform – policeman, sailor, army captain; Leatherman – Black leather motorcycle jacket, trousers and cap, studded leather belt and wristband. (Cole 2000: 138)

The clone persona enabled gay men to act out established fantasies and role models. Ironically, clones could both signal their gay identity to other gays yet pass in public as unremarkable American blokes. In other words, cloning allowed gay culture to proliferate from subcultural gay haunts into the mainstream. The already-mentioned success of The Village People attests to the invisibility of the sexual and erotic underpinnings of cloning. As Cole notes:

> Perhaps ironically, the new gay macho styles began to have an influence on straight fashion. Dennis Altman notes that

the "diffusion of the macho style through advertising (for jeans for example) and entertainers like The Village People led to its being adopted by millions of straight men unaware of its origin." Rather than welcome the move, "straight" men felt threatened by the new overtly masculine homosexual . . . Straight men began to copy homosexual styles, and leather became commonplace (Cole 2000: 134)

From now on, there were arguably public *and* subcultural gay dress codes. Some were instantly recognizable in the mainstream (e.g. exaggerated femininity, dykes, effeminate men) but other required semi-secret knowledge involving "a strict codification of dress and a new system of signifiers, most notably coloured handkerchiefs in a back pocket, specifying particular sexual interests" (Cole 2002b: 2; see also Wilson 1985: 201–3; Holliday 2001; Winn and Nutt 2001). By the 1990s, gay and straight dress were intertwined as designers – many of whom were gay – deliberately juxtaposed, parodied and subverted the tenets of couture style and aesthetics.[20] Moreover, the influence of street and subcultural dress on catwalk and high street design became palpable.

It was also during this time that debate about sexuality became more inclusive and acknowledged gay, bisexual, queer and cross-dressing identifications including the "trans" categories – transvestite, transgender, transsexual, and so on. Transgression had become encoded in the very discourse of sexual identity. The transgressive use of uniforms in sexual performance had itself become normative.

Finally, this chapter turns to the fetishization of Japanese school uniforms in Japanese popular culture (McVeigh 2000; Kinsella 2002; Richie 2003). Despite the obsession with picking up western modes and being ultra modern, Japanese culture is still highly rule bound and structured by a web of minutiae. This is the reason why the institutionalized uniform is so pervasive. As Richie (2003) argues:

In Japan . . . the institutionalized costume is everywhere. All Japanese cooks wear a "cook suit," white with a big, puffed hat; most younger Japanese students wear the black serge high-collared Prussian schoolboy suit; day-labourers concoct typical outfits from rubber-soled socks, pegged pants, cummerbunds. Even ordinary men or women off for a day of skiing or hiking fit themselves out in full skiing or hiking

ensemble. The conclusion is inescapable. Japanese are truly
at home with western dress only if it is some form of livery.
(Richie 2003: 48)

Rather than the quest for individuality and uniqueness that obsesses
westerners, Japanese present themselves as the social body and
dress accordingly: "The Japanese response to [the question 'Who
am I?'] is: 'I am what I appear to be; I am the function that I am
dressed for.' (Richie 2003: 49). Kinsella (2002: 215) relates the love
of the uniform to Japan's modernization, suggesting that the
"military-style uniform is understood as being both distinctively
Japanese *and* distinctively modern." Military uniforms were
adopted as part of the Meiji period transition to a modern society
as a sign of citizen formation and of military discipline and pre-
paredness. According to Kinsella (2002), this visible reference of
the modern state became an icon of the modern Japanese body:

> It is not difficult to see why the military uniform cladding the
> body of the Japanese soldier, on display to the world, became
> highly significant – and peculiarly eroticized – under the
> watchful gaze not only of Japan's own intelligentsia and
> governing elites, but those of foreign powers also. (Kinsella
> 2002: 217)

Of all the Japanese uniforms it was the school uniform – the
Prussian boys suit and the English naval (sailor) – suit of the girls
– that has become most fetishized. School children – in their
uniforms – came to symbolize modern Japanese society. But whereas
the official reading of these uniforms was one of discipline, authority, hierarchy, order and purity, their uptake in popular culture
is redolent of other characteristics – the underside of the uniformed
body. As Kinsella (2002) notes:

> The presence within post-war pornography of the same
> wholesome and innocent schoolgirls in sailor suits is almost
> certainly related to their officially chaste character. Uni-
> formed schoolgirls have appeared in novels. Erotic *manga*,[21]
> illustrations, photo magazines, and videos, and on internet
> sites. Pornographic novels about schoolgirls unbuttoning
> their blouses have been a staple of the pulp publishing mill
> since the 1950s. (Kinsella 2002: 219)

In all this material there is an oscillation between the intended meaning of uniforms and their erotic potentialities and associations with sexuality, unrestrained excess, violence and masochism. The public obsession with cuteness in Japan underlines this tension between official and popular culture (see McVeigh 2000: 135–81; Richie 2003: 53–62).

In addition, however, uniforms – especially school uniforms – have come to markedly influence fashion trends in mainstream and subcultural Japan. This has occurred in a variety of ways. One that attracted considerable media attention and government approbation was the 1990s mushrooming of "bloomer sailor shops" that catered:

> to men with a sexual fixation on the paraphernalia of high-school girls' uniforms . . . Schoolgirls were selling off items of their school uniforms, their own used knickers, and gobs of their saliva, to the proprietors of these makeshift shops, for quick cash. (Kinsella 2002: 227)

Other schoolgirls engaged in more direct selling of the lure of their uniforms working as part-time prostitutes or in pornography (as "H-baito") (Kinsella 2002: 227; Richie 2003: 79–82). During this period, a virtual obsession with the image of high-school girls dominated Japanese popular culture and girls responded by developing their own subculture, known as "kogal" or "prostitute chic" – a form of overt display and sexual provocation (Kinsella 2002: 229–32). In short, the connotations of uniforms in modern Japan has been turned upside down in a carnivalesque parade of otherness:

> Whereas previously Japanese subjects in military-style uniforms were seen to dedicate themselves passionately to the defence of Japan, in *fin-de-siecle* Tokyo high-school girls in military-style uniforms were seen to have nothing at all of meaning to dedicate themselves to but market forces. (Kinsella 2002: 235)

The model "uniformed citizen of the early twentieth century" had been transformed "into the specter of the high-school girl prostitute in a sailor suit in the 1990s" (Kinsella 2002: 236). According to McVeigh (2000) this is because the elision of children with adult women through the school uniform places "females in a control-lable social position":

> This is most clearly seen in the portrayal of women in com-mercials, *manga* (comic books; read by all ages in Japan) and pornography (pornography cuteness). Somehow childlike women are less threatening to men. Since cuteness is part and parcel of the discourse surrounding gender definitions, it is not surprising to find cuteness so much a part of pornography, including child pornography. When portrayed as sexually charged images, women are, to a remarkable degree, pre-sented as very youthful, innocent and naïve. (McVeigh 2000: 147)

This Japanese use of uniforms in sexual transgression differs from uses in western transgressive sexuality. Uniforms are also a major component of sexual excess but the codes seem to be more parodic and specific to behavioural subcodes than to cuteness, childishness and citizenship. Dressing up is a precondition for sexual fantasy whether it be in the form of bondage, discipline, sado-masochism, fetishes, erotic fantasies, role play, cross-dressing or master–slave contracts. The costumes employed range from uniforms – of authority (police, military – frequently Nazi or sailor suits, domi-natrix, nanny) to ones of servility and subservience (maid, nurse, school boy/girl, baby) as well as devising a customized black leather/latex/plastic array of uniforms of sexual excess adapted for particular peccadilloes. The latter includes black bodices, bus tiers, corsets, G-strings, jackets, gloves, boots, stilettos, collars, hoods and fishnet leg body stockings, fastened with a multiplicity of chains, zips, straps and buckles.

The behaviour almost licensed by wearing these costumes per-mits clients to engage in all manner of erotic acts – or, as one provider puts it: "The Ultimate Erogenous Zone is the Imagina-tion!" (Salon Kitty's 1997). Essentially, it involves contractual relations between participants revolving around power (authority, discipline, punishment or inflicting pain) on the one hand and accepting another person's power (servility, submission, humilia-tion or accepting pain/delivering pleasure to the authority) (Artemis 1997; Jaivin 1997). This entails a contract between pain and pleasure, on the one hand, and consent versus limits, on the other. Above all, it involves the exercise of power or abrogation of responsibility to accept whatever comes. In these scenarios, clothing the body in specialist uniforms enables the enhanced performance of the self in these invented personae.

Uniforms, then, are now almost tired props in pornography, prostitution, S&M, mardi gras and explicit stage shows. Their role is to destabilize normative identities and create new ones through the literal donning of another mantle of sensibilities – of power, authority, servility, debasement, punishment and so on. The uniforms become a primary part of the performance of self. Transgressive deployment of uniforms permits unstable identities and multiple personae to explore other possibilities and reinvent identity.

Notes

Chapter 1 Uniforms, Body Techniques and Culture

1. I am indebted to Margaret Maynard for alerting me to this example and sharing information about it with me.
2. The *Kuomboka* ceremony is part of a festivity at the end of the rainy season when the Litunga, king of the Lozi people, returns to his winter palace high above the flood plains. It is a spectacular event with the king and his entourage crossing the river accompanied by drums, dancing and singing.
3. Recently, there was discussion about making the ceremony more accessible to western tourists as a focal point of Zambian cultural tourism.
4. Sumptuary laws were legislation designed to limit expenditure on extravagant forms of conspicuous consumption, in particular, clothing and modes of dress. They were passed in a number of European countries between the twelfth and eighteenth centuries, and were flirted with in North America in the eighteenth century (see Hunt 1996: 29).

Chapter 2 From Military Uniforms to Codified Civility

1. The British Household Division currently consists of several regiments who wear bearskin "beehive" hats, including the Scots Guards (1642–), the Coldstream Guards (1650–), the Grenadier Guards (1656–) and the more recent Irish Guards (1900–) and Welsh Guards (1915–) (Army 2001).
2. In Vivienne Westwood's 1981 Pirate collection, she featured a brown check jacket with slashed sleeves revealing a red embroidered silk lining. This was a deliberate historical borrowing (Hume 1997: 56).
3. A pikeman was a seventeenth-century soldier armed with a pike, a weapon consisting of a long wooden shaft with a pointed head of iron or steel.
4. The term colback referred both to the high bearskin headdress or busby worn by the Grenadiers and the astrakhan version worn by the Hussars (David 2003: 12–13, 34).
5. A shako was a cylindrical hat with a peak and an upright plume sabre (Schick 1978: 246; Abler 1999: 44–6).
6. A forage cap was originally worn by cavalrymen when collecting "forage" for horses and later adopted as "undress" caps replacing the full headdress. Initially round and stiffened with or without a peak, after 1898 it was modified as "a broad topped peaked cap based on the naval pattern" and remains a staple of military dress to the present day (Carman 1977: 59).
7. Slouch hats were broad-brimmed felt hats worn by South African, Australian and New Zealand forces. These hats "afforded a lighter and more practical alternative" (Barthorp 1978: 155–6).
8. In another twist, Hitler's elite bodyguard, the Leibstandarte, dressed up as showgirls to form a pyramid of angels for the 1942 film, *Die Grosse Liebe* (The Great Love) – ostensibly because insufficient statuesque female extras could be found (Hooper 2001: 20).
9. Quentin Crisp (1908–99) was a witty author (perhaps best known for his satiric memoir, *The Naked Civil Servant*). He became a gay icon before it was acceptable for homosexuals to openly declare their sexual preferences. Crisp was as outspoken as he was excessive in his dress, behaviour and writings: "He tinted his hair lilac, wore eye shadow, pert scarves and silk blouses, and transformed himself into a walking, quipping objet d'art", recalled an obituary, describing him as "the late 20th century embodiment of a turn-of-the-century archetype: the bohemian flaneur, the arty, outrageously dressed stroller of the boulevards who negotiates a hostile world, surviving on his guile and witticisms" (Speed 1999).
10. When a trooper of the Blues and Royals was thrown from his horse outside Buckingham Palace during a procession for a foreign

dignitary, he could not get up from the ground because of his uniform and had to be helped up by a bearskinned Guardsman and two uniformed policemen (bobbies) (AFP 2004. "Bearskins and Bobbies to Rescue After Royal Dismount", *The Australian* (7 May): 10.)

11. AFP 2004. "Re-arranging of the Guard", *The Sydney Morning Herald* (8–9 May): 21.

12. Sources on the Salvation Army include Salvation Army 2003a; Wikipedia 2004a; *Warcry*, the magazine of the Salvation Army Australia, 123(17) (24 April 2004); personal communications with Salvation Army officers.

13. The official Salvation Army website explains that wearing a uniform has several advantages: identifies the wearer as a professing Christian who can give practical or spiritual help, enables the wearer to be recognized and accepted, protects the wearer in dangerous situations and establishes fellowship with other Salvation Army members (Salvation Army 2004).

14. British Empire 2004. "Robert Baden-Powell (1857–1941)", 13th Hussars, Colonels 1861–1922, www.britishempire.co.uk/forces/ armyunits/britishcavalry/13thhussars, accessed 7 May 2004.

15. Ibid.

16. There have been some idiosyncratic deviations. In 1980 Oscar de la Renta was commissioned to redesign the American scouting uniforms and produced something "curiously resembling a French uniform of about 1960" (Wagner 2003a). At the world scouting jamboree in January 2004 held in Adelaide, Australia, scouts were dressed in a specially designed blue polo-necked shirt with overall abstract design, blue shorts and the trademark kerchief and toggle.

17. Indeed, Australian Aboriginals found the sights of white administrators in shorts and long socks hilarious and adopted the nickname "the longsocks" to refer to them (personal communication, Ciaran O'Faircheallaigh).

18. Michael Pratt (photographer) 2004. "Graduates Overcome Hardships." *Westside News* (Brisbane) (24 March): 3.

Chapter 3 School Uniforms and Docile Bodies

1. TEE is a secondary school graduation mark in an Australian state.

2. Docile here is used in its traditional *OED* sense: teachable, submissive, tractable and easily managed – not just passive but primed (ready and alert) for instruction.

3. For example, a mother wearing a "hippie" skirt and cheesecloth top on a school excursion in contrast to the tailored sportswear worn by all the other mothers, the "gym-junkie" mum in her leotards and bike pants in an old model sedan among the exquisitely turned out private school mums (in their four-wheel drives), or the installation artist mum whose avant-garde outfits and tattooed limbs stand out among the casually dressed stay-at-home mums of a state school.

4. Uniform regulations are enforced in a variety of ways. A teacher may inspect every student each morning; or nominated teachers called "sweepers" might visit classrooms to find students out of uniform and send them to an office to change; or a school may do "spot" checking for particular items each day or week (correct hats; socks, shoes, etc.: see Kahl 1997).

5. Many charity schools were badly managed and in the 1850s became the focus of a photographic campaign to address the appallingly conditions of malnourishment and deprivation (Strong 1998: 413–14).

6. Christ's Hospital website: www.christs-hospital.org.uk/main.html, accessed 26 May 2004.

7. Frank Ledwith, "The Best Of All Possible Worlds", cited by BSU, "Bluecoat Boys and Their Peculiar Uniform", *Bluecoat Schools*, www.archivist.f2s.com/bsu/ch/memoirs.htm.

8. "Some Up To Date Comments From A Pupil Who Recently Left The School", *Bluecoat Schools*, www.archivist.f2s.com/bsu/ch/memoirs. htm.

9. I recall an event commemorating the construction of a new building at an Australian university where the British High Commissioner was the special guest. Although only recently arrived in the country he was immediately put at ease on discovering that the vice chancellor and heads of two research centres were all wearing their *alma mater* Oxford University ties. They immediately bonded as a special elite group – a positive for the occasion but alienating many others at the event.

10. "Finished" is a term appropriated in the development of "finishing" schools for young "ladies" deemed suitable for "good" matrimonial matches and motherhood. The "finished" young lady would "come out" as a debutante at a special presentation ball, visibly displaying her command of feminine attributes (and charms).

11. See, for example, the history of the uniform at an elite private girls' school in Sydney, Australia (Abbotsleigh School n.d.).

12. For one of the more informative sites, see Canadian Broadcasting Corporation 2000.

Chapter 4 Uniforms for Women

1. Hunt (1996: 246–7) gives all manner of examples: yellow cloak trimmed with blue (Leipzig); plain yellow cloak (Bergano); red cap (Bern and Zurich); gloves and bell on the hat (Florence); white badge (Avignon and Dijon); and – despite social concerns about cross-dressing – even a man's hat and scarlet belt (Castres).
2. An early female police officer, Dorothy Peto, claimed that the first appointment of a woman constable actually occurred in the reign of Elizabeth I (Ewing 1975: 97).
3. See Anime 2002; "Japanese School Uniform", TheFreeDictionary 2004. encyclopedia.thefreedictionary.com/Japanese%20school%20 uniform, accessed 11 May 2004.
4. For example, the internationally syndicated photograph of Private Lynndie England (wearing a khaki T-shirt, camouflage cargo pants, leather belt and army boots) holding a dog lead tied to the neck of a naked Iraqi prisoner became the iconic image that defined the wide-spread perception that US involvement in Iraq had become a debacle (Coorey 2004; McKenna 2004).
5. An Australian soccer referee was threatened with disciplinary action for banning a player from the field for not removing her hijab (Abdo 2004).

Chapter 5 Uniforms at Work

1. When former model, Jerry Hall, was tried for drug possession, she chose demure Chanel suits to project a suitably stylish yet contrite impression.
2. While some retailers cater for all occupations, others concentrate on certain types of work clothes. For example, some specialize in hospitality and healthcare (e.g. Kristen Uniforms and Linens, All About Uniforms, Banner Uniform Center, Eva's Uniform Shoppe); others in aprons for the workplace (American Apron), some in military, law enforcement and security (e.g. Marlow White Uniform Company, Jim Brown Uniforms, Quartermaster, S&R Uniforms, Security Uniforms); while some supply specific niche professions (such as aviation apparel, e.g. Morningstar Business group, or postal wear, e.g. Keystone Uniform Centers, Postal-Uniforms).
3. "Flight Refreshments!" was the slogan from a 1940s Ansett Airways advertisement referring to the role of flight attendants (McRobbie 1986: front inside cover illustration).

4. Personal communication from Qantas steward. Moreover, the shirt-dress's pattern of kangaroos and dots led to the passenger sport of counting the number of kangaroos across the stewards' bottoms – the larger the steward, the more numerous the kangaroos.

5. One nurse recalled the labour involved in maintaining the veil in its pristine state lest staff incur the wrath of the charge nurse. As nurses were allocated only a couple of veils, they had to be maintained rigorously by hanging up high when off duty and constantly washed, restarched and folded correctly. They also had to be worn perched upright on the head and were not allowed to slip down or off, even when lifting patients. When veils were discarded, the number of back injuries among nurses dropped substantially, because nurses no longer had to hold their heads up straight while lifting.

6. Toques are also worn by some quasi-chefs such as master bakers.

Chapter 6 Sports Uniforms to Sportswear

1. See Cunnington and Mansfield 1969; Schreier 1989; Fussell 2002; Pratt 2002.

2. See Kidwell and Christmas 1975; Joel 1984; Wilson 1985; Davidson 1990; Routh 1993; Laver 1995; Joel 1998; Wolfe 2001; Maynard 2002.

3. See Ewing 1975; McCrone 1987; Schreier 1989; Sims 1991; Okely 1993; Warner 1993; 1995; Horwood 2002.

4. For example, Reebok, Nike, Adidas, Puma, Ripcurl, Billabong, Hot Tuna, Quiksilver, Speedo, Jantzen, Canterbury, etc.

5. For example, mambo, gymwear and clothing for aerobics, disco and clubbing outfits. See Schulze 1990; Li 1998; Skoggard 1998; Sawyer 2002; Taffel 2003; Zamiatin 2003c.

Chapter 8 Uniforms in Fashion and Popular Culture

1. The Australian designer, Alex Zabotto-Bentley, uses warehouses of former military wear and reshapes garments by printing and customizing into high fashion – camouflage trousers become a miniskirt, for example.

2. AFP photo, *The Courier-Mail* (11 August 2003): 14; AFP photo, *The Australian* (11 August 2003): 13.

3. AFP/Pierre Verdy photo, *The Sydney Morning Herald* (24–25 January 2004): 13.

4. Molitorisz's (1998) specifically Sydney-based list included homeboys/girls, teenyboppers, dorks, web geeks, indie kids, yuppies, Goths, bikies, surfies, skaters, lager louts, kombi-driving crusties, manga boys/girls, ravers.

5. This distinctive wear became something of a joke when a string of gangland killings occurred in Melbourne. Press reports (e.g. Shand 2004; Stewart 2004) quoted one underworld figure's wife as "lashing out at . . . underworld rivals . . . as posing as Godfather wannabes, with their black suits and dark glasses" at a victim's funeral, commenting "It's like something from *The Sopranos* – did they watch *The Godfather* that morning?". The consensus was that life imitated art.

6. Crocodile Hunter, Steve Irwin, earned media censure for not wearing the quasi-uniform. Instead he wore his trademark khaki shirt and shorts with elasticized boots (that he wears on all media appearances) to Australia's 2004 Logie Awards ceremony with one commentator chastising him: "Steve, mate, you're not a police officer. It's not a uniform. Others managed to wear black tie without breaking out in a rash" (Butler and McCullough 2004).

7. For example, the preferred wear of female actors at the Academy Awards (Krum 2004).

8. For example, 1930s musicals with military themes or the use of uniforms as costume included *Footlight Parade* (1933), *Flirtation Walk* (1934), *Born to Dance* (1936), *Follow the Fleet* (1936), *Rosalie* (1937) and *Give Me a Sailor* (1938).

9. Rebecca Arnold (2002: 58–9) also relates the importance of fashion photography to the emergence of a distinctive American sensibility and national identity during the 1930s and 1940s. While enlisted women wore military uniforms during the war, they were reminded of their "feminine" identity via lunchtime fashion parades and offered new post-war models of femininity (a return to domesticity but prospect of an active lifestyle) at the end of the war.

10. Covers of *Vogue* that used repetition, movement and disassociated body parts included George Hoyningen-Huene's 1930 cover (FV July) of bodies lying on a beach (like corpses?); Eduardo Benito's 1931 cover of a woman's body dissected by an autumn leaf in an archery pose (AV September); Horst Horst's 1940 cover of woman in a pillbox hat multiplied like the petals of a flower (AV August); Erwin Blumenfeld's 1945 cover of a woman and (sinister?) shadow (AV May), a Clifford Coffin 1954 cover of a "snazzy party girl in a short red Dior evening dress and coat . . . repeated like rows of dancing stamps" (AV

December); a 1959 Norman Parkinson cover of two "two highly energetic young dancers from the Royal Ballet" (BV April); a 1962 Helmut Newton cover of a model in black and white set in an angular pose against a black triangle (FV November); a 1965 William Klein cover of a girl in Courrèges' Mondrian print dress dissected geometrically (FV March); and a 1983 Patrick Demarchelier cover of a model in an "angular, loose-limbed masculine stance conveying well the current relaxation of women from their previous sexually stereotyped roles" (BV May) (Packer 1983: 234, 237; Lloyd 1986: 5, 49, 57, 85, 87, 108, 132, 138, 217). Note: FV=French *Vogue*; AV= American *Vogue*; BV=British *Vogue*.

11. Women as or with machines were also common, for example, Georges Lapape's 1930 cover of a woman by a car (BV 25 June); Pierre Mourgue's 1932 cover of a woman reaching for *Vogue*'s plane (BV 16 March); and Jean Pages' 1938 cover of a ship on the horizon bellowing out a huge smoke stack (leisure or war?) (BV 14 December). This convention of illustration was adopted also in photographic covers, for example in Erwin Blumenfeld's 1948 cover of a woman against scaffolding (AV 15 February); Helmut Newton's 1967 cover of a woman sprawled on a safari jeep flanked by a cheetah (BV 15 April); Albert Watson's surprisingly contemporary (shades of Issey Miyake?) 1954 cover of a woman in a black and white outfit posed like the working blades of a machine (BV August); Anton Bruehl's 1936 cover of a woman firing a (hunting) gun (AV 15 October); Bruehl's 1936 cover of a woman in shirt and slacks and masculine pose on a yacht (AV 1 July); Hoyninen-Huene's 1934 cover of a woman leaning on a sports car (AV 15 December); Bruehl's 1937 cover of a woman (in shirt and dark pants – almost a uniform) apparently pushing a plane (AV 15 June); and Toni Frissell's 1941 cover of a female trainee pilot in uniform about to step into the cockpit (AV 1 July) (Packer 1983: 226, 232, 248; Lloyd 1986: 7, 11, 12, 27, 28, 28, 29, 47).

12. Women in uniforms or fashions influenced by elements or the cut of uniforms became common, for example, Jean Pages' 1940 poignant if threatening cover of a woman looking wistful but dressed in "defiant Parisian chic on the eve of the fall of France" with two soldiers marching through a grey smoky background (BV March); Cecil Beaton's 1949 cover of a woman in a uniform-inspired outfit (AV 15 March); Horst's image of a woman in military-style coat (AV 1 August 1943); John Rawlings' covers of a woman in business-like suit "worrying" about the war and her man (AV 15 September and 1 September 1943); Rawlings' and Edward Steichen's covers of a woman with a globe (referencing theatres of war) (AV November 1943; AV 1 February 1940); and Toni Frissell's prescient 1940 cover

of a woman in uniform holding a monkey dressed also in a brown uniform (AV 15 March); Irving Penn's and Horst's images of women in trenchcoats (AV 15 November 1944; AV 1 August 1942); Parkinson's, Coffin's and Penn's similar covers of a woman in a uniform-inspired grey suit (AV 1 October 1949; FV September 1954; AV 1 August 1951) (Packer 1983: 254; Lloyd 1986: 7, 34–5, 44–5, 61, 93–4; cf. Mulvey and Richards 1998: 114–16).

13. *Vogue* (Italy) June 1976, photographer Hans Feurer, and *Vogue* (Australia) February 1979, photographer Patrick Russell (Lloyd 1986: 184–5).
14. The China issue was shot by Alex Chatelin.
15. Photograph by Patrick Russell.

Chapter 9 Transgressive Uniforms in Contemporary Culture

1. Despite the central gay/queer focus, the Sisters have been involved in many activist campaigns, including opposition to nuclear energy, pro-refugee policies, sex education, AIDS management, disaster relief fundraising, street violence and community projects.
2. Thanks to Annita Boyd for ideas and examples in this section.
3. The younger sister of songstress Kylie Minogue, Dannii has complained that she was always younger, chubbier, darker haired and less talented than her sister. She has sought to rectify this by a stringent regime of diet, exercise and cosmetic surgery that has vastly altered her appearance.
4. Lolo Ferrari was a French actress who had successive breast implants; she died prematurely, probably from a drugs overdose.
5. A colleague has kept her musician father's diaries that record his band's gigs with annotations such as "penguin" or dinner suit, "mauve shirt", "Hawaiian", "smart casual", "cravat", "red shirt and white strides", etc. (personal communication) to ensure that the band was coordinated and appropriately clothed for the venue and occasion.
6. More often, Jimi Hendrix wore flower power psychedelia (e.g. Afghan-style jacket, velvet trousers and American-Indian-style buckskin boots: Costantino 1997: 106–7) and later juxtaposed this with uniforms and an Afro hairdo to produce "psychedelic military": www.xanaduonline. com/search-products.php4?item=11.
7. This was despised by Mick Jagger, who parodied Pete Townshend in the song, "Get Off My Cloud" (1965). However, the Union Flag became the motif of The Who and accompanied them on all their tours.

When a band member, John Entwistle, died unexpectedly in 2002, a shrine at the intended concert venue (the Hard Rock Casino in Las Vegas) erected a shrine "with a Union Jack flag hanging over the entrance": www.cathedralstone.net/Pages/TheWho.htm.

8. The intended customers were Calvin Lockhart, "this most beautiful black actor", and Lord Lichfield, a society photographer who became the darling of the pop generation (before settling down with an aristocrat's daughter). Lichfield was put off when a friend remarked: "You'll look like a big girl's blouse wearing that" (Sims 1999: 114).
9. www.rollingstones.cwc.net/1969.htm.
10. "Mick About Style", www.stonesplanet.com/biography.htm.
11. Perhaps the Uncle Sam hat was a rejoinder to Pete Townshend's Union Flag suit.
12. "Mick Jagger became a client of Ossie Clark's in the late 1960s. Clark then made some of Jagger's stage costumes, like this (white skin-tight central zipping with panels revealing nipple and underarms) python-skin jumpsuit designed for the Rolling Stones' 1973 tour. It was intended to unzip onstage": www.vam.ac.uk/vastatic/microsites/1250_ossieclark/designs/clients/.
13. His "fantasy coat" from Body Worship was constructed "from a dozen pairs of shredded jeans, scraps of leather and silk printed with design motifs from previous tours, and featuring the new tour's logo – a Jeff Koons rendition of lips – the coat was a history of the Rolling Stones" (Parker 2003).
14. "Dressing for pleasure", Mystery Channel, www.pharo.com/mystery_channel/pleasure/articles/tvdp_01mc_dr.
15. www.officialvillagepeople.com/History%20page.html.
16. This coincided with the "clone" period of the gay movement when gay men adopted "the epitomes of American masculinity – the Cowboy, the lumberjack, the construction worker . . . and moved to large cities, where it was possible to live an openly gay lifestyle" (Cole 2002b).
17. en.wikipedia.org/wiki/The_Village_People.
18. www.officialvillagepeople.com/History%20page.html.
19. See, for example, *The Academy*, a TV series made about the Australian Defence Force Academy in Canberra, Sydney: Australian Broadcasting Corporation (2001).
20. Examples of gay designers include Christian Dior, Yves Saint Laurent, Giorgio Armani, Gianni Versace, Karl Lagerfeld, Calvin Klein, Tom Ford, Jean-Paul Gaultier, Dolce & Gabbana. Their "gay aesthetic . . . influenced fashion in both obvious and subtle ways" (Cole 2002b: 3).
21. *Manga* are erotic and sexually explicit cartoons featuring schoolgirls (see Richie 2003: 101–9).

Bibliography

Websites are listed in a separate section following the main Bibliography.

Abdo, Feda. 2004. "Aspirations." *The Australian 40 Years: Identity* (27 July) Part 9: 15.

Abler, Thomas. 1999. *Hinterland Warriors and Military Dress. European Empires and Exotic Uniforms*. Oxford and New York: Berg.

Ackerman, Elise. 2004. "US Parades New Uniform." *The Courier-Mail* (16 June): 12.

Adie, Kate. 2003. *Corsets to Camouflage. Women and War*. London: Hodder & Stoughton.

Alderson, Maggie. 2002. "Status Sneakers." *The Sydney Morning Herald* (18–20 April): 29.

Anon. 1994. "Girls Just Want to Have Funds." *World Press Review* (January) 41(1): 24.

—— 2001. "Guns 'R' Us." *The Australian Magazine* (30 June – 1 July): Cover image.

—— 2003. "ICC Cricket World Cup South Africa 2003. All the Contenders and the Pretenders." *The Courier-Mail* (6 February): 10–11.

Arborneli, Caroline and Anderson, Curtis. 1997. "The Wrong Trousers." *Times Educational Supplement* (10 October) 4241(TES2): 14.

Arnold, Rebecca. 2002. "Looking American. Louise Dahl-Wolfe's Fashion Photographs of the 1930s and 1940s." *Fashion Theory* 6(1): 45–60.

Artemis, Mistress. 1997. "Contractual Obligations." *Fetish Australia* (Nov.–Dec.) 2: 22–7.

Aspesi, Natalia. 2000. "Military Style. The Reappearance of Uniforms in the Icon of Masculinity." In Giannino Malossi (ed.), *Material Man. Masculinity, Sexuality, Style*, pp. 148–53. New York: Harry N. Abrams.

Associated Press. 2004. "Final Resting Place at Last for Confederate Sub's Crew." *The Courier-Mail* (19 April): 16.

Australian Broadcasting Corporation. 2001. *The Academy*, Episode 1, Sydney: ABC (video).

Bakhtin, Mikhail. 1968. *Rabelais and His World*. Cambridge, MA and London: The MIT Press.

Barnes, Ruth and Eicher, Joanne (eds). 1997. *Dress and Gender. Making and Meaning*. Oxford and Providence, RI: Berg.

Barrowclough, Nikki. 2004. "The Good Fighter." *The Sydney Morning Herald Good Weekend* (24 April): 25, 27.

Barthorp, Michael. 1978. "Britain's Colonial Wars in the Nineteenth Century." In I. T. Schick (ed.), *Battledress. The Uniforms of the World's Great Armies: 1700 to the Present*, pp. 137–56. Boston, MA: Little, Brown.

Baudot, Francois. 1999. *A Century of Fashion*. London: Thames & Hudson.

Bean, Susan. 1989. "Gandhi and *Khadi*, the Fabric of Indian Independence." In Annette Weiner and Jane Schneider (eds), *Cloth and the Human Experience*, pp. 355–76. Washington, DC, and London: Smithsonian Institution Press.

Beaton, Cecil. 1965. "Fashions and Royalty." In Mary Ellen Roach and Joanne Eicher (eds), *Dress, Adornment, and the Social Order*, pp. 265–6. New York and London: John Wiley.

Bell, Quentin. 1976. *On Human Finery*. New York: Shocken.

Bickman, Leonard. 1974. "Social Roles and Uniforms. Clothes Make the Person." *Psychology Today* (April): 49–51.

Black, Prudence. 2003. "Flying High: Flight Attendants' Performative Fashion." Paper presented to the "Making an Appearance Conference." (10–13 July). Brisbane: University of Queensland.

Bleckwenn, Hans. 1978. "European Wars of Eighteenth-Century Absolutism 1700–63." In I. T. Schick (ed.), *Battledress. The Uniforms of the World's Great Armies: 1700 to the Present*, pp. 13–44. Boston, MA: Little, Brown.

Bleckwenn, Ruth. 1978. "Prologue." In I. T. Schick (ed.), *Battledress. The Uniforms of the World's Great Armies: 1700 to the Present*, pp. 8–12. Boston, MA: Little, Brown.

Bloom, Amy. 2003. "Frill Seekers." *The Sydney Morning Herald Good Weekend* (20 September): 34–7.

Bolton, Andrew. 2003. *Men in Skirts*. London: V&A Publications.

Braddock, Sarah and O'Mahony, Marie. 2002. *Edge: The Influence of Sportswear*, Catalogue. Copenhagen: Oksnehallen.

Breward, Christopher. 1995. *The Culture of Fashion*. Manchester: Manchester University Press.

Bridgewater, Carol Austin. 1985. "Police Uniforms: Navy is Good." *Psychology Today* 19(1): 72.

Butler, Dianne and McCullough, James. 2004. "Steve Gets Away with Safari Suit." *The Courier-Mail* (20 April): 20.

Callaway, Helen. 1997. "Dressing for Dinner in the Bush. Rituals of Self-definition and British Imperial Authority." In Ruth Barnes and Joanne Eicher (eds), *Dress and Gender. Making and Meaning*, pp. 232–47. Oxford and Providence, RI: Berg.

Capon, Edmund. 1982. *Qin Shihuang. Terracotta Warriors and Horses*. Sydney: Art Gallery of New South Wales.

Carlsen, Clifford. 1996. "The Gap May Salute School Uniforms." *San Francisco Business Times* (31 May) 10(41): 21.

Carman, W. Y. 1977. *A Dictionary of Military Uniform*. London: Batsford.

Chalmers, Emma. 2003. "Sneak Up on Style." *The Courier-Mail* (25 February): 14.

Charles-Roux, Edmonde. 1995. *Chanel*. London: Harvill Press.

Chen, Tina Mai. 2001. "Dressing for the Party: Clothing, Citizenship and Gender-formation in Mao's China." *Fashion Theory* 5(2): 143–72.

Chenoune, Farid. 1993. *A History of Men's Fashion*. Paris: Flammarion.

Clark, Hazel and Wong, Agnes. 1997. "Who Still Wears the *Cheungsam*?" In Claire Roberts (ed.), *Evolution and Revolution. Chinese Dress 1700s–1990s*, pp. 65–73. Sydney: Powerhouse.

Clinton, William. 1996. "Memorandum on the School Uniforms Manual." *Weekly Compilation of Presidential Documents* (4 March) 32(9): 368–9.

Cocks, J. 1988. "What the Kids Are Wearing." *Time* (26 September): 87.

Cohn, Bernard. 1989. "Cloth, Clothes, and Colonialism". In Annette Weiner and Jane Schneider (eds), *Cloth and the Human Experience*, pp. 303–53. Washington, DC and London: Smithsonian Institution Press.

Cole, Shaun. 2000. "'Macho Man': Clones and the Development of a Masculine Stereotype." *Fashion Theory* 4(2): 125–40.

Collins Pageant of Knowledge Series. 1966. *A Pageant of History*. London: Collins.

Colls, Chris and Smith, Naomi. 2003. "Uniformity." *Marie Claire* (Australia) (March): 142–9.

Cook, Stephanie. 2000. "Do School Uniforms Stifle Expression or Protect Students?" *Christian Science Monitor* (8 August) 92(180): 12.

Coorey, Phillip. 2004. "Torture Crisis Deepens." *The Courier-Mail* (7 May): 1.

Cosgrove, Stuart. 1989. "The Zoot Suit and Style Warfare." In A. McRobbie (ed.), *Zoot Suits and Second-Hand Dresses*, pp. 3–22. London: Macmillan.

Costantino, Maria. 1997. *Men's Fashion in the Twentieth Century*. London: Batsford.

Cowley, Michael. 2004. "Revealed at Last: How Hackett Dominates the 1500m." *The Sydney Morning Herald* (6–7 March): 69.

Craik, Jennifer. 1994. *The Face of Fashion. Cultural Studies in Fashion*. London and New York: Routledge.

—— 2003. "The Cultural Politics of the Uniform." *Fashion Theory* 7(2): 127–47.

Cunnington, Phillis and Mansfield, Alan. 1969. *English Costume for Sports and Outdoor Recreation*. London: Adam & Charles Black.

Danielsen, Shane. 1999. "Sporty but Nice." *The Australian* (1 February): 15.

David, Alison Matthews. 2003. "Decorated Men: Fashioning the French Soldier, 1852–1914." *Fashion Theory* 7(1): 3–38.

Davidson, Alexander. 1990. *Blazers, Badges and Boaters. A Pictorial History of School Uniform*. Horndean, Hants: Scope.

Dawson, Chester. 1997. "A Sock to the System." *Asiaweek* (11 July) 23(44): 42.

De Teliga, Jane. 1995. "Rough Cuts." *The Sydney Morning Herald* (2 May): 33–4.

Doneman, Paula. 2003. "Magistrate Refuses Protective Custody." *The Courier-Mail* (6 June): 7.

Edwards, Penny. 2001. "Restyling Colonial Cambodia (1860–1954): French Dressing, Indigenous Custom and National Costume." *Fashion Theory* 5(4): 389–416.

Elias, Norbert. 1983. *The Court Society*. Oxford: Basil Blackwell.

Engelmeier, R. and Engelmeier, P. 1997. *Fashion in Film*. Munich and New York: Prestel.

Ewing, Elizabeth. 1975. *Women in Uniform: Through the Centuries*. London and Sydney: Batsford.

Finkelstein, Joanne. 1994. "Neckties." In *Slaves of Chic*, pp. 219–23. Melbourne: Minerva.

Finnane, Antonia. 1999. "Military Dress and Chinese Dress in the Early Twentieth Century." In V. Steele and J. Major (eds), *China Chic: East Meets West*, pp. 118–31. New Haven, CT, and London: Yale University Press.

Fogg, Marnie. 2003. *Boutique. A '60s Cultural Phenomenon*. London: Michael Beazley.

Fordin, Hugh. 1984. *The Movies' Greatest Musicals. Produced in Hollywood USA by the Freed Unit*. New York: Frederick Ungar.

Forest Lake College. 2004. "Uniform Shop." Brochure. Brisbane: Forest Lake College.

Frederick, William. 1997. "The Appearance of Revolution: Cloth, Uniform, and the Permuda Style in East Java, 1945–1949." In H. Schulte Nordholt (ed.), *Outward Appearances. Dressing State and Society in Indonesia*, pp. 199–248. Leiden: KITLV Press.

Frith, Simon. 1989. "Only Dancing: David Bowie Flirts with the Issues." In A. McRobbie (ed.), *Zoot Suits and Second-Hand Dresses*, pp. 132–40. London: Macmillan.

Fussell, Paul. 2002. *Uniforms. Why We Are What We Wear*. Boston, MA: Houghton Mifflin.

Fynes-Clinton, Jane. 2003. "Tune in, Turn on to Smarter Fashion." *The Courier-Mail* (5 February): 16.

Gaines, Jane and Herzog, Charlotte. 1990. *Fabrications. Costume and the Female Body*. New York and London: Routledge.

Garber, Marjorie. 1992. *Vested Interests. Cross-Dressing and Cultural Anxiety*. New York and London: Routledge.

Garner, Philippe. 2003. *Sixties Design*. Cologne: Taschen.

Green, Eileen. 2001. "Suiting Ourselves: Women Professors Using Clothes to Signal Authority, Belonging and Personal Style." In A. Guy, E. Green and M. Banim (eds), *Through the Wardrobe*, pp. 97–116. Oxford and New York: Berg.

Greer, Germaine. 1999. "Pantomime Dames." In *The Whole Woman*, pp. 64–74. London: Doubleday.

Guenther, Irene. 1997. "Nazi 'Chic'? German Politics and Women's Fashions, 1915–1945." *Fashion Theory* 1(1): 29–58.

—— 2004. *Nazi Chic*. Oxford and New York: Berg.

Gulf Air. 2003a. "Sydney to the Middle East Daily." Advertisement. *The Weekend Australian Magazine* (18–19 October): 40.

—— 2003b. "We Believe Everyone Should Enjoy Their Journey, No Matter What Their Age." *The Weekend Australian Magazine* (29–30 November): n.p.

Hall, Carolyn. 1983. *The Twenties in Vogue*. London: Octopus.

—— 1984. *The Thirties in Vogue*. London: Octopus.

—— 1985. *The Forties in Vogue*. London: Octopus.

Hall, Marian, Carne, Marjorie and Sheppard, Sylvia. 2002. *California Fashion*. New York: Harry N. Abrams.

Handley, Susannah. 1999. *Nylon. The Manmade Fashion Revolution*. London: Bloomsbury.

Harkin, Fiona. 2002. "Smarty Pants." *The Weekend Australian Magazine* (9–10 November): 42–3.

Hart, Avril. 1998. *Ties*. London: V&A Publications.

Haymes, Nick and Lafitte, Havana. 2001. "Off Duty. Because Every Girl Loves a Uniform." *Nova* (April): 108–19.

Healey, Murray. 1994. "The Mark of a Man: Masculine Identities and the Art of Macho Drag." *Critical Quarterly* 36(3): 86–93.

Hollander, Anne. 1978. *Seeing Through Clothes*. New York: Avon.

Holliday, Ruth. 2001. "Fashioning the Queer Self." In Joanne Entwistle and Elizabeth Wilson (eds), *Body Dressing*, pp. 215–32. Oxford and New York: Berg.

Hooper, John. 2001. "SS Joined Chorus Line in Showtime for Hitler." *Guardian Weekly* (14–20 June): 20.

Horwood, Catherine. 2002. "Dressing like a Champion: Women's Tennis Wear in Interwar England." In Christopher Breward, Becky Conekin and Caroline Cox (eds), *The Englishness of English Dress*, pp. 45–60. Oxford and New York: Berg.

Hume, Marion. 1997. "Tailoring." In Amy de la Haye (ed.), *The Cutting Edge. 50 Years of British Fashion: 1947–1997*, pp. 36–61. London: V&A Publications.

Hunt, Alan. 1996. *Governance of the Consuming Passions. A History of Sumptuary Law*. New York: St Martin's Press.

Hurlock, Elizabeth. 1965a. "Sumptuary Law." In Mary Ellen Roach and Joanne Eicher (eds), *Dress, Adornment, and the Social Order*, pp. 295–311. New York and London: John Wiley.

—— 1965b. "The Arbiters of Fashion." In Mary Ellen Roach and Joanne Eicher (eds), *Dress, Adornment, and the Social Order*, pp. 346–57. New York and London: John Wiley.

Inchley, Natasha. 2003. "Flight Patterns." *Vogue Australia* (August): 117–21.

Jaivin, Linda. 1997. "Confessions of an S & M Virgin." *Fetish Australia* 2 (Nov.–Dec.): 74–81.

Jeffrey, Nicole. 2004a. "Just Don't Do It, 'Cool' Olympians Told." *The Australian* (16 June): 3.

—— 2004b. "Sharkskin Suits Our Olympic Hopefuls." *The Australian* (10 March): 3.

Jobling, Paul. 1998. "Who's That Girl? 'Alex Eats', A Case Study in Abjection and Identity in Contemporary Fashion Photography." *Fashion Theory* 2(3): 209–24.

Jobling, Paul. 1999. *Fashion Spreads. Word and Image in Fashion Photography since 1980*. Oxford and New York: Berg.

Joel, Alexander. 1984. *Best Dressed. 200 Years of Fashion in Australia*. Sydney: Collins.

—— 1998. *Parade. The Story of Fashion in Australia*. Sydney: HarperCollins.

Johnston, Linda. 1996. "Flexing Femininity: Female Body-builders Refiguring 'the Body'." *Gender, Place and Culture* 3(3): 327–40.

Jones, Sam. 2004. "Muslim Pupil Loses Battle to Wear Jilbab." *Guardian Weekly* (25 June – 1 July): 10.

Joseph, Nathan. 1986. *Uniforms and Nonuniforms. Communication Through Clothing.* New York: Greenwood.

—— and Alex, Nicholas. 1972. "The Uniform: A Sociological Perspective." *American Journal of Sociology* 77(4): 719–30.

Kaiser, Susan, Chandler, Joan and Hammidi, Tania. 2001. "Minding Appearances in Female Academic Culture." In A. Guy, E. Green and M. Banim (eds), *Through the Wardrobe*, pp. 117–36. Oxford and New York: Berg.

Kanter, Larry. 1997. "New Popularity of School Uniforms Boosts Designers." *Los Angeles Business Journal* (9 August) 19(36): 11.

Keenan, W. 1999. "From Friars to Fornicators: The Eroticisation of Sacred Dress." *Fashion Theory* 3(4): 389–410.

Khan, Naseem. 1992. "Asian Women's Dress. From Burqah to Bloggs – Changing Clothes for Changing Times." In Juliet Ash and Elizabeth Wilson (eds), *Chic Thrills. A Fashion Reader*, pp. 61–74. London: Pandora.

Kidwell, Claudia and Christmas, Margaret. 1975. *Suiting Everyone: The Democratization of Clothing in America.* Washington, DC: Smithsonian Institution Press.

Kinsella, Sharon. 2002. "What's Behind the Fetishism of Japanese School Uniforms?" *Fashion Theory* 6(2): 215–38.

Klessmann, Eckart. 1978. "The Napoleonic Wars 1800–15." In I. T. Schick (ed.), *Battledress. The Uniforms of the World's Great Armies: 1700 to the Present*, pp. 97–136. Boston, MA: Little, Brown.

Kohn, Marek. 1989. "The Best Uniforms." In A. McRobbie (ed.), *Zoot Suits and Second-Hand Dresses*, pp. 141–9. London: Macmillan.

Krum, Sharon. 2004. "Putting on the Ritz." *The Australian* (2 March): 11.

Langner, Lawrence. 1965. "Clothes and Government." In Mary Ellen Roach and Joanne Eicher (eds), *Dress, Adornment, and the Social Order*, pp. 124–7. New York and London: John Wiley.

Lant, Antonia. 1991. *Blackout. Reinventing Women for Wartime British Cinema.* Princeton, NJ and Oxford: Princeton University Press.

Laver, James. 1995. *Costume and Fashion* (revised edn). London: Thames and Hudson.

Lawson, Valerie. 2003. "Qantas Gets Out Its Little Black Dress." *The Sydney Morning Herald* (28–29 June): 2.

Lehnert, Gertrud. 2000. *A History of Fashion in the 20th Century.* Cologne: Konemann.

Li, Xiaoping. 1998. "Fashioning the Body in Post-Mao China." In Anne Brydon and Sandra Niessen (eds), *Consuming Fashion. Adorning the Transnational Body*, pp. 70–89. Oxford and New York: Berg.

Lloyd, Valerie. 1986. *The Art of Vogue Photographic Covers.* London: Octopus.

Locher-Scholten, Elsbeth. 1997. "Summer Dresses and Canned Food: European Women and Western Lifestyles in the Indies, 1900–1942." In H. Schulte Nordholt (ed.), *Outward Appearances. Dressing State and Society in Indonesia*, pp. 151–80. Leiden: KITLV Press.

Lovegrove, Keith. 2000. *Airline. Identity, Design and Culture*. New York: teNeues.

Lunn, Jacqueline. 2003. "Anyone for Tennis?" *The Sydney Morning Herald* (2–3 August): Metropolitan 9.

Lurie, Alison. 1981. *The Language of Clothes*. London: Heinemann.

McCrone, Kathleen. 1987. "Play up! Play up! And Play the Game! Sport at the Late Victorian Girls' Public Schools." In J. A. Mangan and Roberta Park (eds), *From "Fair Sex" to Feminism. Sport and the Socialisation of Women in the Industrial and Post-Industrial Eras*, pp. 97–129. London and Totowa, NJ: Frank Cass.

McDowell, Colin. 1997. *The Man of Fashion. Peacock Males and Perfect Gentlemen*. London: Thames and Hudson.

McIntosh, Llyris with others. 2003. *Pax, Slips and Dunlops. 65 Years of Qantas In-flight Service*. Sydney: Watermark Press.

McKenna, Michael. 2004. "Storm Chaser Finds Herself in the Eye of One." *The Courier-Mail* (8 May): 1.

MacLeod, Alexander. 1999. "A British Girl's Bold Bid: Dress Like the Boys." *Christian Science Monitor* (14 June) 91(138): 1.

McRobbie, Margaret. 1986. *Walking the Skies. The First Fifty Years of Air Hostessing in Australia 1936–1986*. Melbourne: Margaret McRobbie.

McVeigh, Brian. 2000. *Wearing Ideology. State, Schooling and Self-Presentation in Japan*. Oxford and New York: Berg.

Mail on Sunday. 2004. "No Skirting School Ban." *The Courier-Mail* (21 June): 14.

Mansfield, Alan. 1969. "General Topics." In Phillis Cunnington and Alan Mansfield *English Costume for Sports and Outdoor Recreation*, pp. 353–62. London: Adam & Charles Black.

Martin, Paul. 1978. "Wars of the French Revolution and the Coalitions 1792–1803." In I. T. Schick (ed.), *Battledress. The Uniforms of the World's Great Armies: 1700 to the Present*, pp. 71–96. Boston, MA: Little, Brown.

Marzano, Stefano (ed.). 2000. *New Nomads*. Rotterdam: 010 Publishers.

Mauss, Marcel. 1973. "Techniques of the Body." *Economy and Society* 2(1): 70–87.

—— 1985. "A Category of the Human Mind: The Notion of Person; The Notion of Self." In Michael Carrithers, Steven Collins and Steven Lukes (eds), *The Category of the Person: Anthropology, Philosophy, History*, pp. 1–25. Cambridge: Cambridge University Press.

Maynard, Margaret. 2002. *Out of Line. Australian Women and Style*. Sydney: University of New South Wales Press.

—— 2004. *Dress and Globalisation*. Manchester: Manchester University Press.

Michelman, Susan. 1998. "Breaking Habits: Fashion and Identity of Women Religious." *Fashion Theory* 2(2): 165–92.

Middelkoop, Norbert. 1997. *The Golden Age of Dutch Art*. Perth: Art Gallery of Western Australia.

Milligan, Louise. 2004. "Silkless in the Spotlight." *The Australian* (26 March): 13.

Moles, Elizabeth and Friedman, Norman. 1973. "The Airline Hostess: Realities of an Occupation with a Popular Cultural Image." *Journal of Popular Culture* 7: 305–13.

Molitorisz, Sacha. 1998. "Tribes of the City." *The Sydney Morning Herald* (4 April) Spectrum Features: 6–7.

Moneera Laennec, Christine. 1997. "The 'Assembly-Line Love Goddess': Women and the Machine Aesthetic in Fashion Photography, 1918–1940". In D. Wilson and C. Moneera Laennec (eds), *Bodily Discursions. Genders, Representations, Technologies*, pp. 81–102. Albany, NY: State University of New York Press.

Morris, Sophie. 2001. "Brandy", Life Lines, photo by Nick Cubbin, *The Australian Magazine* (24–25 February): 11–12.

Mrozek, Donald. 1987. "The Habit of Victory: The American Military and the Cult of Manliness." In J. A. Mangan and James Walvin (eds), *Manliness and Morality. Middle-Class Masculinity in Britain and America 1800–1940*, pp. 220–41. Manchester: Manchester University Press.

Muir, Hugh. 2004. "Parking Wars: Wardens Want Body Armour." *Guardian Weekly* (20–26 May): 10.

Mulvey, Kate and Richards, Melissa. 1998. *Decades of Beauty. The Changing Image of Women 1890s – 1990s*. London: Hamlyn.

Mulvey, Laura. 1989. *Visual and Other Pleasures*. London: Macmillan.

Murdoch, Graeme. 2000. "Dressed to Repress: Protestant Clerical Dress and the Regulation of Morality in Early Modern Europe." *Fashion Theory* 4(2): 179–200.

Murphy, Padraic and Madden, James. 2004. "Gangland War's 'Next Victim' in Gunsights." *The Australian* (25 March): 1.

Myerly, Scott. 1996. *British Military Spectacle. From the Napoleonic Wars to the Crimea*. Cambridge, MA and London: Harvard University Press.

Newark, Tim, Newark, Quentin and Borsarello, J. F. 1998. *Brassey's Book of Camouflage*. London: Brassey's.

Nicklin, Lenore. 1993. "Surreal Estate." *The Bulletin* (24 August): 40–1.

Oberhardt, Mark. 2003. "Prosecutor Forges a Celebrity Career." *The Courier-Mail* (6 June): 7.

Okely, Judith. 1993. "Privileged, Schooled and Finished: Boarding Education for Girls." In Shirley Ardener (ed.), *Defining Women. The Nature of Women in Society*, pp. 93–122. Oxford and Providence, RI: Berg.

O'Mahony, Marie and Braddock, Sarah. 2002. *Sportstech. Revolutionary Fabrics, Fashion and Design.* London: Thames and Hudson.

Packer, William. 1983. *Fashion Drawing in Vogue.* London: Thames and Hudson.

—— 1985. *The Art of Vogue Covers 1909–1940.* London: Peerage.

Poncet, Dell. 2000. "Do Clothes Make the Student?" *Philadelphia Business Journal* (12 May) 19(14): 58–60.

Pratt, Sarah. 2002. "Fair Game." *The Weekend Australian Magazine* (16–17 November): 16–18.

Purves, Libby. 1992. "Trouser Girls, Boys in Frocks and Sequin Envy." *The Times* (6 May), Life and Times: 5.

Quataert, Donald. 1997. "Clothing Laws, State, and Society in the Ottoman Empire, 1720–1829." *International Journal of Middle East Studies* 29(3): 403–25.

Quinn, Bradley. 2002. *Techno Fashion.* Oxford and New York: Berg.

Ramamurthy, Anandi. 1997. "Constructions of Illusion." In L. Wells (ed.), *Photography; A Critical Introduction*, pp. 151–98. London and New York: Routledge.

Reid, Anthony. 1988. *Southeast Asia in the Age of Commerce 1450–1680.* Volume 1. New Haven, CT and London: Yale University Press.

Reiss, Tammy and McNatt, Robert 1998. "Haute Couture Hits the Playground." *Business Week* (17 August) 3591: 6.

Ribeiro, Aileen. 1999. *Fashions of the Past.* London: Collins and Brown.

Richie, Donald. 2003. *The Image Factory: Fads and Fashions in Japan.* London: Reaktion.

Roach, Mary Ellen and Eicher, Joanne (eds). 1965. *Dress, Adornment, and the Social Order.* New York and London: John Wiley.

—— and —— 1973. *The Visible Self.* Englewood Cliffs, NJ: Prentice-Hall.

Roberts, Claire. 1997a. "Fashioning Cultures: Contemporary Chinese Dress." In C. Roberts (ed.), *Evolution and Revolution. Chinese Dress 1700s–1990s*, pp. 87–102. Sydney: Powerhouse.

—— 1997b. "The Way of Dress." In Claire Roberts (ed.), *Evolution and Revolution. Chinese Dress 1700s–1990s*, pp. 12–25. Sydney: Powerhouse.

—— (ed.). 1997c. *Evolution and Revolution. Chinese Dress 1700s–1990s.* Sydney: Powerhouse.

Robinson, Julian. 1986. *The Fine Art of Fashion. An Illustrated History.* Sydney: Bay Books.

Roche, Daniel. 1996. *The Culture of Clothing. Dress and Fashion in the Ancient Regime.* Cambridge: Cambridge University Press.

Rosignoli, Guido. 1978a. "The First World War and the Restless Peace 1914–1939." In I. T. Schick (ed.), *Battledress. The Uniforms of the World's Great Armies: 1700 to the Present*, pp. 201–16. Boston, MA: Little, Brown.

——— 1978b. "The Second World War 1939–45." In I. T. Schick (ed.), *Battledress. The Uniforms of the World's Great Armies. 1700 to the Present*, pp. 217–31. Boston, MA: Little, Brown.

——— 1978c. "The Armies of the Atomic Age – the World after 1945." In I. T. Schick (ed.), *Battledress. The Uniforms of the World's Great Armies: 1700 to the Present*, pp. 232–43. Boston, MA: Little, Brown.

Roth, Julius. 1965. "Ritual and Magic in the Control of Contagion." In Mary Ellen Roach and Joanne Eicher (eds), *Dress, Adornment, and the Social Order*, pp. 117–23. New York and London: John Wiley.

Roufos, Anna. 1997. "School Uniforms Go Public." *Parenting* (November) 11(9): 30.

Routh, Caroline. 1993. *In Style. 100 Years of Canadian Women's Fashion.* Toronto: Stoddart.

Russell, Penny. 1994. "Recycling Femininity: Old Ladies and New Women." *Australian Cultural History* 13: 31–51.

Russo, Mary. 1986. "Female Grotesques: Carnival and Theory." In T. de Lauretis (ed.), *Feminist Studies/Critical Studies*, pp. 213–29. Bloomington, IN: Indiana University Press.

Safe, Mike. 2004. "Fields of Dreams." *The Weekend Magazine* (20–21 March): 12–15.

Salon Kitty's. 1997. "The Ultimate Erogenous Zone is the Imagination!" Advertisement, *Fetish Australia* (Nov.–Dec.) 2: 3.

Sandrejko, Nick. 2004. "Reversal of Fortune for Heroes and Villains." *The Australian* (8 March): 5.

Sawyer, Miranda. 2002. "Suiting Themselves." *The Sydney Morning Herald Good Weekend Magazine* (7 December): 72–3.

Schick, I. T. (ed.). 1978. *Battledress. The Uniforms of the World's Great Armies: 1700 to the Present.* Boston, MA: Little, Brown.

Schreier, Barbara. 1989. "Sporting Wear." In Claudia Kidwell and Valerie Steele (eds), *Men and Women: Dressing the Part*, pp. 92–123. Washington, DC: Smithsonian Institution Press.

Schulte Nordholt, H. 1997a. "Introduction." In H. Schulte Nordholt (ed.), *Outward Appearances. Dressing State and Society in Indonesia*, pp. 1–37. Leiden: KITLV Press.

——— (ed.). 1997b. *Outward Appearances. Dressing State and Society in Indonesia.* Leiden: KITLV Press.

Schulze, Laurie. 1990 "On the Muscle." In Jane Gaines and Charlotte Herzog (eds), *Fabrications. Costume and the Female Body*, pp. 59–78. London and New York: Routledge.

Scott, A. C. 1965. "The New China." In Mary Ellen Roach and Joanne Eicher (eds), *Dress, Adornment, and the Social Order*, pp. 127–35. New York and London: John Wiley.

Scott, Clive. 1999. "The Language of Fashion Photography." In *The Spoken Image. Photography and Language*, pp. 131–60. London: Reaktion.

Sebring, Steven and Coleman, David. 1996. "Classroom Couture." *George* (August) 6: 76.

Seeling, Charlotte. 2000. *Fashion. The Century of the Designer 1900–1999*. Cologne: Konemann.

Sekimoto, Teruo. 1997. "Uniforms and Concrete Walls: Dressing the Village Under the New Order in the 1970s and 1980s." In H. Schulte Nordholt (ed.), *Outward Appearances. Dressing State and Society in Indonesia*, pp. 307–38. Leiden: KITLV Press.

Shand, Adam. 2004. "Belle of the Bullets." *The Bulletin* (27 April): 28–9.

Sims, Joshua, 1999. *Rock/Fashion*. London: Omnibus.

Sims, Sally. 1991. "The Bicycle, the Bloomer and Dress Reform in the 1890s." In Patricia Cunningham and Susan Voso Lab (eds), *Dress and Popular Culture*, pp. 125–45. Bowling Green, OH: Bowling Green State University Popular Press.

Singapore Airlines. 2003. "Fly Spacebed to Europe. The Only Way to Do Business." Advertisement, *The Weekend Australian Magazine* (18–19 October): 2–3.

Skoggard, Ian. 1998. "Transnational Commodity Flows and the Global Phenomenon of the Brand." In Anne Brydon and Sandra Niessen (eds), *Consuming Fashion. Adorning the Transnational Body*, pp. 57–70. Oxford and New York: Berg.

Sladen, Christopher. 1995. *The Conscription of Fashion. Utility Cloth, Clothing and Footwear 1941–1952*. Aldershot, Hants: Scolar Press.

Sparke, Penny. 1986. *An Introduction to Design and Culture in the Twentieth Century*. London and Boston, MA: Allen & Unwin.

Spicer, Jonathan. 1993. "The Renaissance Elbow." In Jan Bremmer and Herman Roodenburg (eds), *A Cultural History of Gesture. From Antiquity to the Present Day*, pp. 84–128. Oxford: Polity Press.

Stallybrass, Peter and White, Allon. 1986. *The Politics and Poetics of Transgression*. London: Methuen.

Steele, Valerie. 1988. *Paris Fashion. A Cultural History*. New York and Oxford: Oxford University Press.

—— 1989. "Dressing for Work." In Claudia Kidwell and Valerie Steele (eds), *Men and Women: Dressing the Part*, pp. 64–91. Washington, DC: Smithsonian Institution Press.

—— and Major, John. 1999. "Fashion Revolution: The Maoist Uniform." In V. Steele and J. Major (eds), *China Chic: East Meets West*, pp. 54–67. New Haven, CT and London: Yale University Press.

Stewart, Cameron. 2004. "If My Husband Dies It Will Be a Police Set-Up." *The Australian* (25 March): 5.

Stone, Gregory. 1970. "Appearance and the Self." In Gregory Stone and Harvey Farberman (eds), *Social Psychology Through Symbolic Interaction*, pp. 394–414. Waltham, MA and London: Ginn-Blaisdell.

Strong, Roy. 1988. *The Story of Britain*. London: Pimlico.

Szeto, Naomi Yin-yin. 1997. "*Cheungsam*: Fashion, Culture and Gender." In C. Roberts (ed.), *Evolution and Revolution. Chinese Dress 1700s–1990s*, pp. 54–64. Sydney: Powerhouse.

Taffel, Jacqui. 2003. "Loosen Up." *The Sydney Morning Herald* (22–23 February) Metropolitan: 9.

Taylor, Jean Gelman. 1997. "Costume and Gender in Colonial Java, 1800–1940." In H. Schulte Nordholt (ed.), *Outward Appearances. Dressing State and Society in Indonesia*, pp. 85–116. Leiden: KITLV Press.

The Collins Atlas of Military History. 2004. London: HarperCollins.

Thompson, Sarah. 2003. "Hey, This One's Got Legs." *The Australian* (7 March): 17.

Van Dijk, Kees. 1997. "Sarongs, Jubbahs, and Trousers." In H. Schulte Nordholt (ed.), *Outward Appearances. Dressing State and Society in Indonesia*, pp. 39–84. Leiden: KITLV Press.

Venables, D. R. and Clifford, R. E. 1973. "Academic Dress." In Mary Douglas (ed.), *Rules and Meanings: The Anthropology of Everyday Knowledge*, pp. 209–11. Harmondsworth: Penguin.

Visser, Margaret. 1997. "Heavenly Hostesses." In *The Way We Are. The Astonishing Anthropology of Everyday Life*, pp. 1–4. New York and London: Kodansha.

Warner, Patricia. 1988. "Public and Private: Men's Influence on American Women's Dress for Sport and Physical Education." *Dress* 14: 48–55.

—— 1993. "The Gym Suit, Freedom at Last." In Patricia Cunningham and Susan Voso Lab (eds), *Dress in American Culture*, pp. 140–79. Bowling Green, OH: Bowling Green State University Popular Press.

—— 1995. "The Gym Slip: The Origins of the English Schoolgirl Tunic." *Dress* 22: 45–58.

Warren, Allen. 1987. "Popular Manliness: Baden-Powell, Scouting, and the Development of Manly Character." In J. A. Mangan and James Walvin (eds), *Manliness and Morality. Middle-Class Masculinity in Britain and America 1800–1940*, pp. 199–219. Manchester: Manchester University Press.

Weinstein, Richard. 2003. "Reboot." *Sport Monthly* (March): 84–93.

Wigley, Mark. 2001. *White Walls, Designer Dresses. The Fashioning of Modern Architecture*. Cambridge, MA and London: The MIT Press.

Wills, Nadine. 2000. "Women in Uniform: Costume and the 'Unruly Woman' in the 1930s Hollywood Musical." *Continuum* 14(3): 317–33.

Wilson, Elizabeth. 1985. *Adorned in Dreams. Fashion and Modernity*. London: Virago.

Winkworth, Kylie. 1989–90. "Women and the Bicycle: Fast, Loose and Liberated." *Australian Journal of Art* 8: 96–121.

Winn, Jan and Nutt, Diane. 2001. "From Closet to Wardrobe?" In Ali Guy, Eileen Green and Maura Banim (eds), *Through the Wardrobe*, pp. 221–36, Oxford and New York: Berg.

Wise, Terence. 1981. *Ancient Armies of the Middle East*. London: Osprey.

Wolfe, Richard. 2001. *The Way We Wore. The Clothes New Zealanders Have Loved*. Auckland: Penguin.

Wood, Alan. 2003. "Australian Airlines Spreads Wings." *The Courier-Mail* (26 February): 26.

Wrigley, Richard. 2002. *The Politics of Appearances. Representations of Dress in Revolutionary France*. Oxford & New York: Berg.

Ye, Sang. 1997. "From Rags to Revolution: Behind the Seams of Social Change." In C. Roberts (ed.), *Evolution and Revolution. Chinese Dress 1700s–1990s*, pp. 40–51. Sydney: Powerhouse.

Young, Malcolm. 1997. "Dress and Modes of Address. Structural Forms for Policewomen." In Ruth Barnes and Joanne Eicher (eds), *Dress and Gender. Making and Meaning*, pp. 266–85. Oxford and Providence, RI: Berg.

—— 2003a. "Future Sexy." *The Weekend Australian Magazine* (3–5 May): 35.

—— 2003b. "Late for School." *The Weekend Australian Magazine* (12–13 April): 46–7.

—— 2003c. "Sole Mining." *The Weekend Australian Magazine* (8–9 February): 36–7.

Websites

Abbotsleigh Girls School. n.d. "The History of Abbotsleigh's Uniform." Archives. http://www.abbotsleigh.nsw.edu.au/archives3.htm.

Anime. 2002. "Seifuku (Sailor Suit)." http://www.tapanime.com/info/seifuku.html.

Army. 2001. "The Household Division." http://www.army.mod.uk/ceremonialandheritage/part_2.htm.

ASIA Travel Tips. 2003. "Qantas Unveils New Uniform Designed By Morrissey." (27 June). http://www.asiatraveltips.com/print03.cgi?file=276Qantas.shtml.

Associated Press. 2000. "Iran Allows Girls to Wear Brighter School Uniforms." *The Times of India Online* (19 July). www.timesofindia.com.

Australian Associated Press (AAP). 2003. "'Trendy' Qantas Uniforms Unveiled." *NEWS.com.au* (13 September). http://www.news.com.au/common/story_page/0,4057,6662261%5E1702,00.html.

Australian Broadcasting Corporation (ABC). 1996. "Do Teachers

Have a Dress Sense?" *Education Report*, host Jane Figgis, ABC Radio National, Transcript (18 December). http://www.abc.net.au/rn/talks/8.30/edurpt/estories/er181296.htm.

—— 2000a. "Schools." *The Comfort Zone*, host Alan Saunders, ABC Radio National, Summary (28 October). www.abc.net.au/rn/czone/s206125.htm.

—— 2000b. "The Green and Gold." *The Sports Factor*, host Amanda Smith, ABC Radio National, Transcript (4 August). www.abc.net.au/rn/talks/8.30/sportsf/stories/s159343.htm.

—— 2003. "Qantas Refreshes Image with New Uniforms." *Business Breakfast* (30 June). www.abc.net/businessbreakfast/content/2003/s890916.htm.

BBC News. 2003a. "Parents Protest over Uniform Abolition." http://news.bbc.co.uk/2/hi/uk_news/england/devon/3020996.stm.

—— 2003b. "Uniforms 'Raise School Standards'." http://news.bbc.co.uk/2/hi/uk_news/education/3186886.stm.

BBC Sport. 2004. "Cameroons Ask for Leniency." BBC Sport Football (13 May). http:news.bbc.co.uk/sport2hi/football/Africa/3708893.stm.

Brunsma, David and Rockquemore, Kerry. 1998. "The Effects of Student Uniforms on Attendance, Behaviour Problems, Substance Use, and Academic Achievement." *Journal of Educational Research*, www.members.tripod.com/rockqu/uniform.htm.

Burgess, Lisa. 2004. "New Army BDU Retains Old Shape, Changes its Colours." *European and Pacific Stars and Stripes* (15 June). http://www.estripes.com/article.asp??section=104&article=22780.

Canadian Broadcasting Corporation. 2000. "Feedback. School Uniforms." www.cbc4kids.ca/general/whats-new/feedback/article12.html.

Cathedral Stone. 2004. "Death of John Entwistle. The Ox Tribute." http://www.cathedralstone.net/Pages/TheWho.htm.

Chaika, Gloria. 1999. "School Uniforms: Panacea or Band-aid?" *Education World* (27 September). www.education-world.com/a_admin/admin065.shtml.

Cole, Shaun. 2002a. "Dolce & Gabbana", Arts, *qlbtq: An Encyclopedia of Gay, Lesbian, Bisexual, Transgender, and Queer Culture*. http://www.glbtq.com/arts/dolce_gabbana.html.

—— 2002b. "Fashion", Arts, *qlbtq: An Encyclopedia of Gay, Lesbian, Bisexual, Transgender, and Queer Culture*. http://www.glbtq.com/arts/fashion.html.

Craik, Jennifer. 2000. "School Uniforms." In Australian Broadcasting Corporation. "Schools." *The Comfort Zone*, host Alan Saunders (28 October) Sydney: ABC Radio National. www.abc.net.au/rn/czone/s206125.htm.

—— 2001. "Why Do Military Uniforms Influence Fashion?" [commentary] In Australian Broadcasting Corporation. "Military Zone." *The*

Comfort Zone, host Alan Saunders (3 February) Sydney: ABC Radio National. www.abc.net/rn/czone/stories/s245608.htm.

De Lange. 2001. "Zappa Story. Some More Pt. III." http://www. thebignote.com/archived/some)more_pt_iii.php.

Embassy of France to Zambia and Malawi. nd. "Tourism, Art and Culture." *Zambia – Tourism in Zambia.* http://www.ambafrance-zm.org/ 3zambie/gb332.htm.

Focus Uniforms. 2004. "Why Have Uniforms in Your Company?" www. focusuniforms.com.au/why.html.

George, Joe. 2003 "The History and Evolution of the Way We Dress." Chef News for Chefs. [chef2chef.net/news/foodservice/Editorial-Chefs_ Corner/The_History_and_Evolu].

Gianoulis, Tina. 2002. "k.d. lang." Arts, *qlbtq: An Encyclopedia of Gay, Lesbian, Bisexual, Transgender, and Queer Culture*. http://www.glbtq. com/arts/lang_kd.html.

Hendrix, Jimi. 2004. "Psychedelic Military." Poster. http://www.xanadu online.com/search-products.php4?item=11.

Historical Boys Clothing. 2003. "Boys' Uniforms: Sports and Athletics." http://histclo.hispeed.com/style/casual/sport/sport.html

Kahl, Kristi. 1997. "Are School Uniforms and Middle School Reform Compatible?" http:/www.middleweb.com/NEWSuniforms.html.

Kane, Ed. 1998. "White Chef's Hat Boasts Colourful History. pp. 40– 51," *Las Vegas Review-Journal* (18 March). www.reviewjournal.com/ lvrj_home/1998/Mar-18-1998/lifest.

Kellerman, Robert. 2002. "Sisters of Perpetual Indulgence." Arts, *qlbtq: An Encyclopedia of Gay, Lesbian, Bisexual, Transgender, and Queer Culture.* http://www.glbtq.com/arts/sisters_perpetual_indulgence.html.

Libakeni, Yuyi. 2004. "Kuomboka at Libonda." *The Lowdown Zambia.* http://www.lowdown.co.zm/2004/2004-03/kuombokaatlibonda.htm.

Luscombe, Stephen. 2004. "Robert Baden-Powell (1857–1941)." 13th Hussars, Colonels 1861–1922, The British Empire. http://www. britishempire.co.uk/forces/armyunits/britishcavalry/13thhussars.

Milbourne, Karen. 1997. "Diplomacy in Motion: Makishi as Political Harmony in Barotseland." *BOABAB*, University of Iowa. http:// sdrc.lib.uiowa.edu/ceras/baobab/milbourne.html.

Mystery Channel. 2004. "Dressing for Pleasure." http://www.pharo.com/ mystery_channel/pleasure/artciles/tvdp_01_dressing.

National Association of Elementary School Principals (NAESP). 1998. "Principals Report on Extent and Impact of Uniform Trend: Benefits to Educational Environment Deemed Significant." NAESP Press Release (20 March) *Principal Online.* www.naesp.org/comm/prss31998.htm.

National Baseball Hall of Fame and Museum. 2002. *Dressed to the Nines. A History of the Baseball Uniform.* http:www.baseballhalloffame.org/ exhibits/online_exhibits/dressed_to_the_nines.

Online NewsHour. 1996. "Uniform Look." http://www.pbs.org/ newshour/bb/education/uniform_4-17.html.

—— 2000. "School Uniforms." wysiwyg://9/http://www.pbs.org/ newshour/infocus/fashion/school.html.

Parker, Ian. 2003. "Chic Mick." *The Age* (4 February). http://www.theage. com.au/cgi_bin/common/popupPrintArticle.pl?path=/.

Polk County School Uniforms, 2003. http://www.gate.net/~rwms/ UniformIntro.html.

Porter, Hugh. 2003. "From Russia with Lust." *TIME Europe Magazine* (10 February). http://www.time.com/time/europe/magazine/article/ 0,13005,901030210.

Rolling Stones. 2004. "1969." http://www.rollingstones.cwc.net/1969. htm.

Rolling Stones Fan Club Office. 2004. "Mick About Style", Biography of the Stones. http://www.stonesplanet.com/biography.htm.

Salvation Army. 2003a. "History of the Uniform." International Heritage Centre. http://www1.salvationarmy.org/heritage.nsf/.

—— 2003b. "The Bonnet." International Heritage Centre. http://www1. salvationarmy.org/heritage.nsf/.

—— 2004. "Salvation Army – FAQ-18-Uniform". The Salvation Army Facts Sheets. http://www.salvationarmy.org.uk/en/Library/ factSheets/ FAQ-18-Uniform.htm.

School Uniform. 2002. http://members.tripod.com/~histclo/schun.html.

Siegel, Loren. 1996. "Point of View: School Uniforms." *In Congress* American Civil Liberties Union Freedom Network. http://www.aclu. org/congress/uniform.html.

Speed, William. 1999. "Quentin Crisp." *Salon.com.* http://www.salon. com/people/obit/1999/12/03/crisp/.

Starr, Linda. 1998. "Can Uniforms Save Our Schools?" *Education World* (11 May). http://www.education-world.com/a_admin/admin065. shtml.

Stevenson, Seth. 2003. "The Way We Live Now; Hamming It Down in Japan." *New York Times* (30 November). http://query.nytimes.com/ gst/abstract.html.

Tapanime. 2002. "Seifuku (Sailor Suit)." http://www.tapanime.com/info/ seifuku.html.

The Free Dictionary. 2004a. "Japanese School Uniform." http:// encyclopedia.thefreedictionary.com/Japanese%20school%20uniform.

—— 2004b. "School Uniform." http://encyclopedia.thefreedictionary. com/School%20uniform.

The School Uniform Galleries. 2002. http://www.school.uniform.freeuk. com.

The Sisters of Perpetual Indulgence. 2002. "Sistory." The Sisters of Perpetual Indulgence, Inc. http://www.thesisters.org/.

The Straits Times. 2004. "US Army Unveils New Combat Uniform." *The Straits Times Interactive*. (16 June). http://www.straitstimes.asia1.com. sg/world/story/0,4386,256461,00.html.

The Traditional English Schoolboy, http://freeuk.net/mkb/SUG/TradBoy. htm.

Townsend, Ian. 2003. "Former Chief Magistrate released from Jail." *The World Today* (3 December). Sydney: ABC News Online. http://www. abc.net/news/newsitems/200312/s1002130.htm.

US Department of Education and US Department of Justice. 1996. *Manual on School Uniforms*. Updates on Legislation, Budget, and Activities, http://www.ed.gov/updates/uniforms.html.

USAREUR. 2004. "Army Unveils New Combat Uniform, Replace Battle Dress Uniform (BDU)." *Public Affairs News Release*. (15 June). http:// www.hqusareur.army.mil/htmlinks/Press_Releases/2004/June20.

USA Today. 2004. "Army Shows First Uniform Redesign since '81." (14 June). http://www.usatoday.com/news/washington/2004-06-14-new-army-uniforms_x.htm.

Victoria & Albert Museum. 2004. "Ossie Clark – Ossie Clark's Designs – Clients." http://www.vam.ac.uk/vastatic/microsites/1250_ossieclark/ designs/clients/.

Village People. 2004. "History", Official Village People website. http:// www.officialpeople.com/History%20pages.html.

Wagner, Christopher. 2000. "Military Uniform Background: Influence on Boys Clothes." Historical Boys' Uniforms (HBO). http://histclo. hispeed.com/youth/mil/mil-styleb.html.

—— 2002a. "Australian School Uniform: Individual Experiences." Historical Boys Clothing. http://histclo.hispeed.com/schun/country/oz/ ia/asu-ia.html.

—— 2002b. "Hitler Youth." Historical Boys' Uniforms (HBO). http:// histclo.hispeed.com/youth/youth/org/nat/hitler/hitler.htm.

—— 2002c. "School Smocks." Historical Boys Clothing. http://histclo. hispeed.com/style/skirted/smock/schsmock.html.

—— 2002d. "Scouting for Boys by Robert Baden-Powell." Historical Boys' Uniforms (HBO). http://histclo.hispeed.com/youth/youth/bib/ org/sco/cou/eng/bp-sfb.htm.

—— 2003a. "Boy Scout Uniforms." Historical Boys' Uniforms (HBO). http://histclo.hispeed.com/youth/youth/org/sco/scout.htm.

—— 2003b. "The History of School Uniforms." Historical Boys Clothing. http://histclo.hispeed.com/schun/hist/schun-hist.html.

—— 2003c. "School Uniform: Australia." Historical Boys Clothing. http://histclo.hispeed.com/schun/country/oz/schunoz.html.

—— 2003d. "School Uniform: European National Styles." Historical Boys Clothing. http://histclo.hispeed.com/schun/country/schun1coueu. html.

—— 2003e. "School Uniform: National Styles." Historical Boys Clothing. http://histclo.hispeed.com/schun/country/schun1cou.html.

—— 2003f. "School Uniform: National Styles—Africa." Historical Boys Clothing. http://histclo.hispeed.com/schun/country/schun1couaf.html.

—— 2003g. "School Uniform: National Styles—Latin America and the Caribbean." Historical Boys Clothing. http://histclo.hispeed.com/schun/country/schun1cousa.html.

—— 2003h. "School Uniform: National Styles—North America." Historical Boys Clothing. http://histclo.hispeed.com/schun/country/schun1couna.html.

—— 2003i. "School Uniform: National Styles—Oceania." Historical Boys Clothing. http://histclo.hispeed.com/schun/country/schun1couoc.html.

—— 2003j. "Uniformed Youth Group Biography: Lord Baden-Powell (England, 1857–1941)." Historical Boys' Uniforms (HBO). http://histclo.hispeed.com/youth/youth/bio/b-bp.htm.

Wikipedia. 2004a. "Salvation Army. " http://en.wikipedia.org/wiki/Salvation_Army.

—— 2004b. "The Village People", http://en.wikipedia.org/wiki/The_Village_People.

Williams, Carla. 2002. "Music: Popular."8, Arts, *glbtq: An Encyclopedia of Gay, Lesbian, Bisexual, Transgender, and Queer Culture.* http://www.glbtq.com/arts/music_popular.html.

Williams, Darlene. n.d. "School Uniforms: The Raging Debate." http://www.gate.net/~rwms/UniformsDWilliams.html.

Willis, Louise. 2003. "The World Today – Di Fingleton Walks Free After Jail Stint." (3 December). Sydney: ABC Online. www.abc.net.au/worldwidetoday/content/2003/s1002630.htm.

Yahoo! Directory Uniforms > Retailers. 2004. dir.yahoo.com/Business_and_Economy/Shopping_and_Services/.

Young, Angus. 2004. "Angus Young ACDC." Poster. http://posters.seindal.dk/p391056_AC_DC_Angus.html.

Index

The Collins Atlas of Military History, 22
The Rolling Stones, 213, 238n12
The School Uniforms Galleries, 12, 59
The Who, 213, 237–8n7
Thomas, Chantal, 180
Thompson, Jenny, 169
Thompson, Sarah, 169
Tinling, Ted, 158
TWA, 113
transgressive uses of uniforms, xviii, 4–7, 16, 137–8, 177–80 passim, 182, 201–28 passim, 237–8n7, 238n16
    see also sexuality, carnival
Travolta, John, 165
types of uniforms, 5–6, 80, 126–7
    see also definitions, occupational uniforms

Ungaro, Emanuel, 198
United Airlines, 115
United States Department of Education, 13, 71
United States Department of Justice, 13, 71

Vandevorst, A. F., 181
Van Dijk, Kees, 42
Vans, 195
Venables, D. R., 123
Versace, Gianni, 198, 238n20
Village People, 204, 219–20
Virgin, 118
Virgin Blue, 117, 118
Visser, Margaret, 110, 112
vivandieres, 84
    see also cantinieres
Vuitton, Louis, 181

Wagner, Christopher, 39, 45–9, 57–61, 231n16
Wahid, Abdurrahman, 48
Warner, Patricia, 147, 152–5, 158, 234n3
Warren, Allen, 46
Watanabe, Junya, 165
Watts, Isaac, 58–9
Weber, Bruce, 198

Weinstein, Richard, 162, 167
West Point, 220
Westwood, Vivienne, 198, 218, 230n2
Whickham Comprehensive School, 99
White, Allon, 209, 210
White, Anne, 158
Who, Harry, 116
Wigley, Mark, 31, 151
Wilde, Oscar, 201, 222
Willhelm, Bernhard, 181
Williams, Carla, 219, 221
Williams, Darlene, 73
Williams, Serena, 158
Williams, Venus, 158
Willis, Louise, 105
Wills, Nadine, 90, 91, 183–4
Wills-Moody, Helen, 155
Wilson, Elizabeth, 141–4, 155–6, 187, 215, 223–4, 234n2
Wimbledon, 154–5, 158
Winn, Jan, 224
Wise, Terence, 22
Wolfe, Richard, 147, 234n2
Women's Royal Army Corps, 133
women's uniforms, 79–99 passim
    domestic staff, 82, 85
    and femininity, 80–1, 84–8, 90–5, 97–9, 140–4, 152–5
    military uniforms, 78–80, 89–94
    police uniforms, 98–9
    and sexuality, 80–1, 84–8, 90–5, 97–9, 140–4, 152–5
    sports, 85, 141, 152, 157
    see also nurse uniforms
Wong, Agnes, 197
Wood, Alan, 118
World Series Cricket, xv, 158
Wyles, Lilian, 87

Yamamoto, Kansai, 198
Ye, Sang, 197
Young, Malcolm, 86–8, 134

Zambia, 9–11, 229n3
Zamiatin, Lara, 138, 167, 173, 234n5
Zouave, 49
Zulus, 22